The Blue Touch Paper

DAVID HARE

The Blue Touch Paper

A Memoir

FABER & FABER

First published in 2015
by Faber & Faber Ltd
Bloomsbury House
74–77 Great Russell Street
London WC1B 3DA

Typeset by Faber & Faber Ltd
Printed in the UK by CPI Group (UK) Ltd, Croydon, CR0 4YY

A CIP record for this book
is available from the British Library

ISBN 978–0–571–29433–6

For Nicole

Contents

Plates

Foreword

In the summer of 2010, I was approached by the estate of Terence Rattigan to write a companion piece to *The Browning Version*. Traditionally, this well-known one-act play had been presented in a double bill with an inept farce called *Harlequinade*. It would be enlivening, the estate thought, if Rattigan's popular piece about masochism and manipulation could for once be matched with something a little less facetious.

I loved the idea of writing about my time at Lancing College in the 1960s, so that Rattigan's version of his schooldays could sit alongside mine on the same bill. Normally a full-length play might take me a year to write, but on this occasion I finished a one-act play in four weeks. All writers dream of a moment when your subconscious dictates and you are able to act as nothing more than a stenographer. It had happened to me only once before. On some nights, I would wake at three in the morning and scribble in a bedside notebook. My wife would stir and ask me what I was doing. 'Writing tomorrow's dialogue,' I would say, before falling asleep.

The result, *South Downs*, was partly fiction. The plot was made up and so were the characters. But the ambience was true to my memory of attendance at an Anglo-Catholic school fifty years previously. The subject, essentially, was the need to fake a confidence you don't feel. It was about the price of pretending you understand when you don't. Everything about the play seemed to delight me, the cast and the director, Jeremy Herrin. Unusually, it was rehearsed and performed without a moment of strain. Anna Chancellor, who played the crucial part of Belinda Duffield, a West End actress who visits the school and thereby transforms the life of the fourteen-year-old hero, remarked that when she first read *South Downs*, it was as if the play had never been brought into being. It simply was. William Empson, praised for his apparent fluency, once said, 'The careless ease goes in last.' But on this occasion it had gone in at the time.

After so many years of anxious struggle, it was an unusual experience for a dramatist to be handed a play for free. I asked myself why it had happened this time and not before. But I also had to answer letters from many contemporaries, most of whom I had not spoken to or heard from for half a century. They, like me, had spent recent years haunted by everything unresolved from their distant adolescence. I kept thinking of William Faulkner: 'The past is never dead. It's not even past.' Or as my friend Wallace Shawn observed, 'They warn you life's short. They don't warn you it's simultaneous.'

Up till then I had taken it for granted that I had lived through a period of little historical interest. Because I was born in 1947, I had spent most of my life feeling that I had missed the main event. The Second World War had ended before I was born, even though over and again it provided the setting for my imagination. But when I wrote *South Downs*, set in the early 1960s, I realised what an extraordinary distance we had travelled. Its world seemed to me closer than yesterday, but for many of the cast it was unrecognisable. I had to explain to the young actors that I had been born into a country the majority of whose population at least professed to believe in God. They also believed in their empire, their institutions, their democracy, their public figures and the essential decency of their civilisation. In particular parts of the country, belief in socialism was also deep-rooted and widespread. Sixty years later, those same people, or their descendants, appeared to have lost faith in everything except private virtue. They ascribed positive qualities to their friends but to almost nobody in large enterprises or public life. How on earth could so radical a change have occurred and how could it have gone so little remarked while it happened?

When writing plays, I've preferred to steer clear of direct autobiography. I may have plundered an incident or a remark, but rarely a storyline or a whole character. Writing about, for instance, the privatisation of the railways or the distribution of aid to the poor, I've tended to find inspiration in the external world. It's difference that has stimulated me, not similarity. So when surprised by a desire to record the circumstances of my own life, I felt a novice. I wanted to be expansive, to move where my memory took me, and I felt this could be best achieved not by writing prose, but by talking. A series of conversations over a year with Amy Raphael followed with the aim of discovering why it was so hard for my generation to put the past to bed. Using as a primary source her edited transcripts – to which, with her exceptional taste, knowledge and literary skill, she made an essential contribution – I have fashioned this book. If, as with my education at Lancing, I have already written about a particular time or place, I have felt free to draw lightly on that previous account.

My hope is to show how a lifelong engagement with two disparate art forms – film and theatre – may reflect at the same time on more diverse questions and on more intimate. This book is the story of my apprenticeship. It seeks to tell how a young man became a dramatist, and to describe the cost and effect of that decision. There are many ways to become a writer and mine is just one. But I suspect certain aspects overlap with the experience of others. I made a series of peculiar choices, but they were in response to common problems.

In an opinion survey, one person in six said what they wanted most before they died was to write a memoir. All of us live lives where we are both large and small: large because of the intense focus of our self-attention – and small because, however fierce our concentration, the universe remains indifferent to us throughout. My life has been no different from anyone else's: both everything and nothing.

DH

London, February 2015

You see, when one's young, one doesn't feel part of it, the human condition; one does things because they are not for good; everything is a rehearsal to be repeated ad lib, to be put right when the curtain goes up in earnest. One day you know that the curtain was up all the time. That was the performance.

SYBILLE BEDFORD

She Could Have Done Worse

When I was growing up nothing excited me more than getting lost. Walking bored me when I knew the way. Until I was twenty-one, my home was on the south coast, firstly in a modest flat up a hill in St Leonards, later in a semi-detached in Bexhill. But when we made our annual family trip to my maternal grandmother's in Paisley, my sport was to get on a bus, close my eyes and then get out. I was barely ten and I had no idea where I was. Sometimes I recognised Love Street, the home of the local football club, St Mirren, for whom my uncle Jimmy was a talent scout, but nothing else made sense to me. My grandmother Euphemia was furious when I got back two hours late for tea – in those days ham, lettuce, tomato and pork pie, followed by a lot of biscuits and cakes. This after a lunch of mince and tatties.

When I disappeared, nobody seemed overly concerned. Children vanished from time to time, that's what happened. A lower-middle-class childhood on the south coast of England in the 1950s became a distinctive mixture of freedom and repression. It was because children were encouraged to make their own way home from school that my nine-year-old friend Michael Richford and I encountered our first sex offender on the Downs, right next to the air-raid shelter which no one had bothered to demolish. The spectral predator was moustached, wearing a grey overcoat and a grey scarf. Our refusal to show him our penises did not seem to lessen his pleasure in showing us his. We two boys hurried home, through the abundant nettles and brambles, up our separate back paths and past the hen-houses that lingered on beneath hedges at the ends of gardens for so many years after the war. Later we were taken by police to line-ups and asked, unsuccessfully, to identify various old men coming out of the Playhouse Cinema after a smoky matinee of *The Dam Busters*. But, in spite of all the dark parental huddles which followed on the incident, I was still allowed at thirteen to go on my own by train to London. Why? At fifteen I was hitch-hiking across England to Stratford in the hope of seeing Vanessa Redgrave in *The Taming of the Shrew*. At seventeen, I left for America. My mother wished me good luck, and no doubt she fretted, but at no point did she try to stop me. I was free. Later I read Nietzsche: 'All truly great thoughts are conceived by walking.'

Over the years I was to convince myself I'd had an unhappy childhood, though I would never have dared say so in public while my parents were alive. Even writing these words causes me a flush of shame. The very over-sensitivity which equips you to be a writer also makes being a writer agony. But in retrospect it's extraordinary how much licence my mother allowed to my sister and me. It goes without saying that after the Second World War, when dealing with their children, adults almost never stooped to our level. Down where we were, we looked up at all times. There was none of today's dippy celebration of children as little unfallen gods. We were not pushed self-importantly through the streets in thousand-pound chariots, scooping up croissants and ice creams on the way. Nobody told us we were wonderful. But on the other hand, even in the stifling atmosphere of suburbia, among those rows of silent, russet-bricked houses and identically tended lawns, adorned with billowing washing lines, strawberry plants, runner beans and raspberry canes, we were granted a level of independence which now seems unimaginable.

Or was that simply because of my mother? Nancy Hare, as she came to be known, had been born Agnes Cockburn Gilmour just a decade into the twentieth century, and brought up as the middle child of three by fiercely puritanical parents who did their best to force upon her a poor opinion of herself. The result, in her mid-twenties, had been a nervous breakdown, precipitated perhaps by the feeling that she was never going to find a husband. She was tall, striking rather than beautiful, with looks which seem typical of their period. Her only escape from what we would now call low self-esteem was her flair for amateur dramatics. She had a good voice and a prized diploma in elocution. The family business was road haulage. Even in my youth, the men stood at lecterns and horses were maintained in stables and sent out on the roads, admittedly as a sort of tribute to past practices, but maintained nevertheless. My grandparents had been the first people in Paisley to own a car, but if that implied prosperity, then letting it show in any way beyond the motor-mechanical would have been frowned on, the subject of ceaseless comment from neighbours never reluctant to pass damning comments on each other. The family religion was judgement.

My mother had been raised in Whitehaugh Drive, a cheerless, rising street of Victorian stone houses, blackened by industry and with back yards the size of handkerchiefs. A few doors up was the spinster Betty Richie, who, on its release, was to see *The Sound of Music* 365 times, once for every successive day of the year. The strong-minded Euphemia had done her very best to make sure that my uncle Jimmy stayed unmarried as long

3

as possible, the better, she hoped, to look after her in her old age. When Jimmy did, at forty, eventually make it out of the house with the inoffensive but marginally vulgar Nan, a childless spinster who bestowed sweet tea, jam and honeyed flapjacks down the throat of any child who came near, his mother refused to allow that the marriage had happened or to admit Aunt Nan to the family house. Only the favoured Peggy, the youngest and brightest of the three children, was lined up to make a brilliant match, and even allowed to go off from Paisley Grammar School to Glasgow University, where she at once fell in love with a medical student who also shone as a rugby player. For my mother, to whom the drunken, violent pavements of Paisley were nightly torture, a fate like Betty Richie's seemed to await.

For the whole of her life my mother was scared. She managed to be scared for forty years in Bexhill-on-Sea, a Sussex dormitory for the retired and soon-to-be-retired which is not, on the surface at least, the scariest of places. I both inherited her fear and tried to reject it. Her mother left Nancy with a strong idea of how things should be done. I only once saw her in any kind of trouser. Respectable women wore skirts. No incident loomed larger in her later anecdotal life than the time when, during the war, while working for the Wrens, she mistakenly drank a china cup of whisky late at night in the belief that it was tea. She made the resulting wreckage of her consciousness in the early hours sound like a descent into un-merry hell. Her horror of alcohol, of men, of violence and of any kind of public disorder seemed to me in my equal primness like a horror of life. My mother was always on guard, always on watch, expecting men, children, neighbours, strangers, and, I'm afraid, her own family to betray signs of their underlying beastliness. Civilisation was a veneer, a pleasant veneer, yes, but not to be trusted. Essential

4

things always came out. I grew used to her favourite rebuke. 'I love you,' she'd say to me. 'But I don't like you.'

Nancy was an intelligent and sensitive woman, born, by bad luck, into the wrong place at the wrong time. She passed her days as a secretary, or as she herself preferred to call it, a shorthand typist, at Coats, the cotton firm, where sometimes, among the reels and bobbins, she wondered whether she belonged with the professional actors like Duncan Macrae who would come from the Citizens' Theatre to Paisley to guest-star in otherwise amateur productions of thrillers and James Bridie's romances. Macrae was an expert in what the Scots of the time called glaikit comedy. We would call it gormless. But if a working-class satellite of Glasgow was not easy for her, then nor, I think, was the suffocating gentility of the south coast of England to which my father transported her after the war. They had met at a dance in Greenock in 1941, and the progress of their mysterious courtship was recorded by my aunt Peggy. In her diary, for reasons not clear to me or to my sister Margaret, Peggy sometimes calls my mother Agatha, even though that was neither her given nor her adopted name.

27 September 1941
My beloved sister went off at 10 o'clock this morning and didn't get back till the minutes before midnight. She was very gay when she came in and announced that she was bringing an Officer for lunch on the morrow. Shrieks from mother.

28 September 1941
Clifford came. He was most charming and an easy talker; he was obviously very fond of Agatha, kept turning round and beaming at her in such an adoring way. Agatha dashed

5

into the back kitchen between courses and asked me what I thought of him. I gave my hearty approval. I think she could do a lot worse, especially at her age. Admittedly, he's queer looking and smaller than she is, but he's kindness itself and very generous.

9 October 1941
Bombshell arrived today at lunch-time. Nancy's letter for this week brought the news that she was going to marry Clifford quite soon. Mother was bowled over by the news and called me all sorts of names for not letting her know sooner. Clifford is coming to see Father at the weekend and Dad is going to ask him gravely if he thinks he can keep her. It's going to be killing.

13 October 1941
Again an ominous date. Clifford arrived tonight to explain his financial position to Father. Then we had some supper and everything seemed to be flowing smoothly until the date was brought up. Both Nancy and Clifford want it soon, very soon; in point of fact, next week. Mother almost fainted.

22 October 1941
It's all over. The whole affair went with a decided swing and passed far too quickly. Everything passed off excellently. There was no confetti to bother Agatha, although the men hoisted Clifford on their shoulders and carried him downstairs, forgetting all about his sore leg.

Reading this diary so many years later, the obvious temptation is to assume that this was the familiar story of a wartime marriage. Two people come together and feel they have no time before the man will go away once more to put his life at risk. Soon after his visit to the Abbey Close Church of Scotland my father was indeed back on the high seas, though not before Betty Richie had sent the happy couple an ambiguous telegram reading simply: 'You have done it now.' But so little in the lives of either of my parents could be called impetuous that this single action stands out as uncharacteristic of them both. Their decision was destined, in subsequent years, radically to transform my mother's life while having remarkably little effect on my father's. You would think that two people could not meet and almost immediately mate unless it was what both of them already had in mind. But what was in my father's mind was never clear to me, and, from her own reckoning, I'm not sure it was ever apparent to my mother either. For all the ceaseless blue flimsies that passed between them while Dad was away at sea, I never read anything in either of their letters which suggested a strong bond of understanding or of passion. My father became necessary to my mother, essential even, without ever becoming adored.

I have in my possession the family Bible which Dad once gave to me, and which, in a pencilled addendum, traces our ancestry back to the Earl of Bristol in the fifteenth century. But by the time the twentieth century began, the Hares were red-brick bourgeois, living in Ilford in a by no means luxurious house, and yet still able to maintain two live-in maids. In quite ordinary streets, servants were still part of the deal. My father was the middle of three brothers, all of them short and all of them soon to be prematurely bald. Both the eldest, christened Sterika but mercifully known as Eric, and the youngest, christened Alan but condemned to be known as Bumper, had posh golf-club accents which embarrassed me when in their company, and which would later make the cinema actor Terry-Thomas sound unaffected. Some of Bumper's adventures were, by repute, not so different from those of exactly the kind of bounder and cad that unusual actor played. But my father, christened Clifford Theodore Rippon but known alternately as Bluey and as Finns, had a much less noticeable accent. He was that rare kind of Englishman who's hard to place. Probably that was because he had run away from England when in his teens. Faced with the prospect of following his father into Barclays Bank as a manager, Finns had left Chigwell School, where he told me he had spent much of his time stealing walnuts from a spreading tree, and made his way to Australia.

At some point in my childhood, Eric told me that during the First World War at St Paul's School he had played cricket, waiting each year to progress upwards. From 1914 onwards, the first XI, he said, had played in the certainty that they would then go off to the trenches. When the season resumed, the likelihood was at least four or five of the year's previous team would have been killed. It was Eric's luck to have been born in 1900, so by the time he enjoyed cricket at the highest level, the conflict was almost over, and at last, in 1918, a full team might hope to survive. When I asked him how young men were so willing to accept the certainty of their own imminent death without question, he replied, 'Nobody questioned. You played cricket knowing you were likely to die. And you accepted it. I can't explain to you. I can no longer explain to myself.'

My uncle's lasting memorial, therefore, was not to be in a cemetery at Ypres or at Thiepval, but rather in *Wisden*, where, playing for Essex as S. N. Hare, he is still credited with holding the record for a ninth-wicket partnership in first-class cricket.

For the rest of his working life, while employed by Shell, he would be allowed back from Baghdad for the summer in order to attend each of the five test matches in the company of the novelist Alec Waugh, who was Eric's rather unlikely best friend. But my father had been born six years later in 1906. His passion was not for cricket but for classical music. When I was little, he would play me Brahms, just as Brad Pitt does for his son in the Terrence Malick picture *The Tree of Life*, and tell me it was the greatest music ever written. The one thing Finns knew, even as an adolescent, was that he had been born into a country in which he did not wish to live.

When, in 1976, I directed the play *Weapons of Happiness* by Howard Brenton, I would constantly repeat to myself a favourite line, when one character says to another, 'You really are something of a perpetual absence, old man.' It stayed with me for years. I did not understand its resonance until I one day realised that the phrase 'a perpetual absence' so perfectly described my own father. Even when Finns was present, he was absent. But he was rarely present. At his best, he was attentive but opaque, happier with anecdotes than with conversation. At his frequent worst, he was self-involved and inconsiderate. Given my mother's naturally nervous disposition, nothing could have been worse for her than marrying a husband who was rarely around. He had gone to Tamworth in New South Wales to work as a jackeroo when he was still under eighteen. In his own account, he had moved from Australia to a tea plantation in Malaya – doing what, I have no idea. He never seemed particularly physical. He had entered the merchant navy, where he played reveille on the cornet every morning to wake the ship, and played again at night to put it to bed. The life suited him fine.

9

During the Second World War, merchant ships were commandeered for the national effort and used to convey troops. Dad was torpedoed twice, once in a troop ship in the Mediterranean early on in the war, and then again as part of a North Atlantic convoy. He had had to climb down nets on the side of his ship in open sea and take a rowing boat to safety. Photos of him in his pre-war freedom show him larking around in easy camaraderie with other men of his own age, standing on each other's shoulders, often near swimming pools which look like half-cut-off oil drums on the decks of ships. He smiles without a care in the world. But by the time he meets my mother, he is seen in a series of framed piano-top photos with his hat still at a jaunty angle, but with a far more serious expression. He usually has an impressive row of braid along the top pocket of his white uniform, because for the length of the war he was in the Royal Navy. At its end, he returned to merchant service, rising to become a full purser with P&O. When attending my first raunchy and foul-mouthed play *Slag* at the Hampstead Theatre Club in 1970, my mother finessed the problem of parental reaction beautifully. 'Yes, we enjoyed it, but your father, having been in the navy, probably understood more of it than I did.'

If I was conscious of wanting not to inherit my mother's timidity, then it was my father's evasiveness I recognised in myself, and also disliked. When Dad died in 1989, my mother was embarrassed by his omission of both his children from his will. I asked my sister if she had been surprised. 'Not at all,' Margaret replied, without any apparent bitterness. 'Dad was never interested in us when he was alive. Why should he be just because he's died?' Asked in 2000 by the Almeida Theatre to adapt Chekhov's 1880 ramblings, usually performed in the English-speaking theatre under the title *Platonov*, I was taken aback when I enquired what the meaning was of this strange word, Безотцовщина, by which the play was known in Russia. 'Fatherlessness,' I was told.

Margaret had been born in Paisley in 1943. After the war the family had moved down to St Leonards in East Sussex, where my father's father had also retired. St Leonards is itself a kind of adjunct of Hastings, in the same relationship as Hove is to Brighton: part but not part. The winter of 1947 was, at the time, the coldest of the century, and my mother, pregnant and alone, pulled Margaret up the steep, icy hill to 23 Dane Road. She lived with my sister on the ground floor of a high unremarkable turn-of-the-century semi-detached which had been chopped haphazardly into flats. The pocket-handkerchief garden was now in front, not behind. My mother loved to joke about the view from the kitchen sink which was nothing but a blank bottle-green wall.

Like many places in Britain after the Second World War, once the sandbags and rusting wire had been removed, St Leonards revealed itself as spectacularly run-down, a vista of crumbling brick and weeping wet windows, lashed by rain from the Channel. A sort of roiling mist seemed year-round to hold the town in its grip. The model village, the chief tourist attraction above the pier, reeked of rot and damp timber. The pier itself was a rusting wreck, occasionally painted but offering no particular attraction at its end to draw the visitor out onto its soaking splintered floorboards. The sea was, on most days, slate grey flecked with turbulent white. The immediate tide of prosperity which was in the next few decades to spread out from favoured London on the wings of colour supplements, restoring and gentrifying nearly every town and village in sight, was not destined to reach the Cinque Ports and their coastal confederation for at least sixty years, and even then intermittently. The word 'conservation' never travelled to the south coast. The Aga never took its relentless advance this far. Buildings were left standing not because they were valuable evidence of the past, but because everyone was too poor to repair them. If you visit Hastings, St Leonards and Bexhill today, you will find only a thin smear of trendiness – pockets of painters, architects and designers, loving the air and loving the sea, going into raptures over the choice little eruptions of modernist architecture – laid over a respectable poverty which has persisted alarmingly. The period costume designer Shirley Russell told me she weekended in Bexhill because the posthumous throw-outs at jumble sales were the cheapest and most dated in the country. There was nothing more artistically opportune for Shirley than a Bexhill death. The average age of the inhabitants of these three towns is still stubbornly high.

I cannot now imagine what it was like for my mother, with one daughter born and a son on the way, to be transplanted from a sheltered upbringing to a town where she knew almost no one, where most people were far older than her, and to be expected henceforth to bear all the burden of family alone. My father had been behaving as sailors do, and conducting an on-board affair with a woman none of us ever met. My sister had even been warned by Mum to ready herself for divorce. One of the nuns at Margaret's Anglican convent school took care to instruct all the girls to do everything they could to keep their parents together. This was advice which, even at the time, Margaret thought particularly pointless to an eight-year-old child. What on earth was she meant to do? Scream?

I don't even know if my father was around when I was born at the Briars Nursing Home, a Gothic Victorian pile, in 1947.

On the very same day, 5 June, the Americans announced the Marshall plan, making me, as so many others, a child of enlightened post-war European reconstruction. I have a clear memory of being pushed around in an enormous blue pram, and I am able to date everything that happened to me in St Leonards by knowing that we moved five miles along the coast to Bexhill in 1952. We did once possess lurid colour film taken on my father's 8 mm camera of Margaret and me playing outside our flat. I can see the images now – Margaret in a candy-striped school dress, the colour of seaside rock, and me in baggy grey worsted shorts, playing with a couple of Polish twins whose oddly spoken refugee father every day wore the same heavy blue striped suit and pebble glasses over his scarecrow figure. I couldn't understand a word he said. Here was a man – there were many such in my youth – who would carry evidence of the war with him for the rest of his life. But some time in the 1970s, just at the point when it might have been possible to transfer such indelible primary images to video tape, my father, retired and finally living at home, with no warning, destroyed them. 'I thought I'd clear out the attic,' he said, telling us proudly that he had also gone on to destroy every Dinky toy, puppet, board game, rail-track and piece of writing from our childhoods. 'I didn't think you'd want them.'

I saw my paternal grandfather, Alan Hare, who lived a mile away, only when we went there for tea on Sundays. In his thick chalk-striped suit, watch-chain in place, hearing aid up to full, he seemed kindly enough, and keen to teach me the game of cribbage, which involved moving the matchsticks he had used to light his pipe up and down a board of holes, while his wife, Rose, in cloche hat and beige stockings, served us tea. I felt I had a reasonable grasp of the procedures. It was only when I was in my teens that my mother asked me if I had never been suspicious about the fact that my grandfather won every week. I told her that I had always assumed he was better at the game than a four-year-old. 'No,' my mother said. 'He cheated.'

As an adolescent it amazed me that a grown man could derive any emotional satisfaction from beating a child at cribbage, and what's more, by doing so dishonestly. Childhood is like going into the jungle without knowing what animals you will meet there. Evolution may have given you some elementary sense to recognise a leopard as a leopard, and a snake as a snake. But recognising dangerous animals is very different from knowing how they're going to behave. Only experience teaches you that. As a child you're at everyone's mercy.

The routine of the early years was established. My father's voyages, though irregular, took up eleven months of the year. So for that time, he would be away, sailing through the Suez canal, to Aden, to Bombay, to Fremantle and thence to Sydney, on a liner called the SS *Mooltan*. While he was at sea, we lived austerely, my mother scrimping on a budget and reminding us every day of what we could not afford. She was what's called a good plain cook, salad being at all times undressed, and meat unsauced. There were a lot of stovie potatoes. When my father's ship returned to Tilbury, Mum would disappear for a couple of days' decompression without us, and then reappear with my freshly suntanned father, who would unroll a rubber band of copious five-pound notes – he preferred to carry cash – and take us for unimagined treats. He would rub his hands together as he ordered rump steak for us all in the Greek-Cypriot Star Café on the seafront in Hastings. He would divert us with stories of the cabaret singers he had seen on his travels. He took particular pleasure in tall dusky women like Kay Starr and

Lena Horne, all of whom sang hip music in a low range. Margaret and I were expected to bask in his largesse. We were all too aware that his abundance contrasted with the life he left us all to lead in his absence. Eleven months of austerity yielded to one month of razzmatazz.

The most exhilarating moments came when the boat was in dry dock, and Dad would summon the whole family up for a few days' visit on board, while he carried out some practical duties as purser. For years, ships like this had serviced the empire, conveying generations of administrators and cricketers to far-flung places. Way into the 1960s they served as the last remaining islands of nineteenth-century British snobbery: deck quoits and dressing for dinner. My sister and I were suitably awed when we were told that on every voyage there were eight chefs from Goa with no other job but to cook curry. My father had a dedicated servant from the same Portuguese part of India. Fernandez was an elegant sweet-natured man, in white jacket and dark trousers. He spent an astonishing amount of his time on his knees on the thick carpet either unlacing my father's shoes or polishing them. Conversation with him was conducted entirely in pidgin. 'You go getty my shoes, me wanty quick,' Dad would say, and off Fernandez would run. One exchange, when my father was dissatisfied with the meal put before us, seemed especially memorable. 'Me wanty curry hot. Me no wanty spicy hot, me wanty heated hot.' 'Yessir, me getty hot hot, not spicy hot.' The two of them could carry on in this vein for hours.

The ship, huge and mysterious, allowed me to indulge my favourite pastime of getting lost. SS *Mooltan* had been built by Harland and Wolff in 1923. It weighed twenty thousand tons and carried over a thousand passengers. All the furniture was ridiculously weighty, in order to cope with the swell. The floral-patterned plump armchairs were attached to the floor with metal hooks and eyes. It took all a child's strength to open a connecting door before it slammed back to secure the long corridors. Even the sight of the vast, empty dining room, in which, my father assured me, passengers were free, if they so wished, to order roast beef, eggs and lobster for breakfast, fired up my idea of what it might one day be like to be adult. I was unhealthily driven by fantasy. Alone at night, I would imitate my father, standing with a glass in my hand and demanding another pink gin and a fresh packet of Senior Service. Miming furiously I would say out loud, 'I'll have one more cigarette, I think, before I go to bed.' The chance to run around empty decks and break into cabins to test out luxurious sheets and eiderdowns gave my imagination a free playground more lavish than anything I knew at home. I came to know the ship inside out and to love it for its unbridled sense of adulthood. Nothing yet intimated to me that I would never take a sea voyage in my life.

Something of my father's attitude to me crystallised on the morning of my fifth birthday. With his sailing dates a lottery, it was rare for him to be around on this, for me, the most important day of the year. Just before breakfast, he got up, put my mother on the back of his Vespa and told me that they would not be staying for the day itself because they were going scootering in northern France. My sister and I could stay home and our grandmother could look after us. He said they had thought of warning me in advance that they were going to be away for the big day, but had decided it would be less hurtful to get up, give me a present and leave. The shock, he said, would be less. My mother was definitely ashamed, my father not. Before they disappeared off into the distance, Dad presented the clinching argument. 'It was much the most convenient day for me.'

A wiser child would have protected himself by adjusting his needs. But for a long time I allowed my father's absence of interest in me to determine my own emotional life. Another time, after a bath, when I rushed back down to kiss him goodnight, he greeted me with the words, 'Oh God, don't say that boy's out of bed again.' Unsurprisingly, I have always been resistant to literature which portrays childhood as a paradise from which we fall. My own experience suggested this view was false and sentimental. Even as a child, J. M. Barrie and Lewis Carroll meant nothing to me, and they mean less today. *Swallows and Amazons* was anathema. I have been Hobbit-hating from Day One. I never bothered myself with film or theatre specifically aimed at children. Even in Bexhill I had discerned that, as a child, things not intended for you are much more rewarding than things that are. So what if you don't understand them? That's how you learn. Although I could hardly have articulated it, nor still less known what lay ahead, I had begun to suspect that a child's radar was often sharper than an adult's, principally, it turns out, because the child lacks the equipment to process the information from that radar. For me, childhood is not defined by innocence but by bewilderment. I remember thinking all the time, 'Someone tell me what's going on.' How could I know what I was meant to do, when I had no clue what anyone else was up to?

In 1952 we made our move out of the flat in St Leonards and into the leafy semi-detached in Bexhill, a town which was later improbably used by Alfonso Cuarón as the last location for those surviving Armageddon in a film called *Children of Men*. My sister has always suspected our parents went there in order to cement their marriage, to make sure there was an investment which together they would have an interest in protecting. They chose a street which backed onto the Downs, and in which everyone lived in houses all constructed by the same local builder. It was almost a parody of suburbia, and, like new suburbanites seeking to pass a national examination, we bought a television set in time for numbers of neighbours to come round to see the Coronation of Queen Elizabeth II in black and white on a tiny screen in the corner of what seems also, in retrospect, to have been a tiny living room. Our house was packed with people staring at a snowy blizzard of imperial imagery, cooked up by Victorians and clothed in music and drapery to suggest a seamlessness in history which the real thing lacks. Peanuts were passed round all day, alongside the filter-tipped cigarettes which my mother favoured but never inhaled. These cigarettes were retrieved from individual pipe-shaped containers within a revolving silver globe, representing the shape of the world. When, in the 1980s, well-born intellectuals deployed the word 'suburban' as a term of abuse against Margaret Thatcher, I always bridled. I thought there were a thousand reasons to oppose our most self-admiring prime minister, but not for her background. That background was not so different from my own.

How do I begin to explain the level of repression obtaining in Newlands Avenue, where to hang your washing out on a Sunday or to fail to polish your car on a Saturday invited – well, what? The opprobrium of your neighbours? Or maybe just the imagined opprobrium, which could well, in the latent hysteria of the silent street, be twice as bad? What exactly was everyone frightened of? As an adult, reading Kenneth Tynan's diaries, I came across his characterisation of the craven drama critic of the *Sunday Telegraph*, John Gross, whom he described as seeming 'to be in fear of being blackballed from some nameless club of which all aspired to be members'. That phrase 'nameless club'

shocked me to my roots, because it so described the threat hanging over the life we had known in Bexhill-on-Sea. James Agate
had once summed Bexhill up as 'bleak and purse-proud'. That's
how it was. It was not a particularly Masonic town, and it had
no dominant institutions. The churches and the golf club did
not seem powerful, nor did the Rotarians and Past Rotarians
hold the town in an iron grip. You couldn't even say there was
a strong social hierarchy or clique, a group of favoured names
who held sway. If there were aristocrats, we never met them.
But nevertheless somehow everyone in the town of twenty-
four thousand white people and one black knew full well by
messages which came only through the air that you might be
damned if you broke the rules. Worse, you might be doubly
damned because you never knew the rules in the first place.

So much, clearly, was to do with sex. How could it not be?
The popular injunction 'Be Yourself' which was to take hold
so completely in the next fifty years would have been meaningless to a majority of the British population in the 1950s. Be
what exactly? On the other side of our semi-detached, 32 Newlands Avenue beside our 34, lived the Yearwood family, Tim,
Sheila and their son Michael, almost my sister's age, who in
their impeccable integration into the morals and manners of the
town seemed to offer some sort of implicit rebuke to all around,
and to us in particular. Sheila, younger than Mum, had been her
petty officer in the WRNS, and it was Sheila who had alerted
the Hares to the vacancy next door. Tim was a snifty solicitor,
at the heart of the town's life, a Freemason and a member of
what in another age was called the Quality. Barbados-born,
Tim had fenced for his university and landed in France with
the Royal Artillery just after D-Day. His well-creased cavalry
twills and weekly game off the back tee with other professional

worthies – 'Straight down the middle, Tim!' – suggested a level of acceptability to which we could only aspire. Sheila, pearls in place round her cashmere sweater, was the daughter of cockneys, and, like my own parents, in a marriage which had only happened because of the war. Sheila ran family life so that the breakfast table was set immediately after the evening meal, in order that everything might be there, waiting, when the family woke punctually at seven. The marmalade, even, had its own lacy cloth with beads, a sort of yarmulke of gentility. Michael himself, pale-skinned and geeky, was for the next fifteen years presented to me and my sister as the exemplar of all we failed to be: studious, hard-working, polite and serious in his dedication to scholarship and discreet advancement. Sheila unfailingly took to her bed every afternoon for a few hours in order to recover from goodness knows what.

Two sides of a semi-detached invite comparison – both sides are hyper-conscious of the other – and it would be fair to say that for many years the Hares defined ourselves by our proximity to the Yearwoods. They became the standard, and we became the satirical failures. Try as we might, we could not live in the orderly manner of our neighbours. Though to their face my mother showed nothing but friendship and respect, though in her heart she craved for nothing but to be accepted by Tim and Sheila, it was to her credit that, when confiding in Margaret and me, she seemed to take a certain kind of raffish pleasure in our supposed social shortcomings. We were not as posh as the Yearwoods – you could tell that as much from our rickety furniture and from our kitsch oriental paintings as from our naked marmalade tops – and that was fine. But we were clearly posher than the Richfords who lived two doors down in – horror! – a bungalow.

The gradations of class grip early and they grip absolutely. You could not exist in this order without knowing your place in it. I was best friends with Michael Richford – it was he who was with me when together we encountered our first paedophile – but the details of our schooling were different. Private education was Bexhill's principal industry. In the twentieth century there were four hundred schools in the town at one time or another, some up for a few years, some longer. Every rambling red-brick mansion with grounds was turned into a preparatory school, and staffed by ex-military personnel whose wars had not gone entirely to plan. First I was sent off to be one of the very few boys allowed at St Francis, a hitherto all-girls' school in West Down Road which boasted an entrance through a mock-medieval castle keep. It was known informally as Fanny's Fortress, in honour of the headmistress, Fanny Fulford. My sister was there, much more senior, and the young Julie Christie, having been dumped by her parents in India on the south coast, was already attracting, in her teens, a certain amount of attention. But soon enough I was moved out of kindergarten and on to Pendragon, a wacky operation down Cantelupe Road, a pleasant residential avenue somewhere between the promenade and the railway station. Pendragon was run by a teacher called Alec Everett who, graffiti in my *Kennedy's Latin Primer* informed me when I turned the flyleaf on my first day in the building, was known to be the owner of 'a great fat steaming cock'.

Mr Everett, in his thirties, in fact lived with a young American friend in the residential part of the school, in a forbidden flat into which we never saw at the end of a classroom corridor. The headmaster went out to get Smarties or jelly babies for his protégé most afternoons, some time after lunch. The blond lounged around doing nothing in canary-yellow crew-neck pullovers, like a useless young man in a Terence Rattigan play. But because Mr Everett wore a blue blazer and flannels and spoke with an impeccably cultured accent, and because he drilled learning into the boys with ruthless efficiency, he was held to be respectable by all the parents, who, to a man and woman, admired him beyond suspicion. The best place to hide is in plain view. Mr Everett was, like most of his class and generation, a disciplinarian, insisting that every boy in school sit on his hands for a whole afternoon until an individual owned up to having left chewing gum under a seat. I learned that the only collective thing people in Bexhill admired was collective punishment. But Mr Everett also drew to him exceptional teachers, so that at the age of seven I was being taught piano by Philip Ledger, a myopic, gentle soul who tried not to wince as I played. 'Try again,' he would say, taking his glasses off, as if cleaning them might somehow polish up my appalling technique. 'Try and play better.' He had already established the connections with Benjamin Britten and with Peter Pears which would one day see him become Director of the Aldeburgh Festival.

My mother was meanwhile gravitating to what would today be called the Scottish community, but which was then thought of as a few stubborn and strongly accented expatriates who happened to have migrated south to Bexhill, and who still wore tartan scarves and waistcoats. On Monday they all received the previous day's copies of the *Sunday Post*. This Scottish newspaper celebrated the home country in sugar-overloaded tones which suited the toffee fudge, tablet and peanut brittle they all liked to eat. They would gather annually for a haggis dinner, and to recite Burns. Weekly, they would meet to dance Highland reels. My mother's most prized records were by Jimmy

Shand and his Band, and she had once met Kenneth McKellar, who, she told me, was a very nice man. I was dragged along to take part in the classes from an early age but unfortunately the white-haired enthusiast in charge of putting the gramophone records on suffered from Parkinson's, which meant that a jumping needle got each dance off to an uncertain start. But if Mum's Scottish identity remained important to her – it defined her, it made her feel she belonged somewhere – so too was her continuing interest in the stage. Mum soon found herself helping out, teaching Scottish accents, sometimes to professionals, at the Thalia School of Drama, a parking spot for tots and aspirants in London Road, ruled over by the formidable Christine Porch, and by Isobel Overton, a markedly intellectual young woman in billowing skirts and gold glasses, who would later publish a book of letters entitled *A Canadian in Love*, and after whom the theatre on the campus of the University of Toronto is now named. Mum went on to appear as a footman, dressed in what looked like a pair of red velvet curtains, saggy round the knee, in amateur Molière. She held one side of the double doors open for Julie Christie to burst through as the soubrette.

I was two years at Pendragon before Mr Everett left. He fled town in the manner of schoolmasters at that time, without notice and for no given reason. My mother did not take to the new owner of the premises, a diminutive man with a thin moustache. She told me there was something 'not right' about him. In that at least, she was correct. There is today a lively internet thread dedicated to his abuses from fifty years ago. And so the decision was made, probably at the Yearwoods' suggestion, to send me instead to what was said to be a more reputable institution on the smarter side of town. Its most famous old boy was Reginald Maudling, a gruesome sort of Conservative archetype, who was to fail as Chancellor of the Exchequer – it was he who left his Labour successor a note about the economy reading 'Good luck old cock, sorry to leave it in such a mess' – before being bought off by the fraudster John Poulson and dying of alcoholic poisoning in 1979.

Harewood was also, by chance, the school which had originally spawned Pendragon. In the early 1950s the Reverend Woodruff had been dismissed as headmaster of Harewood for gross indecency. In the wake of the scandal, Mr Everett had left his teaching job at Harewood in order to tempt angry parents to put their boys in a completely new school, Pendragon. Now, in a backward twist of fortune, I was to return to the mother ship.

2

Mignon

Harewood was set in fabulous grounds in Collington Avenue with its own cricket and football pitches, and only shamed by its immediate proximity to Normandale, an even better endowed building whose bronzed headmaster, Mr Palmer, spent most of the day and a good part of his nights, pipe clamped between teeth, driving his state-of-the-art petrol lawn mower over his velvet turf. His Christmas card portrayed him on his machine. By contrast, our own red-haired head, Michael Phillips, spent his day in a torment of self-feeding ill temper, clawing compulsively at his crotch and driven mad, it seemed, by his pupils, his staff, his wife, his children, the workers, General Gamal Abdel Nasser, and the general state of disrespect towards entrepreneurs and educators like himself. I remember him standing in the school corridor, dealing with some ungovernable itch deep inside his trousers, while at the same time brandishing a Beaverbrook newspaper and fulminating to a sympathetic Mr Mulvihill and Mr Morgan about how Frank Cousins and the trade unions ran the country unopposed. Fifty years later, he was to send me for my professional advice his film script drawing an analogy between the EU bureaucrats in Brussels who had de-manned our native isle and the conquest of Britain by William and the Normans in 1066. Would I be willing, he asked, to help him get it made?

My new school, it turned out, was savage, a place where

teacher-on-pupil violence was as common as pupil-on-pupil. From the perspective of the twenty-first century, Harewood, with masters twisting ears and whacking skulls, feels far closer to Dickens than to how we live now. Most of us were day boys, but the ethic, like the luridly striped green and red blazer, was that of a traditional boarding school. After tea, as we returned to our classrooms, there was an ominous silence each day. Some small boy was put on lookout in the corridor while inside the classroom, on the dusty wooden floor, one of the new boys was laid out, his trousers pulled down and his forked nakedness exposed to the screams and derisive laughter of forty or fifty older pupils. You could choose to fight back or not. The purpose for each newcomer was not simply to humiliate you, not simply to introduce you to the idea of visceral male force, but also to classify you into one of two teams, in which you remained for the rest of your days at the school. A foreskin or the absence of it marked you out as a Cavalier or as a Roundhead. At that time I did not even know there had been a civil war in England, let alone what its political intricacies might have been, so the terms meant nothing to me. Nor had I thought to begin the unhappy business of dividing my peers into friends and enemies. That came later. A couple of weeks after my own initiation rite – my trousers and underpants had been round my knees, my thighs scratched from the nails in the floor – an older boy called Hugh Bishop gravely informed me that in life it was better to be a Cavalier. They were carefree and happy-go-lucky, whereas Roundheads were dour and humourless. But at Harewood, Hugh said, it was better to be a Roundhead. They were more powerful, and larger in numbers.

Even this slight migration from chaotic Pendragon to regimented Harewood – from outside to inside, as it were – brought out in me, no doubt inevitably, a repellent consciousness of class status. Meeting my friend Michael Richford on the Downs one evening on my way home from Harewood, I remarked that my father had recently bought a Vauxhall Cresta, a car whose chrome bumpers and giant tailfins were the justifiable envy of all. On his rare visits home Dad was taking us motoring on Sunday afternoons for teas with meringues, sandwiches and éclairs down what Mum called 'leafy lanes' to far-flung Sussex villages. That was the kind of life we lived. Whereas, I said, everyone knew that the Richfords did not have a car because they could not afford one.

I went home like an animal that has swallowed another, sated by this rodomontade but expecting no consequences. At seven the Richfords rang. I was in my dressing gown when they appeared at the door in person at eight. Mr and Mrs Richford came into our living room and sat down – a full entry not lightly undertaken in Newlands Avenue. They wanted to make clear in person, they said, that their decision not to have a car was a choice. It was most definitely not, they said, because of any economic problem, but simply, they said, a question of how they preferred to live. The idea that they did not have enough money to buy a car was pure slander. In the circumstances, it was impossible, they said, that Michael and I could continue to be friends. I had, they insisted, unintentionally revealed my true feelings towards the whole Richford family. From now on, they said, no Hare or Richford was ever to speak to one another.

Unpleasant incidents like these were, in a sense, red days in Bexhill's calendar. They were the moments at which the gears of class crashed and the engine jerked to a halt. The unspoken finally became spoken. There were such feuds and long, unreasoning silences all over town. I say this not to excuse my loathsome behaviour. Nothing could do that. Among other things, I was a nasty little boy. But it was also odd to live in an atmosphere where nobody really could speak about anything very much. My uncle Alan, who as a young man and shining rugby player had been Aunt Peggy's perfect Glasgow University groom, turned up around this same time in Newlands Avenue with two Paris prostitutes whom he had just smuggled across the Channel in the boot of his car. He had fallen from being a prosperous doctor to recently being struck off the medical register for supplying drugs to whores. Between Dover and Bexhill he had moved both the girls into the back seat, and at this point he unloaded them, unlikely arrivals on a hitherto entirely respectable pavement. Margaret and I watched from upstairs windows as Alan led them, chattering happily, down the short pathway to our front door. The six of us ate a cheerful lunch, in which conversation flowed freely in two languages, without any of us making the slightest reference to the oddness of the situation, in spite of the added fact that my uncle was incapably drunk. When he staggered back into the car to resume what would presumably be a terrifying journey back to London, nothing was said. I do remember asking who on earth my uncle's friends were, and, as usual, receiving no answer.

The 1950s began as a period of political stasis, at least as experienced by the young. If, as Doris Lessing was later to claim, Earls Court was jumping, Bexhill, like large swathes of the country, seemed to be in a sort of dormitory coma, as though John Wyndham's triffids had just passed through and stunned the population. No sound was heard, except the tomatoes liquefying on the vine or the chickens adjusting their snooze-position in the straw. Even the cawing seagulls seemed stunned into silence after lunch. Down by the English Channel you could still go shrimping in the rock pools and come home with small fry admittedly, but fry nevertheless. Mum regularly bought Sussex dabs, a delicious kind of diminutive lemon sole, from the fisherman who sold them each morning on the beach. She made sure to clean the house first before the cleaning lady came, lest we be thought dirty. In our house we read the *Daily Express*, and it presented, in particular through its cartoons, a continuing view of white England in which nothing much was allowed to change. A featureless strip on the back page called *The Gambols* portrayed an archetypally uninteresting family which, I felt, resembled my own more closely than the characters created by the anarchic Giles. But then in 1956 the Suez crisis impinged even on a nine-year-old. There was in adults' conversation the turbulence of a real event, and one briefly disastrous for the Hares. The SS *Mooltan* was once more called into service by the Royal Navy to ferry troops down towards Aden. In the wake of the self-inflicted humiliation caused by a trumped-up invasion of the canal, the popular press was in a posturing bad temper, looking for scapegoats, and in particular for anyone who did wrong by 'our boys'. There had been some terrible failure of hygiene in the ship's fabled kitchen which had precipitated a mass outbreak of food poisoning among the ranks. Forewarned, my mother returned ashen from the paper shop. On the front page of the *Daily Sketch* was a characteristically enigmatic picture of my father, in uniform, apparently at ease in his floral armchair. A screaming headline provided the exact charge: 'The Man Who Served Our Troops Soapy Potatoes'.

Such public visibility clearly violated our family ethic. It was at the very centre of my mother's beliefs that you should under no circumstances do anything to draw attention to yourself. Scottish, she had a stubborn faith in education – a faith to which I owe a large part of my subsequent prosperity – but for her the purpose of education was to burrow your way more successfully to a place of absolute security. Meaning, privacy. The front page of the *Daily Sketch* was no such place, even if, luckily, fellow members of the Highwoods Golf Club and Mum's bridge partners were unlikely to take that particular paper. When I chose to become a playwright, it seemed to Mum like a tempting of the gods. It could only end badly. Why would any member of a family dedicated to survival choose to do anything so conspicuous? Life was dangerous enough even if you kept your head down. Why on earth would you stick it up? 'I see Bernard Levin's attacking you again,' she would say to me over and over in later life, as though it were my fault. 'He really doesn't like you, does he?' 'No, Mum, he doesn't.' 'What did you do to him?'

My father was continuing to visit for at least four weeks a year, unloading whole frozen New Zealand lambs and small plastic pots of papaya, lychees and pineapple which he had acquired as some sort of kickback for his huge shipboard purchases. While in the UK, he traded frequently with a chain-smoking woman called Grace who lived in the Dorchester, dealing in fruit and vegetables from Covent Garden. She wore black sequinned numbers cut low across the powdered bosom, and croaked out suspiciously hearty laughter at all Dad's jokes. He also brought crackerballs, little exploding fireworks from Hong Kong which made me briefly popular at school. Occasionally one of my family would wind up the clockwork ballerina who danced inside a bottle of gold glitter-filled Bols gin, placed on the sideboard to remind us of the donor's existence. But Dad was actually on one of his rare visits home, and quite as surprised as my mother, when the headmaster called them in to the school. Naturally, they were apprehensive. Instead Mr Phillips asked them whether they realised that they had an unusually clever son. One day, he said, I might gain a scholarship to a public school. Since they themselves, one out of indifference, the other out of nervousness, had never dared to detect any particular aptitude in me, they were taken aback. They had rather tended to credit my grandmother's view that I was soft in the head. Meanwhile, my sister was sent off to Bexhill Grammar, where the syllabus included compulsory home economics, i.e. cooking. Margaret was dispatched there in spite of my mother's misgivings that the local school might have an unfortunate effect on her accent. In their view, Margaret could only reasonably aspire to be a secretary, or, at a pinch, a teacher. It was part of the ethos of Bexhill that you might get away with having one clever child, but to claim to have two would have been classed as showing off. Margaret would go on to collect a postgraduate science degree from London University and make her life as a patent lawyer. But for now, the far more important priority, to a certain amount of resentment from the daughter, was to smooth the passage of the son.

I cannot say I felt any crushing pressure of expectation. I was that lucky kind of boy who enjoys learning. I particularly enjoyed being taught by John G——, a charismatic musician who had recently come out of the army in Egypt in his early twenties. He had spent his National Service playing in a military band. He had an unusual approach to his job, often beginning French lessons by reading out that day's editorial from the *Daily Telegraph* on the grounds that it was a model of how we might one day wish to write English. My best friend was a boy of my own age, Keith Lamdin, who was to provide the first of my many friendships with the kind of cheerful, capable people who find life easy – among my favourite companions at all times. Mr G—— was assumed by the whole class to be in love with Keith. We took it for granted. The signs were unmistakeable. He returned Keith's homework with tousled, blushing violence, often throwing the deep-hued book through the air in his direction while telling him he was lazy and a disgrace, but in such a way that the whole class knew it was an act.

Many of the teachers at all my schools had chosen their profession for a reason. They wanted to pass the whole day in the company of young boys. While most of the prep-school masters, untrained and washed up from the war, wished us no harm, there was nevertheless in the very intensity of psychological game-playing between boys and masters the possibility that their sexual gaskets would one day blow. One popular teacher at Harewood did indeed find the pressure intolerable, stepping dramatically forward and pulling the towel off some tiny boy after a shower. For this he was quickly dismissed. To call such tortured and impossibly unhappy souls paedophiles is to make them sound predatory. At the time, they just felt like landmines you must step around.

John G—— was everything schoolboys most enjoy – wild, unpredictable and easy to imitate. His shockingly bad teeth were stained deep brown by the constant cigarettes which left strands of tobacco on his lips. He loved telling our class, presumably following Jean Brodie, that Form 2A were special, and that he expected us therefore to behave as if we knew it. He drove up each morning in a green pre-war Austin 7 with ill-fitting plastic windows, and then, thick shock of curly hair to the fore, he swept past the eager young art mistress, Yvonne Soundy, and the sweet young matron, Miss Homer, who both coloured at his very presence, before he presented himself to us in a force field of unprompted quotations from Dylan Thomas.

It was therefore an astonishment to me, when, out of the blue, one of my regular French essays was returned with a single word written at the bottom next to the mark, nine out of ten. The word – in red ink, I can see it clearly – was '*Mignon*'. It had then been crossed out, but lightly, so that it was still visible. Since I had no idea what this judgement meant, I had to go home to consult a dictionary. I remember when I first saw the translation I thought there had been some mistake. But no, there it was. I looked several times. '*Mignon*'. 'Darling'.

I had a feeling akin to stepping into a lift shaft. I felt myself travelling to the heart of childhood. Looking at the word '*Mignon*' and at the scratching-out confirmed what I had always suspected. Irrational, adults were in the grip of strong and uncontrollable feelings which, under impossible pressure, might occasionally erupt and which mere children could not hope either to foresee or to understand. Me? He thought me '*Mignon*'? Or was it just my French? I had been at Harewood for a couple of years, I was probably eleven. I did not mention the exercise book and nor did he. But soon after, Mr G—— was ill, with nothing more serious than bronchitis. The message came that he would like a sickbed visit. His younger brother led me up to his bedroom, in a large Victorian house in Bexhill Old Town. John was lying in pyjamas in the bed, reading the paper, and with a big circular tin of fifty Players untipped cigarettes within easy reach. He hugged me at once, drawing me to him. He hugged me harder than anyone had hugged me in my life. He told me how much it meant to him that I had come to see him. But, at some deeper level, I felt completely safe. This man needed me. He had profound emotional needs which were very important to him. But even then I felt a flood of relief when I sensed that these needs were not going to be overtly sexual.

We began a programme of cultural education. I had already acquired a strong taste for the cinema, lapping up with delight all the mythologising films which insisted the British had fought the Second World War with unfailing grit and courage. There was a great deal of bobbing about in small boats full of actors with boot black on their faces and woollen hats pulled over their brows. The murky tanks at Shepperton were built for heroes. I identified more strongly with the impossibly glamorous Dirk Bogarde as the medical student Simon Sparrow in the *Doctor . . .* films, sweeping round the wards of grateful patients and getting to kiss nurses. But Mr G—— started taking me, after school, to a far more diverse programme of concerts, films and plays.

At the time there was a repertory company permanently resident at the De La Warr Pavilion, a badly maintained modernist building designed in 1935 by Serge Chermayeff and Erich Mendelsohn, the latter a Jewish refugee from Nazism who had been taken up by the English aristocracy. A second company played Devonshire Gardens during the summer season. In 1957, the company presented a total of forty-seven plays – over twice as many as now offered annually by our National Theatre. From time to time their undemanding repertory of thrillers, light comedies and farces was stretched to include work by Anouilh, Sheridan, Wilde, Maugham, J. B. Priestley, Arthur Miller, Ugo Betti and Graham Greene. Both theatres had ashtrays on every seat so any children attending could complete a full day's passive smoking. The Penguin Players were run by a married couple, Richard Burnett and Peggy Paige, while their juvenile leads, Vilma Hollingbery and Michael Napier Brown, also shared a bed. Even Donald Wolfit and his wife Rosalind Iden came visiting with a Shakespearian programme which ended ominously with the ham actor threatening to reward our response by doing the whole thing again. 'But Time, the great master, calls,' he added, to the relief of all. For music, we could go to concerts in the White Rock Pavilion in Hastings. For films, there was a choice of three cinemas in Bexhill, and a further five within a few miles.

John had a deeply romantic view of art. It was about access to massive, mysterious forces, it was about greatness. But he also had a *faiblesse*, which I shared, for all the hick little black-and-white comedies, a lot of them starring Peter Sellers, which presented adult Britons as petty, posturing and ridiculous. The only response any halfway sensitive person could have to British life in the 1950s was to laugh at it. Meanwhile, a lot of the stuff we saw from the Penguins, he told me, was not very good. This was a weekly rep, after all. Rehearsals were just line-learning. The actors provided their own costumes from a travelling trunk which had to include dinner dress and a police uniform. But Mr G—— also told me that you could sometimes learn as much from bad theatre as from good. I had no intimation that this was a proposition I would test to destruction in the coming years.

This period of my life probably lasted a few months, and made me uneasy. It was clear to other boys at school that Mr G—— had moved his attentions to me, and the response was a mixture of mockery and jealousy. Keith Lamdin, on the other hand, was glowing with relief that the spotlight was no longer on him. But again, as so often in later life when I appeared in other people's eyes to be receiving more than my fair share of favours, I had no reason to be disloyal. Far from it. This man was opening my eyes and ears to all the things which were most interesting to me. Why on earth would I object to that? Each time we went out – a man in his mid-twenties accompanied by

35

a boy aged eleven – I had to ask permission from my mother, which at all times she automatically gave. The plan one Saturday afternoon was that we should drive in Mr G——'s car to Hastings to see *Our Man in Havana*, a Carol Reed picture with Alec Guinness and Noël Coward. We were both looking forward to it. But this time, when I asked her, Mum unexpectedly refused. She was standing at the sink, and I was in the kitchen behind her, when she went on to say that it was wrong for me to take so much from Mr G——. I said that there was nothing wrong in our friendship. He was simply being kind. My mother replied, in a tone which brooked no argument, 'Mr G—— has been kind enough.'

It was, you may say, a perfectly pitched Bexhill remark. It was loaded with insinuation but at the same time free of it. To this day, I can't tell whether Mum truly disapproved of my teacher's generosity – nobody should be unusually kind – or, more likely, suspected the motive for it. All I knew was that there was no way past it. It was, I think, one of only two or three times I ever heard my mother say anything which was completely final. People who rarely lay down the law have a special authority when they do. After that one sentence, there would never be any question of my going anywhere with Mr G—— again. Feelings of guilt had already consumed me when the elderly gentleman had exposed himself a couple of years earlier to me and Michael Richford. The more people reassured me that the incident was in no way my fault, the more disturbingly certain I became that it was. When a police car drew up in Newlands Avenue outside our house, and I was summoned down from my bed in my dressing gown to answer exhaustive questions, when I was given a special mug of hot chocolate and a plate of digestive biscuits, I felt, in the very lowering of everyone's voices and the elaborateness of their concern, that I was judged complicit and judged bad.

Is this why I became a Christian? I don't know. Something inside me was susceptible when I started reading the Old Testament and believed it to be true. Maybe I just inherited my mother's Presbyterian guilt about daring to exist at all. I remember weeping on my knees beside my bed in terror at some of God's bloodier threats, and believing that I fell clearly in the group singled out for eternal damnation. Fifty years later, an incumbent Archbishop of Canterbury would make me happy by praising the perceptiveness of my writing about the Church of England, but the original reason for my six adolescent years as a believer had not been at all high-minded. Simply, I was impressionable. I was vulnerable not to Christ, but to His Father. The prospect of hell seemed real.

Religion was one of the many things my mother approved of in principle, but did little about in practice. So it was at my own initiative that I started attending Sunday School at St Stephen's Church up the road, and then, more enthusiastically, Crusader class in the afternoons. There I enjoyed weekly evangelical uplift. Under Crusader auspices I could also go off to annual summer camp – white cloth tents pitched in fields twice outside Aviemore, and twice at Studland Bay in Dorset, both bracing locations well suited to lung-filling open-air hymns and frying sausages. I even once stepped forward, in a moment of miserable foolishness, at the end of a Baptist service to declare myself for Christ, à la Billy Graham. Walking home, even I apprehended that this had been an embarrassing thing to do, and I avoided the follow-up meetings which were scheduled to make sure that I would stay born again. When I was pilloried at school by a boy who claimed to have seen me coming forward,

I lied and denied it had ever happened.

The onset of religion made me sanctimonious. My insecurity, my own deep certainty that I was unlikeable, was now lacquered with a glossy layer of stupid ideology. My sister and I had a fight on the stairs at home over ownership of a Bible and I screamed at her, 'It's the word of God.' She laughed and said it wasn't one word, it was many. Religion to me was an alternative, a second life which might vitiate the pain of the first. I liked being in a relationship with Our Lord because it meant I had something which nobody else could touch. It didn't give me immunity, but it did mean that what I regarded as the dismal story of my life wasn't the only story. But piety also offered me a shield against the discomforts of class. To a group of rough boys who assaulted me on the way home from school for no other crime but going to a private establishment and wearing its distinctive blazer, I shouted again, 'Christ would be ashamed of you.' Looking back, it's hard to say who Our Lord would disown quickest in that encounter, but I would be the leading candidate. Christ would certainly have had something to say about my mother's fear of being thought common. To be fair, it grew not out of a dislike of the working class but out of a heartfelt fear of them, fuelled by so many nights as a young woman in Paisley scurrying past drunks. But considering how little money we had, and how insecure was our own social status, it's amazing that so much effort went into dissociating ourselves from manual workers. Margaret was forced to go to visit the Botwrights at No. 36 twice weekly to watch *Emergency Ward Ten*, since we were not allowed to have ITV in the house. It was vulgar. Only the BBC for us. And we were particularly forbidden to pick up penny chews and Wagon Wheels from the Cosy Café in Sea Road, a place of abundant runny egg sandwiches and steamed-up windows, which filled my mother with a horror which was all the more real for being ridiculous.

The shortage of money in our family meant that it would be essential for me to get a scholarship in order to continue in private education. As I moved past the age of ten, I began to become affected, trying out attitudes I thought fitting for advanced and superior people. My grandmother Euphemia had described football as 'eleven grown men chasing a wee bit of leather', and I reported her description to the referee one day, who looked back at me as if he had heard it all before. This contempt provided me with convenient cover for my own uselessness. I did have a brief, unlikely interest in boxing, which turned out to be one of the most practical elements of my education. The blinding shock you suffer when hit full on the nose by a boxing glove is electric. Since I possessed neither strength nor agility to avoid pain, I had instead to learn how to manage it. I found this priceless in later life. But even more useful than learning how to sustain blows was learning how to dodge them. Even today, I am expert at swerving. As the years went by, I was able to see the aggressor coming from an ever greater distance, thanks to the radar I acquired in the boxing ring. At some enduring level of consciousness, I also know that I can take the blow and survive.

For any young person, the words 'Bexhill' and 'boredom' were joined at the hip. That was what older people liked about it. I slowly became aware that adults were recovering from a traumatic event. It was called the Second World War. Whatever psychological damage it might have done was never referred to. The only available therapy was silence. The whole nation agreed that what was needed now was a bit of peace – something which Bexhill was in prime position to provide. The words 'nice' and 'quiet' were tautologous. When Marty Wilde, an insipid rocker of the mid-fifties, was scheduled to appear in a leather jacket and singing 'Teenager in Love' at the De La Warr Pavilion for one night only, the protests to the local paper briefly sprang the whole town from its deckchair. The sharp-elbowed old ladies who muscled their way to the front of the queues in Sainsbury's were in uproar against his swaying hips. But far more dangerous than Marty's moral turpitude was the fact that he dared to make a loud noise.

In Newlands Avenue, time moved achingly slowly, whole summers seeming to last a decade, no house ever changing its appearance, no inhabitant ever changing their characteristics. Everyone in the street – Sparrowhawks, Botwrights, Hares, Yearwoods or Richfords – simply continued like characters controlled by the mechanical story-book of a soap opera. They clucked with disapproval at any element of change. So it was paradoxical that, by some unlikely affinity, only the game of cricket could joyfully speed things up. Simply by walking onto a cricket field I was able to stop looking at my watch. Time used to deliquesce in the most sensual way, so that sun, grass and linseed oil would become a druggy concoction in which whole afternoons passed without noticing. I may not have been very good as either batsman or bowler, but that was not the point. Better just to linger on the boundary, and wake when it was evening. Even now, as a playwright, there is no compliment I treasure more than when an audience member remarks, 'The two hours flew by.'

In April 1956 my mother had taken me to Glyndebourne, not to the opera but to the off-season East Sussex Youth Drama competition. Among the entries was a supposedly hilarious play in which Shakespeare hid in a trunk. It was received in arctic silence. In spite of this chilling initiation into the unmistakeable sound of a flop, I had begun to have ambitions for my gallery of Pelham puppets. They were wooden-blocked characters with eight strings leading to a starfish-shaped hand control. At the suggestion of Michael Yearwood next door I helped form my first theatre company, which was called PHY, after the initials of the three puppeteers, Porch, Hare and Yearwood. Michael Yearwood's advanced tastes spurred us to attempt dramas we scarcely understood, just as he had inveigled me into the hopeless venture of trying to make pinball machines out of cardboard. Now we built a puppet theatre and painted little sets to present in our living room a version of Dorothy L. Sayers' snobbish thriller *Busman's Honeymoon*, with Lord Peter Wimsey, Harriet Vane and their devoted valet Sergeant Mervyn Bunter, who had seen his master through the horrors of shell-shock at the end of the First World War. Unfortunately, there was some complicated and unreliable string-work in the climactic murder which involved dropping a miniature flowerpot and cactus on the back of an unsuspecting puppet block-head. This rarely worked. But the ambition of staging wooden Sayers was as nothing to our next project, full-scale wooden Wilde. *The Importance of Being Earnest* was presented at the Thalia School theatre. Because we performed it at numbing length for charity, our initiative and altruism were praised in a glowing editorial in the *Bexhill Observer*. P, H and Y were, apparently, exactly the kind of young citizens Bexhill needed more of. The hopeless tangle of strings caused by trying to hand over the cucumber sandwiches in the first act was generously overlooked.

Up till then, my taste in reading had been largely for Richmal Crompton and Agatha Christie. They both cleverly appealed to a child's desire for a world more solid, more substantial than the one the child knows. But aged twelve I had taken to Oscar Wilde big-time, no doubt because of his witty outsiderism. One of the first features of the school magazine which I started with my friend Christopher Hudson was a serialisation, painfully transcribed from the original, of *The Canterville Ghost*. But our publication hit the buffers with the third issue. We had begun to go round Harewood with clipboards, doing an opinion poll to discover who was the most popular master, though most of us suspected it was the ageing and arthritic Colonel Doughty, whose idea of teaching history was to sit on the edge of his desk and recount the strategic details of various twentieth-century battles he had taken part in. News of this plan to award rankings to our teachers reached the headmaster, who reacted badly, as he did to almost everything except mass executions of trade unionists. He knew perfectly well that he was personally unlikely to excel in any such exercise.

By this time, I disliked Mr Phillips with a passion. His temper had not been improved by the events around the Suez canal, and even less by the petrol shortages that followed. A man who had divided his school into houses named after three historic British military victories, Trafalgar, Blenheim and Waterloo, was unlikely to take kindly to our government being thoroughly outwitted by socialist Egyptians. Phillips had been revealed to all his pupils as the worst kind of bully and boor, who liked to put a smiling face on for parents, while behind their backs hitting their children as often as he could. Somewhere Philip Roth argues that 'a writer *has* to be driven crazy to help him to *see*'. Well, Harewood was the experience which first drove me towards the edge. One evening, while we were all in silent ranks doing homework downstairs, we heard on the ceiling the sound of struggle from his study above us. A boy called Larkin, rather than accept some arbitrary punishment, had had the courage to take on the thirty-year-old Mr Phillips in a knock-down physical fight, man to man. After some time, Larkin, a burly lad, appeared bleeding from the nose, his shirt torn to the waist, and with blood running from scratches all the way down his chest. He moved back silently to his place and resumed his work. I have always had too easy an access to anger, but generally my aim is good, and my feeling for justice as deep on another's behalf as on my own. Larkin became not just my hero but the hero of the whole school. Mr Phillips, presumably marked from the fist-fight as Larkin was, did not appear for a day or two. Nothing further was said.

Ever the bright kid, I was taking all my learning in my stride and was untroubled by the prospect of sitting for a scholarship for Winchester. Everyone promised me that it was regarded as the most academic of Britain's private schools. Winchester did not offer its examination until the very end of the scholarship season, implicitly daring only those who thought they might succeed to pass over their chance of going to easier schools. Only one school in the country, Lancing College, was so keen to attract brains that it would hold a scholarship for a boy while he went off to sit the later exam for Winchester. So for no other reason, I was put down to try first for a school of which neither I nor my parents had ever heard. We certainly had no notion of its High Anglican traditions. Nor indeed did we know that the famous character of Lady Bracknell had originally been named Lady Lancing, and that, auspiciously, our puppet play had been redrafted many times under that title until it was eventually immortalised as *The Importance of Being Earnest*.

The night before the written exam, my mother was dangerously ill. From the room next door, I could hear the most terrible groaning and wailing, followed by her screaming, 'Don't come in, don't come in.' My sister finally disobeyed, and found her distraught. Mum had lost all balance in her inner ear, and thereby control of her bowels. A doctor was called, who was mercifully quick to diagnose, but the memory of that awful night henceforth added to her generally fraught nerves. I was supplied with a letter of explanation which was slipped in with my exam papers and sent on to Lancing. It said, 'This boy may not have done as well as expected. That's because he spent the night cleaning up his mother's bed.' Such a message might have caused suspicion among more cynical souls, but at Lancing it aroused compassion. Although I was myself biliously, rackingly sick in a ditch outside Polegate on the way to my interview, I was awarded a major scholarship.

In my last term at Harewood I was required to become a weekly boarder, in order to get into practice for leaving home. One afternoon, I malingered, faking an illness I only faintly sensed, when in fact I wanted to skip football. I was sent home, where I woke up next morning with scarlet fever. It was a satisfyingly dramatic illness, which involved high temperatures, projectile vomiting, peeling skin, complete isolation and the need, for some reason, to burn my sheets, my books and indeed anything with which I came into contact. The attempt to send me to Winchester was at once abandoned, on the grounds that I could not be expected to emerge from my fastness. The suggestion of putting Winchester exam papers under the bedroom door was vetoed on the grounds that they would be returned contagious.

So there it was. Providence.

There were two immediate effects of my being sent away thirty miles along the coast to somewhere I had no intention of going. First, it aroused in me a feeling of sustained excitement at being out in the world. This has stayed with me for the rest of my life. Although I have spent much of my time depressed, i.e. dissatisfied with myself, I have almost never been bored, i.e. dissatisfied with the world. I have never lost the feeling that my surroundings are exciting and interesting because they are part of a long journey from Bexhill's cold pebbled shore. A psychologist may feel that I went on to become a writer of fiction because my resentment of my father's absence had so strong an influence on my growing up. To me, it's likelier that my imagination was wildly overstimulated by the exceptional dullness of my early environment. In a classic provincial childhood, the writer dreams because he or she has to. There was nothing to do in Bexhill except fantasise about getting away. While I was growing up, I spent so much time longing for a place, any place, which was not where I was. But second, I was also, to my sorrow, at the age of thirteen, exiled from a life principally shaped by women. I moved out of the life I was used to, sharing everything with my mother, my sister and our Siamese cat, Susie, and into a life with 420 other boys.

For my preference for putting women's lives at the centre of my writing, I would later receive an amount of attention which often embarrassed me – attention, after all, for doing what came naturally. My first full-length play had an all-female cast, and most of the best-known leading roles I have written have been for women. For years, my name has been deployed, particularly by actresses, as a stick with which to beat other male playwrights. But in writing as I did I was merely reflecting my own temperament and upbringing. Women have remained far more present to me than men throughout my life. They shaped me. But I was also well aware, right from the 1970s, that the moment was long overdue to begin to correct a ridiculous imbalance. From the beginning I wanted to give women the play or film's point of view and not simply to imprison them as objects of manly love. How could a dramatist not want to give half their stage time to half the human race? The regular testosterone-fuelled stage revolutions of the last fifty years have left me indifferent.

I would eventually take part in a number of appropriate and timely political movements – against the American presence in Vietnam, for universal nuclear disarmament, and against the allied invasion of Iraq – even if, to my shame, I failed in the mid-1980s to recognise the historic importance of the miners' strike against the Thatcher government. With Howard Brenton, writing our newspaper satire *Pravda* in 1985, I was able to add to the gaiety of nations by warning just how completely British public life would be soiled by the lethal nihilism of Rupert Murdoch, some twenty-five years before such a view became conventional wisdom. And yet wherever I turned, I was aware that many of contemporary history's most important changes were being wrought by feminism. From the start, that feminism would inform my writing. How will we remember the late twentieth century? As a time when the role of women in the developed world, at home and at work, changed decisively. Not to reflect that would have been unthinkable.

3

Lear on the Cliff

No military plan survives first contact with the enemy. I was dropped off by my parents at Lancing in the expectation that a change in my fortunes would also bring about a change in my personality. How wrong can you be? The reason that Simon Sparrow had made such a deep impression on me in *Doctor in the House* was that he was always busy. Yes, he was humorously busy, the victim of all sorts of stumbles and mishaps. But did he ever stop to think how lucky he was to live a life which offered a steady stream of events?

At that level, things were indeed livelier at Lancing. There was more to do. A religious school was succumbing to the infection of humanism. Harold Macmillan had woken up, looked around and responded to the moral authority of independence movements in large parts of a world hitherto coloured pink. As a result, all institutions which had been founded for one purpose – the manning of the empire – were beginning to creak and groan as they adapted to a mission much less clearly defined. Christianity in England had allowed itself to be used as the ethical clothing for imperialism – we weren't abroad to conquer, oh no, we were there to convert – and it had disgraced itself by providing moral gloss to justify the slaughter of the First World War. The Second World War had postponed the crisis but not averted it.

Now, as harder questions were being asked about the character and purpose of the British Establishment, 'Service to the Community' was replacing 'Service to the Empire' as the ingratiating banner under which the public school sought to march. Anglicanism was paying the price. Culture, which had long been seen by public schools as only a tributary of religion, was, for an increasing number of boys and staff alike, coming to represent value in its own right. People of ideas were beginning to prevail over people of beliefs. The resident clergy were appropriately threatened. Although the school still had all the *Tom Brown* trappings – beatings, bullying, fagging and prefects, all the stuff of empire/religion – the newer teachers, fresh from post-war universities, were no longer recruited from the shires or the deeper recesses of *Debrett's*. So struggles of adaptation made Lancing interesting in a way that my bull-headed preparatory school had never been. The school debating society would take on subjects which were much more far-reaching than anything in today's insipid discourse. 'Should advertising be banned?', 'Should private schools be abolished?' and 'Should the church be disestablished?' were all argued with a passion that suggested that, were the motions carried, there might be a sporting chance of action. Everything, rightly or wrongly, felt as though things were in play. But unfortunately I was not, on contact with a far more stimulating prospect, turned at once into the popular chap that I had hoped. Nurture was to be no more successful at making me easy-going than nature had been.

The school was approached from a rickety toll bridge over the charmless River Adur and up a long drive. Behind lay the mud-flats of Shoreham with its perspective of massive brown-brick power stations. The flat fields were criss-crossed with freezing ditches into which you had to plunge when doing three- and five-mile runs. Looking west, the landscape was thrown out of proportion by the scale of Lancing Chapel. The

Centre Point of the South Downs, it had been flung up to a ridiculous height in fourteenth-century Gothic style by the Victorian founder, Nathaniel Woodard, who had created both school and chapel to do something about what he saw as 'the ignorance and ungodliness of the middle classes'. He made sure from the off that even if the building were incomplete in his lifetime no sensible compromise would ever be possible. The chapel was going up and no one could take it down. Howard Roark could scarcely have done better. The chapel is still three million pounds short of being finished a hundred years later, the subject of endless reconsecrations, financial appeals and changes of architectural plan. Even in its present state, without the projected 325-foot tower at its end, it is the largest school chapel in the world. Attendance for all pupils was compulsory: a service every evening at six, and on Sundays a full Sung Eucharist in the morning, followed by Evensong at night. A lone Jewish pupil was excused kneeling and praying, and allowed to sit at the back, but never excused one minute of the endless offices.

The first thing that struck you about British public schools in the 1960s was how cold and dirty they were. Nowadays education has become a commodity like any other, a place you flog rather than a place where you're flogged. Lavish brochures are mailed to prosperous addresses at home and overseas to suggest to ambitious Russians and Chinese the Sheraton-like luxury in which your child may acquire the practical knowledge to smooth his or her path to future advancement. Websites gleam with images of happy harmony. Like everything else, education is offered as a consumer deal, idealised through advertising. Come here, do well, move on. But fifty years ago schooling was neither utilitarian nor comfortable. Lancing's conditions were as austere as its purpose. A wartime ethic, both of economy and of dedication, prevailed. Detachable collars were the school's crafty way of ensuring they didn't have the expense of washing our shirts too often. There was a thick ring of grime on the fold as we threw them, three times a week, into the basket. Electric waxing machines embedded filth into the extensive parquet but rarely removed it. Any kind of snivel, wart, growth or adolescent eruption was treated by matrons with their stinking cure-all: the sloshy application of a purple antiseptic called 'gentian violet'. The overall impression was of dirty fingernails and dirty laundry. Little wonder that many of the boys were, in that evocative Australian phrase, 'on the nose'.

Lancing had its share of famous old boys and the best known was Evelyn Waugh, a devastating English stylist, who had arrived in 1917, discontent not to be somewhere more elevated. He noted that 'wind, rain and darkness possessed the place'. Waugh also observed that 'the food in Hall would have provoked mutiny in a mid-Victorian poor-house'. By 1960, little had changed. Most offensive, a sock was used nightly as a kind of primitive teabag and lowered, full of leaves, into a steaming urn. We ate a great many curried eggs, slimy fish roes, soggy toast with margarine, cold sardines and twisted slabs of rank haddock. Everything came with a crust, a skin. The weather was as filthy as the food. In particular, towards the end of 1962, a brutal winter took hold. The snow never left the ground for eight weeks. Your face ached, rigid in the icy wind, as you braced yourself turning a cloister corner. Wrapped in scarves, gloves and extra pullovers you rushed back at break to your house – mine was called Field's – in order to clamber as best you could onto the hissing radiators, or to hold white sliced bread on a toasting fork against the dimpled white elements of the communal gas fire. An industrial tin of Nescafe stood close.

To this day I can judge twenty minutes perfectly in my head to within a few seconds, thanks to the memory of that daily break.

In his letters, Graham Greene has fun with the convention that whenever he wants to make a character in one of his books dishonest or unpleasant, he makes him a graduate of Lancing College. For Greene it was a private joke, a piece of mischievous biography intended to amuse his best friend Waugh. There was, Greene claimed, a particular sort of aspiring public school which produced a young man full of facile sociability and doubtful morals. He loved stressing the word 'minor' in that resonant term 'minor public school'. Certainly at Lancing there was a definite sense of pretence, a feeling that we were in some way being asked to ape an unseen original. We had all been cast as walk-ons in a seaside repertory version of *Goodbye Mr Chips*. The bigger, more famous schools all had their eccentricities. It was therefore essential that we must have ours, including special names and conventions which made no sense outside the walls. Teachers had to be known as Tiger, Monkey or Dozy. Fags were known as underschools and lavatories were groves. Everything was in code, and the code had to be learnt. Some of the rules seemed to defy explanation. Maybe that was the point.

For me, the place was a challenge from the start. Inside the classroom, I was fine. In lessons, even with the more self-consciously eccentric teachers – teachers who loved playing up to the quirky characters long service had assigned them – there was a sort of order, a world I understood and in which I had always prospered. But outside the classroom, in the big farty dormitories of ranked beds and wanked-in handkerchiefs, I was lost. The other boys, a lot of them from Surrey, seemed to have a social ease, a basic understanding of how the world worked which I entirely lacked. The children of clergy who made up a third of the school's intake may have lagged behind in material prosperity, but they all had a sense of belonging which I could only envy. They gave the impression, false of course, that they had arrived at the school knowing each other already.

Within the first term, after a certain amount of half-arsed ridicule, I adjusted my accent. Tones which had been regarded as highfalutin in Bexhill were mocked as plebeian when aired at Lancing. My first few weeks were rough, as I struggled to smooth my own corners rather than to have them knocked off by others. I knew enough never to mention that my family lived in a semi-detached, but I also knew that the reasons for my disorientation were more than social. I didn't know what attitude to take. Did I like this place or didn't I? Harewood had been easy to deal with – a brutal and stupid school against which all self-respecting pupils rebelled. It was that simple. But Lancing was not simple.

Halfway through my first term, I realised that I would be less unhappy if I had the right friends. My motive was not snobbery but understanding. I needed sympathetic companions who might help me get some insight into how this foreign culture – part Stanley Matthews, part Benjamin Britten – worked, and where I might fit in it. The problem was, I had no idea how to acquire friends, and failing made me unhappier still. I couldn't get in with the right people, because, self-ignorant, I had no idea who the right people for me might be. This feeling persisted throughout my adolescence. In the 1980s, I would feel a strong identification with the work of John Hughes. Films like *The Breakfast Club* and *Pretty in Pink*, released for teen enjoyment, fascinated me because they detailed the agonies of social exclusion. The films were usually about girls, but my own dilemmas resonated closely enough with those of Molly Ringwald or Ally Sheedy. Everywhere at Lancing were enviable cliques of cheerful and self-confident young men, laddish in grey flannels and herringbone jackets, hands in pockets, ties casual at half-mast. I would see them lounging together, laughing in the school tuck shop, eating Flat Harrys and drinking Coke. They didn't even bother to look up before dismissing the idea of my anguished and unconvincing company out of hand. My first friend, inevitably, was the lone Jewish boy, Peter Konig, because he too was contemplating Lancing in bewilderment. At least in Konig's case there was a simple explanation – religious upbringing. In mine, what? Rank stupidity?

My housemaster was Patrick Halsey, a humane and decent man. Then in his fifties, he had been a central pillar of the school's hierarchy since before the war, when Lancing had been forced to migrate deep into the patrician country wildness of Shropshire to avoid the bombs. If Michael Phillips was the worst kind of Tory, Patrick was the best. A celibate bachelor, often come upon unexpectedly in corridors with a pipe in one hand and a glass of whisky and a copy of the *Spectator* in the other, he was married to his vocation. His quarters were immediately above his charges. He lived and slept school, leaving only occasionally between terms to visit his ageing mother in Berkhamsted. Religiously devout, he wore his love of teaching with an infectious light-heartedness which, we were told, dismayed his more pompous colleagues, especially the churchy ones, but which delighted boys. He had a weakness for practical jokes, the most obscure of which involved one night putting the whole house on alert because, he said, someone had stolen the amphetamines of a visiting monk. Since, innocents, we had no idea even what uppers were, the joke was lost on us.

Patrick was proud of having been at Eton with a fellow pupil called Lord Remnant. It seemed to him a symbolic name for a world he believed was unlikely to survive much longer. Similarly, he admired another Etonian, the future prime minister Alec Douglas-Home, for daring to admit to doing his economics with matchsticks. Patrick himself taught matchstick history. He worked within an unashamedly amateur tradition. Goaded on by a willing audience, his classes were peppered with well-loved Adolf Hitler imitations, screamed at full pitch and accompanied by elaborate foot-stamping and arm-raising. He could reel off whole speeches, often ending with his dentures becoming unfixed. The memory of them has sustained me subsequently in the darkest moments of play- and film-making. How often, in the stalls, have I muttered to myself what became in Patrick's impersonation Hitler's catchphrase, '*Meine Geduld ist zu Ende.*' My patience is at an end.

It was Patrick's personal kindness to which I clung during some desperate days of adjustment. The main highlight of my early time at the school was the obligation to write a weekly letter home. For me it was not a burden but an opportunity. I continued corresponding well into my thirties, partly because Mum was so conscious of the cost of the telephone that conversation with her was rushed and unsatisfactory, but more seriously because it was good for me to bring order to chaos. Writing to my mother offered a lifeline, a welcome chance to process my experiences and present them, not perhaps exactly as they had really happened, but in a way which might take some of the sting out. Everything was safer once it was set down. From pride, I never gave any intimation of the anguish or the loneliness. Enemies of literature will say that this is what professional writers do for a living. They seize hold of the complex reality of the world and reorder it the way they might wish it to be, rather than the way it is. My letters were not particularly interesting, nor were they well written. There was no sign of any early aptitude. It would be another ten years before, for the first time in my life, I stumbled on a gift for writing dialogue. The discovery of that gift would change my whole life. But discovery it was.

My problem for now was that at Lancing I hadn't found a role. I needed a mask to hide behind. I began to find it through my cultural journeys to London in the holidays when I would stay with my aunt Peggy, who had fallen on rough times. Before her marriage to the promising young doctor had ended unhappily, they had moved from a large house in Bath to a cramped flat above the surgery in the heart of Brixton, in which Peggy was now bringing up four children alone. My mother had been deeply unsettled when she was forced to testify as a witness to the physical damage done to Peggy by domestic violence. On more than one occasion Alan had thrown her down the stairs. But although she had so little money, Peggy treated me with extraordinary hospitality, cooking up beautiful meals of roast chicken, stuffing, gravy, peas and roast potatoes – meals on occasions more lavish than anything she was offering to her own children. 'We're having sausages.' She and they, my cousins Ann, Lindsay, Lesley and Graham, were cheerful and welcoming, a sort of second family, knocked around by ill fortune and finding good grace to survive the kind of unforeseen hardship my branch of the family had never known. Life had kicked the gentility out of them, and they seemed more robust and warmer for it.

Going warily down Landor Road after such a feast, I would catch the tube from Clapham North to the West End. I was thirteen when, alone, I saw Harold Pinter's play *The Caretaker* in its first production at the Duchess Theatre. I have a strong memory of sitting in the Upper Circle as the curtain went up and Alan Bates stood, feral, alluring, in a leather jacket, waiting to pounce, as sharp in mind as in dress. Bates was my first sighting of those dangerous young men – James Fox, David Hemmings, Terence Stamp – who by paying a British debt to Brando were, alongside their gleaming counterparts – Julie Christie, Vanessa Redgrave, Charlotte Rampling – to give the best sixties cinema its glittering edge. In the interval I looked down amazed as full afternoon tea in good china was served on trays in the stalls to patrons remaining in their seats. Had they been watching the same play as me? But at that age it made little difference what I saw. Just being in London was enough.

The mask I was reaching for, inevitably, was that of an intellectual. And I was helped in this ambition by my first real friendship with a boy from another house at school. Nigel Andrews, though from a far more confident family, spent his holidays as I did, buying cheap day returns and trailing round theatres and cinemas. Pretty quickly, we decided we might as well do it together. Often we would meet at 10 a.m. to take in an early film, then go to two plays before heading off from Victoria or Waterloo to our separate homes. If there were any spare time at all on the concourse, we would also dip into the news theatres which offered newsreels, cartoons and, best of all, Edgar Lustgarten reconstructions of famous murders, gloatingly recounted, and always ending with the resonant words, 'And then he was hanged by the neck . . . until he was dead.' For me at least, film and theatre were never fantasy. They were welcome relief from fantasy.

Although our enthusiasm was equal, our tastes were widely divergent. Nigel's passion for the 1960 film of *The Fall of the*

House of Usher with Vincent Price meant that he rushed me at the first opportunity to a morning showing of Price's *The Pit and the Pendulum* a year later, every moment of which he relished like fine wine. At fourteen, he could already discourse on the superiority of Roger Corman films to Hammer. In the evenings, he took special pleasure in watching plays with actors like Margaret Lockwood and Nigel Patrick, whose Palaeolithic creakiness held him spellbound. In between he liked to re-fuel in Wimpy Bars, where his favoured dessert was a Banana Pretty, a pastry loaded up with baby mash and synthetic cream. I, in contrast, was trying to get us, underage, into *Never on Sunday* and *La Dolce Vita*. From my standpoint, Nigel's preference for the garish over the good was perverse, but I could already feel something spontaneous and touching in his pleasure. Susan Sontag had not yet written her 'Notes on "Camp"' – 'No. 56: Camp is a *tender* feeling . . . No. 58: The ultimate camp statement: it's good *because* it's awful' – but if, for any reason, she had chosen to do her early research among Sussex schoolboys, Nigel, a pathfinder by genuine instinct not by imitation, would have been on hand to help. It would have been impossible for any of us to guess that Nigel's willingness to go into raptures about trash would later gain him sustained tenure as the chief film critic of the *Financial Times*. In those earnest times, how could anyone have imagined that it would one day be thought unexceptional for someone as clever as Nigel to spend their time writing hagiography on the films of Arnold Schwarzenegger? The post-modern revolution which would fashionably advantage the unknowing over the intentional lay a long way ahead. As a repentant Pauline Kael admitted at the end of her life, 'When we championed trash culture, we had no idea it would become the only culture.'

Following Nigel, I had the equipment and a little of the knowledge to act out a part. I was the kind of boy who woke up in the morning feeling fine. But because I had resolved to be an intellectual, I knew that the first qualification was to behave as if mornings were difficult. I would stagger out of bed as though life were a burden, in what I imagined to be the approved egg-head manner. If I had been allowed to wear dark glasses to the first lessons of the day, I would have done it like a shot. Other pupils started calling me a pseud, but being a pseud bothered me far less than being a nothing. Rather than be an individual idiot, I could be a generic idiot. It was progress. I was encouraged in this decision by the example of a new French teacher. In a school full of masters in grey turn-up flannels, leather patched jackets and panama hats, Harry Guest materialised, not long out of Cambridge. He had published Sylvia Plath and Ted Hughes in an undergraduate magazine, and was himself a practising poet in drainpipe trousers, chic button-down shirts and slim knitted ties.

With his loping walk, Harry didn't look like his colleagues and his eloquent enthusiasm for all things continental meant that he most certainly didn't sound like them either. The names coming from his lips – Rimbaud, Baudelaire, Mallarmé – were not at that time common currency in West Sussex. Nor had Lancing ever before had a master offering to host evenings of poetry and bebop with the Inigo Kilborn Quintet. Harry was also responsible for the maintenance of an Art Film Society which allowed sixth-formers to meet in the chemistry labs four times a term for the projection of films by Buñuel and D. W. Griffith. At the end of each term, I would ask Harry for a reading list, which he would set down in his immaculate handwriting. Back at home, I would lie on my bed, working my way through Forster, Balzac, Koestler, Wells, Camus and Ford Madox Ford, without understanding much of what I was reading, but aware that, come the new term, Harry would want to know what I thought of them. When, towards the end of my time at Lancing, Cyril Connolly published a list of the '100 Greatest Books of the Century' in the *Sunday Times*, I had read sixty-two. Entirely thanks to Harry.

I never felt that Harry was as keen on me as I was on him – he had favourites among boys and I was not one of them – but it never bothered me. What he was giving me was far too important for me to worry about whether my feelings were hurt in the process of getting it. A defining moment came some years on when I was in the sixth form and Harry decided with his glamorous American fiancée Lynn to give a dinner party for some pupils in his flat above a shop in Shoreham. At a certain point, Harry pulled down a book from a shelf. It was a paperback copy of *The Death of Tragedy* by George Steiner, a volume of literary criticism which was enjoying a distinct vogue. Its egregious badness seemed to consume him. 'How can anyone take this seriously?' he kept asking. I had noticed as he opened it that Harry's copy was already ominously disfigured, both with scrawling in the margin and with thick black lines through whole paragraphs of Steiner's prose. But by the time pudding came, and perhaps a certain amount of red wine had gone down, Harry was becoming more and more agitated. 'This book', Harry said, 'is taken seriously. It's taken seriously. And it's full of schoolboy howlers. Referring to Shakespeare's *King Lear*, Steiner writes of the blinded Lear standing on what he believes to be the cliffs of Dover, and falling. And yet everyone knows' – Harry climaxed with tremendous emphasis – 'everyone *knows* it was not King Lear who was blinded, it was

Gloucester. How can anyone take seriously a book which confuses King Lear with the Duke of Gloucester?' At this, Harry took the book and threw it into the wastepaper basket. At the same moment, he burst into tears.

I had seen enough to grow used to the idea that adults' passions tended to erupt unexpectedly, but never had I seen anyone driven to such lengths by a mere book. The lesson I learned that night was that, for good or ill, there were people who thought literature enormously important, as important, it seemed, as life or love. Since school I have witnessed a good few pieces of violent behaviour brought on by real or imaginary deficiencies in works of art, but I have never seen a reaction so pure and purely devoid of self-consciousness. Harry could not endure a book he thought bad.

Back at home, my parents had long realised that I had grown into a bookish adolescent, but also one who was becoming mysterious to them. I could see my father once or twice looking at me and asking himself whether I really could be his son. He was transferring to ever bigger ships, finishing up on the SS *Oriana*, which alongside the *Canberra* became the pride of the P&O fleet. But with no intimation yet of how popular cruising would become from the 1970s onwards, Dad would repeatedly tell me that aviation had destroyed the merchant navy. On no account should I consider following his trade. He had become obsessed with a full-length parody LP of *My Fair Lady*, which, with Zasu Pitts' and Reginald Gardiner's help, became *My Square Laddie*. 'I've Grown Accustomed to Her Face' became 'I'm Kinda Partial to Her Puss'. He played it every day he was home, Brahms now taking second place. As I became less fearful of his worldliness, so my relationship with Dad was heading for a crisis. It duly arrived one Christmas evening when we were seated round the table finishing turkey sandwiches. Dad was giving us the details of his latest voyage, and railing against a particular passenger whom he kept describing as a 'typical flashy Jew-boy'. He had used the word 'Jew-boy' several times before I burst, screaming semi-audibly, 'Do you have any idea how fucking offensive you're being?' and then running out of the room before I could see how much damage I had done. Inevitably, my mother was more upset than my father, who was simply puzzled. What on earth had he done wrong? But for me the moment was significant. When Dad's leave in the UK coincided with my being at school, he and my mother would still take me for roast lunch in the Old Ship Hotel in Brighton. He still rubbed his hands together as he ordered. 'And a nice Bordeaux.' But something had shifted in the balance of power between us. His indifference no longer defined me.

My political education was running alongside my cultural. Again there was a crisis of sorts, this time brought on by my sending off a postal order to the Campaign for Nuclear Disarmament to buy myself a badge. I remember the expectation of slipping it out of its tiny brown envelope and fixing the familiar symbol, designed from a combination of the semaphore flag signals for the letters N and D, proudly to my jacket. I was ordered by a prefect to take it off, an order later confirmed by a master. When I then wrote anonymously to *Peace News* to tell them that I had been prohibited from wearing evidence of my most profound beliefs at a place of learning where Christians were freely allowed to display theirs, to my amazement, the organ of the peace movement not only published my letter but also responded by offering to send down an investigative reporter to give more comprehensive coverage to this obvious outrage. It did not take long at Lancing for my anonymity to be unmasked, and I was hauled in front of the headmaster, William Gladstone. He told me I had done a very dangerous thing. It was, he said, easy to destroy a school. All you had to do was go to the North Field and set fire to the corn. With a following wind, you would soon burn down every building. It was only by the exercise of common restraint that institutions survived at all. I had abandoned that restraint.

In return, I questioned Mr Gladstone's sense of proportion. I did not think it likely that a single unsigned letter of complaint to *Peace News* had threatened the long-term future of Lancing College. But I kept my scepticism to myself. How on earth could an institution which I had imagined to be strong be revealed in its own imagination to be so weak? Previously I had assumed that authority was sure of itself. That's why it was authority. Now I could see authority was an act, a pretence. Underneath it all, its representatives were often as insecure as I was. My mother had ingrained in me the idea that we must pay particular attention to men in suits who occupied official positions. We must obey them for no other reason but that, when it comes down to it, they know and we don't. Teachers, bank managers and solicitors are to be respected and feared. But with this fatuous line of argument from an incumbent headmaster, the scales fell from my eyes. I did not become anti-authority, but I did henceforth expect authority to be able to produce convincing arguments. I remain uniquely unimpressed by men from public schools who sit across desks. Because of my own education, attempts at class bullying and blackmail by a David Cameron or a George Osborne fall flat. I am immune to the assumption of command such people adopt when they attempt their familiar trick of asking the poor to pay the bill for the rich.

My schoolboy politics were best summed up by a remark I had

memorised of Françoise Sagan's: 'In any given case of injustice, the man or woman of the right will say it's inevitable. The man of the left will say it's intolerable.' I had not been overdramatising when I had described my desire for unilateral nuclear disarmament as my most profound belief. In the 1950s and after, intelligent thinkers worried principally about the bomb and overpopulation. Recently, politicians have surrendered themselves to more fashionable concerns and these two existential threats have plummeted way down society's anxiety list. I have no idea why. They still seem to me far more important than any others. At Lancing we were thrown further off kilter by the Cuban Missile Crisis in October 1962 – one boy told me in complete seriousness that there was no point to doing our homework that night because we were all going to be dead tomorrow – than we were by news of Kennedy being shot in the head the following year. That potentially lethal stand-off between two, as it turned out, posturing superpowers ended with a climbdown more by luck than by design. It was thinking about the divine futility of a world containing the means of its own obliteration which started my move away from the Christian faith. But my departure from the Anglican church was accelerated by the pending service of confirmation, which was filling me with misgiving. When I had arrived at Lancing, I had sometimes acted as server to the chaplain in a side-chapel at unimportant services, often at six thirty in the morning, with only a few worshippers. Once I was confirmed, the chaplain said, I would be able to serve the far more important function of sacristan at the Sung Eucharist in front of five hundred people. When, he asked, would I be coming for my pre-confirmation confession?

It sounds shallow if I say that I ceased to be a Christian because I didn't want to confess my sins to the school chaplain.

That reluctance is in itself, I suppose, the sin of pride. But that's how I felt. The idea of parading my faith also disgusted me. Faith must by definition be private. I had already been thrown out of the Eastbourne ABC for laughing myself silly at Audrey Hepburn in *The Nun's Story*, so it was clear which way the wind was blowing. If I did have any relationship with God – and now, after reading Sartre, Camus and Bertrand Russell, it was tenuous and frayed – the last thing I wanted to do was walk up an aisle, turn round and be seen to help administer the host. Later, it turned out that my entire professional life would be dedicated to the act of scrutiny which is at the heart of public performance. The theatre would be valuable to me for precisely that act. In the theatre as nowhere else, the authenticity of a thought or feeling may be examined and judged by the process of acting out. How often have I stopped a rehearsal and said of my own writing or directing, 'Sorry, but I don't believe it'? I was aware that if ever I consented to become a performing sacristan, with an audience's eyes upon me, I would be revealed as the biggest hypocrite alive.

I went through with the service of confirmation, which served as a convenient final staging post for my loss of faith. By the time I was fifteen, I was changing fast. I was no longer desperate to ingratiate myself. When I had arrived at Lancing, a certain jostling proximity in the way of life had been attractive to me – the rough and tumble contrasted with Bexhill – but after a year or two any slim crevice of privacy had become more valuable. We all lived in an environment where total nakedness seemed to be expected half the day. We slept in dormitories together, we showered together and in the evening we took baths together. The lavatories were often lockless and some had no doors. Whatever age, pupils were also required to go unclothed in the swimming pool on the unlikely pretext that if we wore trunks the fibres from our garments would clog up the pool's filters. It was noticeable that visiting clergy never missed an opportunity to cruise the swimming pool on their school tour, however brief. They would stand on a high, chlorinated balcony in intense theological conversation, lingering longer than in other, less exposed parts of the school, kneeling to do up that pesky shoelace, or once more elaborately wiping that stubborn speck of dirt from their glasses. So it was a relief, in these ogling circumstances, when I came upon one thing at least that we involuntary bathing belles could do alone and unobserved. I took up smoking. I found its solitary rituals and necessary secrecy comforting.

After a couple of years I had also befriended a pupil in my own house, a little older than me, and sometimes he and I would stroll together up past the sanatorium and into the woods to have a couple of crafty cigarettes. James Watson was sardonic, a touch anguished, right out of the heart of the English middle class but trying to work out whether his easy assumption of the qualities of a natural leader was going to be a trap or an asset in later life. It was with James that, after O levels, I hitchhiked to Stratford and slept in a haystack until, exhausted by the cold and the surprising hardness of bundled hay, we joined the queue to get day seats at the very back of the theatre. In the next couple of years, we would often sneak out to permissive working-class pubs nearby to enjoy a pint of mild or of Watney's Red Barrel on a Saturday night. Some of my best times at Lancing were spent taking tea in a weird cottage where an old biddy seemingly out of Thomas Hardy, standing in an apron and slippers, still served soft-boiled eggs and buttered soldiers from a blackened stove in what looked like her front room. Or on blazing days, lying on our backs in a cornfield, staring at the sun, smoking a Player's Medium and leaving our exam revision neglected in the long grass. Walking away from the school came to be a greater pleasure than walking towards it.

Unsurprisingly, a lot of our talk was about girls, and how hard it was, within our designated way of life, to meet any who were not family friends. James and I had both cottoned on to the fact that one of Lancing's principal educational assets was its closeness to Brighton. Every generation has a Brighton of its own, but ours was still convincingly bohemian. The town was less tarted-up and less prosperous than it is now. The early sixties were not that far distant from 1938, either in time or spirit, and you could still catch the reverberations from the random bursts of violence which had made Graham Greene the great Brighton poet, with Patrick Hamilton his crapulous equal. In side-streets, we were told, there were basement nightclubs for both transvestites and transsexuals, but we never saw them. Our time was spent at the Continentale in Kemp Town watching Jeanne Moreau movies – the best was one in which you could see her right breast in the bath – then going on for vindaloos and chop suey in the first Indian and Chinese restaurants of our lives. Later, we hung out at dances under the pier. The acned bands playing there modelled themselves more on the Swinging Blue Jeans than on the Beatles, all in neat little suits and polka-dot shirts, kicking their legs in rhythm like Tiller Girls whose batteries had run down. On the floor, the girls were wonderfully made up, with soft pastel sweaters and slacks in minute checks. I was a useless dancer, but an OK conversationalist. When today I come upon agony aunts in newspapers advising that wit is the most attractive quality, and that, from a woman's perspective, nothing is more seductive in a man than the ability to listen, I think, 'Hmm, maybe, but not in Brighton in 1964.' I spent many long hours listening.

It was in Brighton that I had another experience which over-turned my future thinking. Of all the commonly cited factors which led to a transformation of social attitudes in the 1960s, the most frequently overlooked is the television series *The Great War*, a documentary narrated unforgettably by Michael Redgrave. With its inexhaustible flow of unseen contemporary footage, it revealed to an angry public the full extent of the military and political establishment's indifference to their own men's lives in the First World War fifty years earlier. Haig and his gang of blood-soaked enforcers were revealed as something near criminals in the scale of their recklessness. Now, with my English teacher Donald Bancroft, I was part of a group of boys who were allowed to go to the Theatre Royal Brighton to see the B cast in a long-touring production of *Beyond the Fringe*, which played on some of the same sensitivities.

We had looked forward to this event for months, since among our Françoise Hardy and Billie Holiday LPs most of us had an original cast album of this much-discussed Oxbridge sketch-show. We knew it and could imitate it more or less word for word. Given that I had been forbidden to do maths at A level because the curriculum would not allow me to mix literary and scientific subjects, I was studying an enjoyable mix of French, English and Divinity. Donald was therefore one of my three principal teachers, and one I hugely liked. A short, pugna-cious Northerner, he had a remarkable gift for taking the most obscure classic literature and laying out a clear understanding of its essential subject matter, and only thereby considering its method. It was an approach to which I responded. There are a thousand ways to approach a work of art, but 'What is it saying?' remains the most useful question you can ask. What other question comes close?

I was therefore astonished when, coming out of the theatre, Donald took violent exception to a sketch by Peter Cook called 'Aftermyth of War', which parodied all those films I had seen at the Playhouse Cinema, in which stiff upper lips are maintained throughout and people go laughingly to their deaths without complaint. Walking away down the street, Donald was puffing at his pipe, saying that the evening was an insult to the brave men and women who had sacrificed their lives for a generation which was now rewarding them with nothing more than mockery and ingratitude. Bewildered, I pointed out the sketch's title. The object of the satire, I said, was not the British military themselves but the ridiculous myths that had been propagated by their phlegmatic misrepresentation in countless bad films and television series since 1945. Famous actors and directors had grown rich by propagating a stupid lie, that there could be such a thing as a war which was moving without being upsetting. In truth, it had been six years of slaughter and violence. It was high time someone came along to point out the difference between reality and fiction. Donald turned to me, unforgiving, still missing the point. 'I doubt if you lot would have done any better . . .'

Taken aback by obtuseness in someone I knew to be perceptive, I realised that night that I was dealing with something more than generational conflict. Donald, whose profession was the seeking out of meaning in literature, could not, on this particular occasion, see past his own value system. It blinded him. I was facing direct evidence of how much we all have invested in the story we tell ourselves about our own lives. In every human being there is a reef of conviction which grows up like a continental shelf. I began to appreciate how rich is the interaction between what happens to us and what we come to believe. I did not at this point have any presentiment that I would spend years fascinated by this subject, or that it would one day lie at the heart of a catalogue of plays. How could I, when I had no intimation that I was going to be a writer? But I did start to examine my own prejudices, and to see how relative they were. Thenceforward, although I would continue to end up alongside father figures, no doubt to replace my absconding biological dad, I would never expect any single man or woman to have all the answers. I would always be alert. In adult life, pompous films of Jungian quest and discovery, a ubiquitous genre after *Star Wars*, would bore me as formulaic – and worse, at the deepest level, inhuman. Everything which generalised about arcs or journeys was by definition piffle. Anything which set spiritual quests in outer space or in oatmeal-robed prehistory was a waste of children's time as much as adults'. I couldn't give a damn who found the rabbit's foot or the magic mug, or where it was buried. The self-importance got up my nose. Anything valuable to be uncovered was likely to lie in the everyday, the specific.

In this mood, I had fallen upon the writings of Raymond Williams, whose last words to me in Cheltenham shortly before he died in 1988 were to be, by coincidence, 'I can't be a father to everyone.' At Lancing, I managed, not without struggle, to fight my way through his two most acclaimed books, *Culture and Society* and *The Long Revolution*. The complications of his style were prodigious, but without always being too sure what he was saying, I nevertheless picked up a flavour which was much more strongly reinforced by anecdote. For obvious reasons, I loved Williams when he said that he refused to take lessons in family values from a class that expelled its own boy children from the home at the age of nine. At the time when men were horrified that the invention of the pill might offer women a degree of independence, I loved him asking, 'When they talk of the permissive society, I always want to ask who exactly is doing the permitting?' I loved the fact that when, at a university seminar, the lecturer L. C. Knights advanced the familiar argument that, because of the dehumanisation wrought by the Industrial Revolution, no modern person could possibly hope to have experienced what Shakespeare meant by the word 'neighbour', Williams interrupted to say that he at least knew perfectly well what 'neighbour' meant because he had been brought up in a working-class community in Wales. But most of all I loved Williams for his essay 'Culture Is Ordinary'. In this he argues that every single person, wherever they are born, already belongs to a culture of some sort. Literature is not created by fine minds at the top of society talking one to another. Culture is not sipped from fine china. No, it is, on the contrary, the outcome of social forces coming up from below, from deep down in society itself. Culture is not an add-on. It's an expression of what society is, and, most of all, of how it is changing. 'There are no masses to save, to capture or to direct, but rather the crowded people in the course of an extraordinarily rapid and confusing expansion of their lives . . . So when Marxists say we are living in a dying culture, and that the masses are ignorant,' he wrote, 'I have to ask them . . . where on earth they have lived. A dying culture and ignorant masses are not what I have known and see.'

A great many schoolchildren fall headlong in love with the essays of George Orwell because their author is fair-minded and lucid. His work acts as a welcome relief from the pretension of normative literary studies, a sort of sorbet, a palate-cleanser for people who read too much jargon. I liked Orwell too. But Williams, though never able to emulate Orwell's clear prose, had two different qualities which were of equal value. First – and important in my scale of values – Williams was witty. He was that rare intellectual who makes good jokes, which gut the heart of an issue. But second, his outlook on matters cultural was in all aspects profoundly generous. He wanted everyone to have access to everything. Orwell was an upper-class refugee who wanted things to be simple. Williams was a working-class migrant who knew things were complicated. He was one of the first academics to be engaged with television, both the programmes and the advertising, because he was especially interested in where ideas came from and how they were distributed and absorbed by people at large. He would be delighted to know he is today the subject of more Google hits than all other New Left thinkers put together. Williams hated the idea of culture as something exclusive, a door which had to be knocked on by supplicants. In his own personal experience, from which, to the disapproval of more conventional scholars, he drew so much of his understanding, culture was already out there, thriving among ordinary people. The job of those who sought to theorise about it was to look around them. They must connect the movement of society to the movement of art.

My excitement at encountering Williams's ideas turned into a practical plan. I noticed on the first page of his books that he taught at somewhere called Jesus College, Cambridge. For that reason, helped by Donald Bancroft who always admired enterprise, I immediately applied for admission, without knowing very much about where it was or what it would be like. In a rare lapse of faith from her governing beliefs, my mother had wanted me to leave school at fifteen because she had secured me

71

a promising position training to be an accountant in one of Bex-hill's leading firms, just a few hundred yards from Pendragon. When she got her annual report from Marks and Spencer, dis-patched to her by right as the owner of several hundred shares, she had noticed that almost everyone on its distinguished board had accountants' letters after their names. So it was at my own insistence I had forgone the chance one day perhaps to sit in the Marks and Spencer boardroom in Baker Street. Now at least I had a counter-proposal. I would go to Britain's coldest, wettest, flattest university and sit at the feet of a clever man.

Once I had stumbled onto a potential path, my interest in Lancing fell away. I enjoyed an eye-opening month in Paris studying an external course at the Sorbonne in preparation for my French A level. I shared a room for seven francs a night in a hotel in the Rue de Verneuil, tuning in to the very last days of a vanishing Left Bank where *ouvriers* still stood in blue uni-forms, leaning on zinc bars at seven in the morning, already drinking white wine and marc. Lunches of savoury sheep's brains *meunière*, or slabs of pork with beans, were two francs fifty. I edited the school magazine without distinction. I stood as the school's Labour candidate in the 1964 mock election and was roundly defeated. This last experience proved to me for all time that standing for public office was yet another on the long list of things, including tennis, debating and carpentry, which I turned out to be useless at.

In previous years Patrick Halsey had invited us down from our dormitories on Saturday nights to sip cocoa in his sitting room in our pyjamas and slippers and to watch *That Was the Week that Was*. It was one of those unmissable shows, common to decisive shifts in public taste, which are more exciting in pros-pect and in commentary than they are in reality. Sketches about open fly buttons didn't seem very radical to me. But somehow on the night of 15 October, in adjacent floral armchairs, it was only Patrick and I who stayed up late into the night to see Alec Douglas-Home, the most delicate flower of English nobility, thrown out of Downing Street. Harold Wilson, talking about the white heat of technology which significantly did arrive, but not, for most people, for another thirty years, was due to take office by a tiny majority. Labour was back in at last. While the one-time Lord Home prepared to concede defeat with aristocratic courtesy, Patrick sank deeper in his chair, endlessly reapplying fresh flame to his pipe which seemed to dampen and die as the evening went on. Patrick sipped from his whisky glass and asked me, 'Aren't you moved by him?' – but in the tone of a man who anticipated the answer 'No'.

4

The Mercedes Symbol

I did what was required and got myself an open scholarship to Jesus. Christopher Hampton was a year above me at Lancing but before he had left for Oxford, he had introduced me to a couple of friends in his house. In future years people would find it remarkable that Christopher, Tim Rice and I, all later known as writers for the theatre, were at school together. But the high cultural tone of the place – Peter Pears would come down with Benjamin Britten and stage concerts always with that weird screeching noise which still gives me the shivers – at least provided us with examples, if not ability. Although soft-spoken, wry and sweetly modest, Christopher had always been distinguished in my eyes with a precocious inner certainty. For all his monologues of comic misfortune, girls who said no and so on – he was as keen on Tony Hancock as I was – he was, ultimately, like a top that couldn't be knocked off its axis. Tim also looked into the future with a degree of justifiable confidence. He was already an expert theologian of the pop charts and scholar of obscurer texts in *Melody Maker* and the *New Musical Express*. He had a pop band called the Aardvarks who played at school concerts. They were strongly in debt to Cliff Richard and the Everly Brothers, who were to remain Tim's lifelong heroes. But the second close friend of Christopher's was Roger Dancey, a handsome, genial fellow with an informed love of cricket and in proud possession of what he claimed was the Sagittarian's gift for getting on with everyone. Those born under this sign, he told me, could call themselves playboys of the universe. I told him I was Gemini. Gemini? Hmm, not so good.

One of the masters, Norman Holmes, had recently hosted the visit to England of an American couple, driving them round to Windsor and Stratford. It had been part of an exchange. Now, in reply to a speculative letter from Roger, this couple were happy to take two schoolboys at a loose end who might be willing to go out and paint their house on Manhattan Beach in Los Angeles in return for food and lodging. Since we both had a spare nine months before going to university, it sounded like an ideal way of passing the time. The only obstacle was that I had no money to get across the Atlantic. So I went along, like thousands before me, to the educational headhunters Gabbitas and Thring. My hope was that some menial posting would become available in a prep school. They had nothing. Then, out of the blue, in the New Year, just when I was about to give up, the agency rang to report that a teacher at Cranleigh School, Lance Marshall, had broken his leg. There was an unexpected vacancy for one term only, starting in just five days' time. I met the head of English, Pat Maguire. He told me that among my other jobs I would be required to teach A level. I pointed out that I would still be seventeen for another six months, and that I myself had only sat the A level the previous summer. 'Good,' he said. 'That means you'll be ahead of the boys.'

Cranleigh was not a great spot for someone without a car. A Victorian red-brick monstrosity, the school sat in the middle of a Surrey village, which itself seemed to sit in the middle of a fair-sized depression, with little ruffling the surface of its wealthy commuter self-satisfaction. This was Lancing without the seasoning, without the challenge. Lodging as I did with the pleasant Mr Maguire in his family home just across from the school in Edgefield Close, I had little chance to do anything at night except drink moodily in the masters' common room, a sort of elevated Portakabin round the back of the building. I tried to play billiards with anyone as lonely as I was on the table which dominated it. Since I still looked and sounded pretty much like most of the pupils they spent all day teaching, few masters cared to oblige me with a game. Anyway, they had lives.

There was a paradox here. I had finally escaped a median English public school to set forth into the world, and yet here I was dumped down for eight weeks in another, only this time on the other side of the electric fence. Cranleigh was in the grip of a boring sort of muscular Christianity, with a rugby-playing headmaster, David Emms, whose knuckles scraped along the ground as he walked. I once heard him address the assembled school on the equal dangers of masturbation and borrowing other boys' bicycles without permission. He had me removed from teaching Divinity when he learned that my notion of how to address the subject included some rudimentary laying out of the principal arguments for and against the existence of God. For him religion was worship, not thought. The state funeral of Winston Churchill at St Paul's Cathedral, happening within a few weeks of my arrival at Cranleigh, brought the school to a stately, deferential halt. The war leader had taken ten days to die. On 30 January Mr Maguire's living room filled to capacity as everyone assuaged their grief with Twiglets and industrial quantities of gin and tonic. The spontaneous lowering of the cranes to half-mast on both sides of the Thames as Churchill's coffin sailed by remains the most indelible public image of my life. Twenty-five million of us were back in front of our black-and-white TVs, tapping for the last time into unifying notions of service and patriotism which, after the duplicity of Suez, already sounded a touch out of date. People were moved, but moved at the passing of value, not at its ascendancy. Appeals to Churchill's memory were from that day on to ring national alarm bells of hypocrisy and manipulation when invoked by the far seedier leaders who saw Britain through to the end of the twentieth century.

I lucked into a couple of friends among the younger masters in the common room, one of whom took me to a few revealing parties, regularly enlivened by his delightful air-hostess girl-friend. And I was taken up by Edward Black, who was probably twenty-two and already a gifted linguist. He had graduated from reading French and Spanish at London University and he enjoyed showing a child-colleague the ropes. He had a Citroën 2CV, and it became our regular custom to go into Guildford at night to listen to jazz. Edward was an enthusiast, alive as only lovers of a disempowered art form can be to all the internal splits and divisions within the British history of the music. Edward's carrier of the New Orleans grail was 'The Guvnor', Ken Colyer, who, unlike the better-known Chris Barber, Acker Bilk, Kenny Ball or Monty Sunshine, was held by purists to have resisted all the temptations of facile popularity. He alone was the real thing. When, red-faced, Colyer blew his uncompromising trumpet, he looked alarmingly as if the prominent boil on his forehead were going to burst. But of more significance to me than how he played was where. The little nightclub we heard him in was right by the bus station, opposite the larger Rikki Tik Club. It was called the Harvest Moon, and just like the Whisky-a-Go-Go which I had come upon next to the Opéra during my stay in Paris, it was full of flighty girls in tightly ribbed woollen pullovers and short skirts. Most were called Sarah or Fiona. In real life, the Harvest Moon was soon after taken over by mods, whose preferred music was the blues. Inevitably when mods arrived, drugs became a more important part of the scene. Jazz was kicked out, as jazz always is. But nine years later, in my 1974 play *Knuckle*, the club was reincarnated in dramatic imagination as the Shadow of the Moon. It became the fictional location for a piece of work which would one day turn my whole life upside down.

Procedure in the classroom presented its own pitfalls. I realised that teaching, like journalism, is something which is dangerously easy to do badly. Thomas Jefferson said you should never quarrel with a man who owns a barrel of ink. In the same way, you should never quarrel with the man or woman who is holding the chalk. They have an unfair advantage. Theirs will always be the last word. As in journalism, there is an imbalance in the power relationship which needs to be admitted if it is to be kept in check. Janet Malcolm's resounding declaration in *The Journalist and the Murderer* that 'Every journalist who is not too stupid or too full of himself to notice what is going on knows that what he does is morally indefensible' should also be pinned on every teacher's blackboard. On the whole I acquitted myself decently. I had a few outstanding students in the sixth form whom I could approach as equals. They were almost my age, after all, and no less bright. For them, I was running something more like a seminar than a class. And I also had junior classes of thirteen-year-olds, full of promise, whose eager desire to express themselves I would never have dreamt of abusing. But once or twice I felt myself, on lazy days, tipping over into something less pleasant, of which I was deeply ashamed. I still hated myself, after all, and teaching played to a flaw in my character – an ability to dominate a situation by showing off. Worse,

I was occasionally more concerned to press home and win an argument than I was to go after the truth.

These were ugly characteristics. I had known for some time that I had acquired a new role, and the role was that of a young man on the make. To be aware of this offered me no obvious way of dealing with it. Who was I? Julien Sorel? A scholarship boy, ascending through society? So it was a relief, after saving £80 from my eight weeks of teaching, to go and join Roger at Heathrow on 9 April 1965, before flying to Glasgow for the first hop to Reykjavik. There we deplaned from a shuddering prop jet at 3 a.m. to eat lukewarm fish and chips in the passenger lounge before continuing on the interminable journey to New York. Icelandic Air was known by everyone to offer the best bargains in the skies, if glimpses of the red-hot engine parts didn't put you off. We had both been supplied with green cards at the American Embassy. In those days they were handed out like jelly beans. So we breezed effortlessly through the recently renamed John F. Kennedy airport before flying on to LA.

I had been abroad a few times – a desolate family holiday in Ostend and Bruges, the educational stint in St Germain, a trip once to eat paella and meet my father's boat in Palma, Mallorca – but nothing in Europe had prepared me for this. The magnificent Californian light, the wide-open sky, the palm trees and, later, the dazzling surf hit me in an eye which was regulated only to English grey. My irises shrunk to pins. I arrived with no particular feeling for American culture. Yes, I read Kerouac and Ginsberg, but I was not one of those people who dreamed of diners and pony tails and barn dances. Europeans like Françoise Dorléac, Romy Schneider and Claudia Cardinale possessed my romantic imagination in a way Marilyn Monroe never could, accomplished comedienne as she was. *Bitter Rice,*

THE BLUE TOUCH PAPER

with Silvana Mangano among rows of Italian women labouring up to their knees in water in the fields, was insanely sexier than *Pillow Talk* with Doris Day. Only the upward inflections of Martin Luther King's aspirational voice had an American melody whose music touched me deeply. But even so, as Roger and I stood at the top of the aircraft steps, looking out at the bubbling tarmac, I did feel an uplift of spirits at visiting a world which was, in every aspect, so wholly different from the one I knew.

Virginia Johnson was there to meet us. A pioneering primal scream therapist and psychoanalyst in her mid-fifties, she was understandably touchy about so often being confused with the Virginia Johnson who was, with William Masters, all over the newspapers as a pioneer in the study of human sexual response. Our Virginia, considering her profession, was rather prim in that regard and, for someone regularly exploring the wilder shores of human depravity, lip-puckeringly right-wing in her social views. She was married to Ed Cornell, a short, silver-haired and tanned electrician who worked every day at Warner Brothers, humping lights and cables. Ed had a talent for chess which in better days had made him the regular on-set partner for Humphrey Bogart. His regular disquisitions, beer in hand, on the decline of the studios sounded pretty much like my father's on the decline of the navy. A few years later, his son from a previous marriage was killed pointlessly on a training exercise in Vietnam. Ed would not be able to recover. Henceforth, a tiny glissade of pain would pass across his face whenever Ed Jr was recalled. We were soon to hear of many such bitter bereavements, bereavements which did so much to change America's idea of itself. People who talk today about America losing its optimism in the new century have surely mislaid memories of the 1960s. Together, Ed and Virginia lived in a house in West Hollywood too small to accommodate us, so Virginia had arranged that, before we started work as house-painters, we should stay with a couple of her patients in Van Nuys, Knute and Phyllis Fritz.

It was to be a continuing problem of our first visit to the US that almost everyone who open-heartedly received us as guests all over the country was either a patient or an ex-patient of Virginia's. Many had done primal therapy. They therefore believed that they had suffered serious trauma either at the time of their birth or soon after. Meeting a succession of such people may have given us a warped view of America, but it certainly gave us a distinctive one. Since, later, it had also fallen to us to reorganise Virginia's extensive filing system, we had acquired rather intimate knowledge of their current problems. We had often read out loud to each other the lurid details, sometimes of the patients' experiences, sometimes of their fantasies. Roger had a sense of humour no less callous than my own, so we would come to spend many of our vacant hours roaring with laughter at the neuroses of the people we were staying with. 'Oh, so that's the guy who can only ejaculate in a plastic bag!' On our very first night in California, after a somewhat halting meal with the Fritzes, Roger and I were put up in bunk beds, where we spoke with misguided freedom about the social shortcomings of our hosts. 'What a couple of weirdos!' Next morning we came down to a chilly reception and were asked to pack our bags. Knute, it turned out, was a technology freak and had wired our bedroom with microphones, no doubt in the hope of overhearing something rather more flattering.

The unexpected thing about this disastrous start to our trip was that it seemed to amuse Virginia rather than dismay her.

We reported back, luggage in hand, thinking she would be furious. But much to our surprise, she took the whole incident in her stride, as though this were indeed one of the acknowledged problems faced by anyone who stayed with the Fritzes. They bugged your conversation. What could you do? But it was also as if it had never occurred to her that the American preoccupation with yourself and the unique problems of your own sexuality – at that time so sharply contrasting with British reserve – was, among other things, hilariously funny. Far from resenting two English schoolboys who were so quick to mock her work, she began to see it through our eyes and to take as much pleasure in laughing at it as we did. Her sense of the ridiculous was liberated. At various times when we were rationalising her paperwork, she would actually call us through to witness the drug-induced birth re-enactment which was at the centre of the treatment. 'Come in, boys, see this!' Virginia would roll her eyes at us as the adult 'foetus' was delivered, bawling and oblivious, onto the carpet. She loved recalling that her most damaged patient had been traumatised for life, he said, by the embedded memory of the obstetrician saying casually to a colleague as the baby emerged, 'Hey, this one's coming out like a pretzel.' How the baby had absorbed sounds he could only four years later translate into language remained unexplained.

At first, Virginia put us up on a sofa and a camp bed in her Westwood office, where we worked to repay her hospitality. We were both pale-skinned and painfully thin from the inadequate British post-war diet. Potatoes and milk had done little for us. Pictures show us looking like albino mice, wearing shapeless cardigans and sandals with socks. So it was a liberation to be moved out to the beach, and to spend the day stripped to the waist, paint-brushes in hand, doing a physical job and

admiring the unselfconscious Californian freedom of bronzed
girls who cut their blue jeans off at the thigh. Wow, what confidence! Teenagers, owning Ford Mustangs! We slept on site,
with the sound of the ocean nearby. We had both got bargain
tickets from Continental Trailways, the rival bus company to
Greyhound, which allowed us to travel as far as we wanted in
the US, without limit, for ninety-nine days, all for ninety-nine
dollars. Once the beach house was spick and span, our first trip
was to San Diego, with a quick visit to the seedy Mexican border town of Tijuana. We then headed straight back up the coast
to Santa Barbara because we had heard it boasted a campus,
part of the University of California, which led down to the sea.
There we made nightly visits to a disco where we watched an
assured student who mesmerised admiring young women with
his impressions of Marlon Brando as Terry in *On the Water-
front*. 'You don't understand, I coulda had class, I coulda been
a contender.' He was, we were told, the son of Kirk Douglas.
His name was Michael. But even more impressively, in Santa
Barbara we also went to a screening of *Shanghai Express* hosted
by Josef von Sternberg himself.

At that stage in his life – he must have been seventy – the
great imposter had forsaken the jodhpurs and riding whip
which he had assumed in the 1920s to make himself look like
a film director, though he had held on to the von. He could
still demonstrate the techniques he had invented for the but-
terfly lighting which made Marlene Dietrich the most alluring
of screen stars. You hang a hanky over a lamp. His dismissal of
all cinema which had followed was absolute. Not a single film
since 1937 had deserved his approval. 'After my films, there
is nothing! Nothing!' Roger, braver than I, stood up after a
half-hour torrent of contempt by von Sternberg for everything

that wasn't von Sternberg, and observed that although he had enjoyed *Shanghai Express* very much, he felt that perhaps the performance of the leading man, Clive Brook, opposite Dietrich, had been a little wooden. Von Sternberg looked at Roger without pity. 'Vooden? Vooden? Of course he's vooden, he's English!'

After a quick trip up to the redwood forests and Seattle via San Francisco, we set off in June on a U-shaped bus journey round the Southern States and on to New York. At an early stop in Texas we stayed with Chuck Bothner, another of Virginia's wilder patients, who worked on the White Sands rocket programme outside El Paso. Inside the house he had a machine for opening doors unaided. When, before a lightning trip across the border to Juarez in Mexico, I casually put my hand on the bonnet of his immaculate Mercedes, I received an electric shock which went through my whole body. When I asked, 'What the hell?' Chuck told me he had wired it to stop anyone stealing the Mercedes symbol. 'They get stolen all the time,' he said. Freeloaders, Roger and I were finding invitations multiplying with every stop. Each billet spawned five more. In those days British teenagers travelling through the more distant parts of America were a welcome rarity, so we were received not so much as individuals but as young ambassadors from a foreign culture. When we got out of the bus in Phoenix it was 112 degrees. We got straight back in. We lived for a week or so in New Orleans on a refined diet of doughnuts, oysters and traditional jazz.

It was only as we stopped going east and turned north that our trip began to become at once both more sinister and more serious. We tended to arrive in towns in the early mornings after fitful sleep on overnight bus rides. One morning we got off in Montgomery, Alabama, and walked straight into a threatening atmosphere as we went to drink coffee in the diner at the bus station. There had been a big race demonstration the day before, and the air was still thick with police violence. The only white people in the area, we moved carefully. This was the South as represented in Michael Roemer's great film *Nothing But a Man*, shot in Birmingham only a couple of years previously. As some sort of joke, our hosts told us to go and say hello to the notorious Governor of Alabama, George Wallace, whose intransigent white supremacism was an international symbol of bigotry. Only two years earlier he had stood at the University of Alabama trying to stop the enrolment of two black students. We walked up the steps of the Capitol and told the attendants that we were a couple of boys from England who wanted to meet him. Wallace came out within a few minutes, and we stood in the splendour of the state legislature exchanging pleasantries. His social awkwardness matched our own.

The idea of meeting Wallace in person had been suggested by two of his most principled opponents, with whom we were staying for a few days. Together they impressed both me and Roger more than anyone we had ever met. Later, I would get to know a few American radicals, and to love them deeply, mostly for the courage they show in the sheer unlikeliness of their cause. Their powerlessness seems to bring forth realism. You find in them a toughness and a sense of humour often lacking in their more pampered British counterparts. The vastness of the challenge for an American socialist evinces a corresponding vastness of soul. That night, among the fireflies, we sat on a Southern balcony drinking mint juleps with Clifford and Virginia Durr. Virginia was the daughter of a Presbyterian preacher and a passionate advocate of equality and voting rights for African Americans. At one point she had been a schoolteacher, then had run for the US Senate on the Progressive ticket from Virginia in 1948. Clifford, her husband, had been a New Dealer, a lawyer in the Roosevelt administration who had played his part in the life-saving financial reconstruction following the crash. He had later set up a law firm in Montgomery which represented civil rights activists. It was Clifford and Virginia together who had, in 1955, bailed out their good friend Rosa Parks when she had been arrested for refusing to give up her seat on a bus to a white man. Clifford had then represented Parks when she had brought her epoch-making case in the state court.

Roger and I were awed by the Durrs' sweetness and eloquence, but also by the knowledge of how close they were to the most important political movement in America. The four of us sat down for dinner. Not long after, the telephone rang in another part of the house. At once, Virginia sprang up to get it. Clifford continued eating and talking, until from the next room we heard Virginia's voice raised in horror and disbelief. The words rang out clear as a bell. 'But Lyndon, what are you *doing* in Vietnam?' When she came back, she was shaking her head. 'That was the president.' It turned out she and Lyndon Johnson had started out as union school organisers in Texas together, and he still regularly telephoned her from the White House to get soundings on what his old friends and contemporaries back in the real world were thinking. When in March 1968 Johnson refused to run again for the presidency, pleading in mitigation for his actions that no one at the time had warned him of how dangerous it would be to expand the doomed American operation in Vietnam, I knew he was lying. I'd heard someone warn him.

It's extraordinary how quickly your view of a whole country can change. Roger and I travelled on up the East Coast, neither of us ever likely thereafter to succumb to the facile anti-Americanism of the European left. At first hand, I would come to know and loathe the crimes of American imperialism, the toll it took on the innocent when in the following years, under Nixon and Reagan, the US enthusiastically sponsored terrorism and dictatorship all over the world, particularly in South and Central America, where it killed many and saved none. But I would also experience the true principles of American dissent and the startling honesty of American dissenters, many of whom had already paid a price for their beliefs unimaginable to leftists back home. In 1965, the US was starting to be a country at war with itself, and the evidence of that war was everywhere. Chastened, we moved on to Atlanta, to Charlotte, to Williamsburg, to Washington and then to Philadelphia, before arriving in Manhattan on our ninety-ninth day. We had nowhere to stay, and my Cranleigh wages were long gone.

I'd suffered from asthma and from its neurotic shadow eczema throughout my upbringing, and the heat and humidity in New York that July were sometimes asphyxiating. They were certainly tiring. I'd never been anywhere before where the thermometer stayed steady at night. It was hard to sleep, and by day it was hard to move. My most urgent need was to get a job. The only available short-term employment was on commission. Within a day, I had signed up to sell vacuum cleaners door to door. Every morning I would report to an office on Third Avenue where all the salesmen would be given an inspirational talk before setting out on the day's trudge. You got a free doughnut and a cup of coffee, so I never missed it. Every day it was explained to us that it was not enough to sell the basic Electrolux. For some extra dollars, the client could buy something called a power nozzle, which, we were told, made the machine even more effective. It was part of the daily uplift to tell us that we should not be ashamed of trying to push the case for the more expensive nozzle. 'Think of it this way,' the instructor would say. 'If you fail to sell it, you're not just depriving the client of a valuable nozzle. You're depriving America of nozzles.'

This kind of speech had already been parodied in movies a thousand times, but there was something splendid about a man – I think he was even called Art – who could deliver it without self-consciousness. Anyway, I was in no position to sneer, because I was hopeless at selling door to door. It was not just that I found it embarrassing. It was also that, when I was lucky enough to get inside anyone's apartment, I referred to the machine as a Hoover, which I wrongly believed was the generic name for any apparatus which sucks up dust. I'd been calling my product a Hoover for some days before a woman, well into her seventies, corrected me. 'What you're selling's an Electrolux. Hoover's your opposition.'

The city was divided up on a grid among Electrolux salesmen, and you didn't stray onto other people's territory without their permission. Because I arrived last, I got the least promising. I spent every day in the insufferable heat up on the Upper East Side, knocking on every single door in every single building around 93rd and 94th. What struck me first was how dark the apartments were. I had imagined New York as a city of light, and from the cinema knew it as a place of towering verticals and shimmering silvers. Instead, when you actually started going inside people's homes, you found tiny, cramped little boxes with cream venetian blinds and ornate table lamps which needed to keep burning all day. Everyone was overlooked.

Large parts of the city were still as described by Richard Yates and Sloan Wilson. Office workers drank Martinis and men wore hats to work. The women radiated a brisk kind of elegance which was formidable without being uppity. But the place Roger and I found to stay was in the less tony part of town. The Lower East Side, where an alternative culture was just beginning to be forged, was by no means the glamorous *quartier* it is now. You looked behind you quite a lot and what you saw made your pace quicken often. I came upon my first dead body on East 6th Street, lying halfway across the sidewalk. The man had a stab wound in his back and the blood, scarlet, was still running into the gutter. We were given bunks, six to a room, in something called the International Student Hospice. At $1.50 a night, it was suspiciously $3.50 cheaper than any other in the city. It turned out there was a reason. The warden was a predator. There were breweries close by, so every morning I would set off to work through streets already sopping with the yeasty stink of warm beer. I used to divert through the hippyish St Mark's Place for no other reason but that I associated it with Bob Dylan. I hoped to catch sight of him. The photograph of Dylan with his arm round the artist Suze Rotolo on the cover of the album *The Freewheelin' Bob Dylan* was, for me, a definitive image of romance, one I had stared at longingly more times than I cared to admit. It represented a perfect fantasy of everything I might wish my life to be.

Unfortunately, I was not making a penny. On 21 July I sold my first packet of carpet shampoo bags, and that was it. Nobody wanted to buy from an emaciated teenager whose unlaundered shirts were darkly patterned with sweat. In the evenings Roger and I would eat the unsold food supermarkets passed on to the hostel owner, and then, according to my diary, we headed off to see what was on offer: as it turned out, *Intolerance*, *The Zoo Story*, *Krapp's Last Tape*, *Les Quatre Cents Coups*, *La Strada*,

Bicycle Thieves, *Citizen Kane*, *Les Amants*, *The Spy Who Came In from the Cold*, *The Informer*, *Great Expectations*, *Darling*, *Paths of Glory* and *Sunset Boulevard* – these last three in a single day. At the Village Vanguard we heard Sonny Rollins play several times. Cecil Taylor, too. The admission charge was $1.

Eventually, in an act of philanthropy which I absolutely associate with Americanness, my senior colleague Mr Baker, who sold four or five Electroluxes a day, gave me a couple of his sales, just so that I would be able to go on living. Baker had been doing the job for thirty years, and he had a notebook with a handwritten record of the state of household machinery within more or less every apartment to the east of the park. He spent as much time updating and consulting the book as he did selling. For him, information was power. He knew when people needed a change.

What Roger and I were exploring, to our surprise, was a nineteenth-century city which took its character from the fact that the working class and the immigrants still lived in the middle of it. You could move around, eat in cheap places, stay in cheap hostels, go to cheap shows, because there were lots of people who lived in Manhattan who were far worse off than you were. It wasn't just the famous racial mix, it was much more a mix of fortune which made life liveable at the bottom, if never as luxurious as it was at the top. From the outside, as you looked across, the skyline was all soaring Gershwin and grandeur. But in its interstices, non-vacuum-buying people hung on, finding ways of getting by.

I stayed about a month, and in mid-August, as Roger headed on to Boston, I went back to fulfil a long-hatched plan. Each year Patrick Halsey took two of the pupils he liked most on a camping trip in Europe. In August 1965 he wanted to take me and another boy, David Ransom, to what Patrick still called Constantinople. My old housemaster's overexcitement at driving his battered Triumph through Salzburg, Otočec and Zagreb was palpable, so progress down through Yugoslavia and Bulgaria to the Bosporus was speedy but hair-raising. We seemed to spend days staring out at women drying tobacco, or bathing up to their waists in mud-holes in the fields. But after a four-day stay on the waterside in Istanbul it was the homeward leg of our long journey which left the more lasting impression. As a historian of the Third Reich, Patrick wanted us to take in as much as possible in a single transit. We travelled in the famous elevator cut out of the rock at the very centre of a mountain to visit the Kehlsteinhaus, the Eagle's Nest. At Berchtesgaden we also went to see the burnt-out site of Hitler's Berghof. But for Patrick the most urgent priority was that we should visit Dachau, the Nazis' first purpose-built concentration camp, where he had regularly been since the war. It was part of what made him such a fine teacher. He did not think a civilised education would be complete unless a pupil visited at least one of the places where civilisation came to a halt.

In the mid-1960s, few tourists took in concentration camps. They were little visited. Acts of commemoration were few. Probably on the day we went there were only twenty or thirty people trooping round, staring at the exhibits which were all the more powerful for being so amateurish and unadorned. The sister of someone who had been killed in the camp haunted the place every day of her life, picking out strangers at random and explaining to them the exact ways in which the rituals of the camp had been organised. Many different reasons have been advanced for the peculiar time-lapse of perhaps a generation after the end of the war before deep curiosity about the nature of Nazi crimes spread wide, and about what it was in Jewish history, or perhaps Israeli history, which freed survivors up to speak out. But on that day in 1965, the three of us left shaken to our roots. Throughout my childhood, the Second World War had been a presence, an essential part of the perspective from which so many events in my life had been seen. But I had known only the war's victors. Now David and I learned a little about its victims. We travelled on up the Mosel because Patrick wanted to attend the annual wine festival. We went from town to town, sampling, in tents. Bands played. The wine, we were told, was especially delicious because it had grown on vines in fields fertilised by so many dead bodies. I stuck to beer.

5

Serious, Not Solemn

From the start, the language of Cambridge was the language of rebellion. We still dressed in ties and sports jackets, we had to wear gowns in the street and to lectures, shoulder-length hair didn't arrive until 1966, and in some crazy affectation, or perhaps because it was the cheapest way of absorbing the most nicotine, I took to smoking a pipe. Like everyone else, I ordered bottles of dry sherry from the buttery to keep in my room. Occasionally, port. But the way I saw the world, with the Vietnam war darkening daily, was increasingly about authority and opposition. The city of Cambridge looked dirty and down at heel, while the colleges had an air of benign neglect. We were all given threadbare rooms of our own, in my case in college, and there was a system in place whereby the young gentlemen's beds were made and their rooms tidied by women from the town. The culture of college servants, Raymond Williams pointed out in his 1970 TV documentary in the series *One Pair of Eyes*, was one which the university studiously ignored. Although a bedder's duties theoretically included letting the college know if their young men had made it back before the 11 p.m. curfew – any later and you had to climb in over railings – it never occurred to me they would take their obligations seriously. I always trusted people. In my first year I was therefore astonished to be hauled before my moral tutor, Bernard Towers, who was a hardline Catholic and a scholar of Teilhard de Chardin. He threatened

93

to send me down because my bedder had reported finding me one morning with a girl in my room. Magnanimously, he said he was going to be lenient and let me off with a fine of £10. I said, 'Oh you mean like a brothel charge?'

Jesus College brought out the glibness in me. Often I took refuge in a sort of exhausting facetiousness which I look back on without pride. California drained out of my bones the moment I arrived, like a suntan which had taken too fast. I was back in the worst of authoritarian, self-deluding Britain, dealing with characters even more arcane than those of my childhood. With teachers like Harry Guest and Donald Bancroft I had already experienced university teaching of the highest standard. Why did I need to go to another? In the outside world, a vigorous burst of working-class energy was transforming the feeling of the country, often giving voice to groups in society which had never been heard. And here I was, contracted to spin my wheels in one of the places that surge of energy was certain never to reach. After scanning only the first page of a Pelican, how was I to know that I would land in a reactionary rowing college, full of resonantly white South Africans and Rhodesians – van der This and van der That – who longed for nothing more than for their college to be Head of the River? Jesus, or more properly, 'The College of the Blessed Virgin Mary, St John the Evangelist and the Glorious Virgin St Radegund', had been founded on the site of a twelfth-century nunnery. It was stuck away down a side-lane, off Cambridge's main strips. From 1503, Thomas Cranmer, the first of a long line of theologians and archbishops, had studied there. The chapel had survived the assaults of both Edward VI and Cromwell. Now we all lived in chilly rooms where we heated tins of baked beans directly on the gas ring, blistering our fingerprints as we took them off. The only glimmer of enlightenment came from a comprehensive modern art collection, from which undergraduates were invited to take loans for a term. So few were interested, let alone excited, that during most of my three years at Jesus I worked with a bronze Barbara Hepworth maquette on my desk. On my wall I hung a Giacometti, which I stared at while listening, day after day, to The Band, Procol Harum and Tom Lehrer.

Before my university life had got underway, there had been a moment of ill omen. Michael Yearwood, who was my senior by a couple of years, had been sent away by his ambitious parents to board at King's School, Canterbury. At Oxford he had switched from reading law to reading theology. Michael followed up this decision by abandoning formal education altogether. As a next-door neighbour who had been the subject of regular unfavourable comparison, I had no doubt about the cause. Michael had read law at his father's insistence. A fellow scholarship boy, he had been forced up through the system like a hothouse plant. Far more than me or my sister, he was expected to perform. Hardly surprising he had buckled under the strain. A few years later, his mother Sheila, the paragon of all respectable virtue, could no longer endure the tangible, desolate silence of red brick. She took off all her clothes, left them on Bexhill beach and walked naked into the sea. Critics, both of left and right, like to look back on the social revolutions of the 1960s and claim that such revolutions were nothing more than surface changes in lifestyle. What, they ask, did a more progressive approach to personal morality, to music, to dress and to youth actually achieve? I knew the answer, because I had experienced at first hand the price of life in a repressed and moralising suburbia. If lifestyle could kill, why on earth was it not worthwhile to change it? If it saved one life? Surely I could never prove that away from the numb panic of 32 Newlands Avenue, Mum's exemplary best friend would not have killed herself. But Sheila would at least have had a chance, which she might or might not have taken.

In those days, thank goodness, culture *was* ordinary. Although the country looked so much poorer than it does now, all governments of whichever party, inspired by the great settlements in health, education and social security of the 1940s, saw it as their duty to pay for students' education. Whatever your background, getting a grant from your local authority was a formality. My latest scholarship, just £60 a year, was an honour, not a serious source of subsidy. The common practice in Cambridge was for students to attend lectures organised by the university but to take weekly supervisions, usually in twos, in their own college. My first supervision partner at Jesus was Humphrey Davies, a thoughtful and mature contemporary who had won the college's other English scholarship. The moment I heard Humphrey talking about poetry, it was clear to me who was truly clever and who wasn't. Within a few weeks of setting off on the English syllabus, Humphrey decided the subject could never be intellectually serious and began studying Chinese in the afternoons to give himself some proper roughage. When, after a few more weeks, he decided to drop English altogether and take up Arabic as his principal study, he continued his Chinese, just as a hobby. The rest of us complained, Humphrey alone did something about it. But he also chose to stay socially among our first-year group. Fellow English students included the amiable Christopher Hudson, who at the age of eleven had helped me transcribe Wilde into the Harewood school magazine. For our first two terms, the undergraduates of our year were stunned into staying close, huddling together as if none of us could quite believe how unrewarding it was going to be to read English literature at Cambridge. We were immobilised by a shared disappointment. The experience inoculated me for life against art which needs a framework of art theory to be understood. I knew the racket of art theory too well: I'd had expert training.

One of the reasons for our disillusion was the absence of Raymond Williams. We saw him on the first day we arrived and never thereafter. It was as if he had a clipboard at the ready, waiting only to dispatch us as fast as possible. Serene, distant, wearing a Bob Dylan cap, he had the desolate formality of a figure from a Pina Bausch ballet. Perhaps it was his experience as a captain in the 21st Anti-Tank Regiment, Royal Artillery during and after the invasion of Normandy which made him seem old before his time. He gave off an unmistakeable air of tweeds and mustard baths. Raymond lost no time in farming us out to be taught by graduate students and making it clear meanwhile that he had no interest in supervising us himself. We found that throughout the university English was being taught in a way of which, had he followed it more closely, Raymond would have heartily disapproved. Kenneth Tynan called the English literary scene 'all wasps and no honey' – a perfect description of Cambridge in the mid-sixties. The teaching at Lancing had been about the discovery of literature's achievements. University teaching was about the punishment of its shortcomings. As far as our captious lecturers were concerned, the purpose of art was to fulfil the expectations of the critic. Unsurprisingly, by those impossible standards – because, believe you me, these were very *difficult* critics – nearly everything flunked. At some point, that most austere of literary figures, F. R. Leavis, had concocted an unlikely but influential theory that society was awash with consumerist rubbish, the notion of community had been destroyed, and that therefore the future of civilisation depended on its universities. The central preoccupation of those universities should, for some reason, be the study of English literature, which alone could provide society with its renewed moral axis. Quite how and why was often asserted but never explained.

Leavis's theories had not, however, generated a spirit of benevolence and inclusiveness in the university faculty. Far from it. As usual, disciples boasted the faults of a hero without practising his virtues. The followers were mean-spirited and envious, as only lifelong academics can be. Leavis himself had gone in for the silliest kind of list-making, which excluded from consideration all writers the critic regarded as less than first-rate. He had even come out with a book called *The Great Tradition*, which listed those few strugglers – Shakespeare, I guess, George Eliot, T. S. Eliot, sometimes Milton, sometimes not – who met with his hard-won approval. Like Thomas Hardy, Dickens was said to lack 'the seriousness and formal control' of a great novelist, though for some reason his most inaccessible work, *Hard Times*, was grudgingly admitted into Leavis's sheltered accommodation. A working-class outsider himself, Leavis nevertheless believed that the ineffable vulgarity of nasty popular culture had destroyed people's ability to relate to each other. Like an aristocrat, he believed in elites, only in his case they happened to be elites of sensibility rather than birth. When he was told that Ludwig Wittgenstein had been seen queuing for a film at the Arts Cinema, Leavis was amused at the philosopher's frivolity. He said that after a day of philosophy you 'perhaps need a period of complete mindlessness to recover'. Interestingly, this was almost the exact reverse of what most students felt. After a pointless day in which a critic tried to bring some errant poet or novelist to heel, we could at least slip off to enjoy the carbonated vitality of the cinema. Stimulation flowed like spring water from the films of Godard, Bergman, Fellini, Antonioni, Malle and Losey. Had Leavis ever been to a cinema? Did he have any idea that in the 1960s, both for content and for stylistic originality, cinema was at least literature's equal if not its superior? What novelist came near?

Towards the end of my first year, two things happened which broke my gloom. First, I found myself more and more in the company of a second-year Jesus student who, with his stubble, dark glasses and packs of Gitanes, bore more than a passing resemblance to Jean-Luc Godard himself. Tony Bicât was an untypical undergraduate. For a start he was a passable jazz drummer, whose godmother, for some reason, had endowed him with a field in Hampshire, planning permission thrown in. From this bequest, Tony had money to dress in chic handmade suits and jackets which were hardly common currency among students. He believed his mother, Packly, to be a White Russian whose family had fled the revolution, though later he discovered that the family was in fact Chechnyan. In the chaos of short-lived governments, his grandfather had even briefly been prime minister. His father, a noted artist, had left school at fifteen to paint scenery and design sets for the Ballet Rambert and the Mercury Theatre. Not only was Tony a welcome breath of cosmopolitan fresh air who opened up worlds of painting and music of which I knew very little, but we also shared the same satirical sense of humour. To us, everything was funny.

The second change in my mood was brought about by my deciding to have a go at acting. I'd done a little at school, usually as a pilot fish to Nigel Andrews. Now here was my chance to move centre stage. After doing a couple of small parts, I was cast in a revue to go to the Edinburgh Festival at the end of the university year. The critic Clive James, then a graduate student and the producer of the Footlights, had been planning to go, but he had pulled out, leaving behind a title – *Best Laid Mice* – and a few sketches. He had given his blessing to the rest of us to get on with it. There were only four people in the show, which went on at the cheerless Lauriston Hall in the rainy, granite back-streets of Edinburgh late at night. It fell to me to pad the evening out with some excruciatingly clumsy skits and songs. When, in a review, the *Scotsman* newspaper described me as 'a real actor in the making' I was genuinely mystified. We all slept together in a sort of barracks in a basement on the Royal Mile, and listened every night to both sides of the Beatles' just-released *Revolver*. Diana Quick, whom I met that year at the Festival and who became a lasting friend, describes me at first encounter as having been 'shy and formal'. Perhaps I was just ashamed.

An accidental feature of the revue was a physical similarity between me and Richard Cork, a fellow undergraduate who was already a gifted draughtsman but who, by the strange rules then obtaining, was forced to idle for two years reading English before he was allowed to move on to his true interest, the history of art. He would later go on to be the popular and well-read art critic of *The Times*. We were both over six foot tall and slender as a switch. Steve Gooch, the chosen director for the following term's Experimental Theatre Group production, seized on this similarity and decided to present Shakespeare's *The Comedy of Errors*, which depends for its plot on a comic confusion between two men, both called Antipholus, and their servants, both called Dromio. Steve's resulting production was fresh as a daisy and full of teenage high spirits, and in December 1966 we were sent off on a high-speed tour of France and Switzerland. In seventeen days, we gave performances in Aix-en-Provence, Grenoble, Lausanne, Fribourg, Berne, Zurich and Lyon, where the local paper described us as 'looking like distinguished herons who could have served in the Guards'. At several venues, much to our surprise, Richard and I were mobbed at the stage door. We were pleased that none of the screaming fans knew which was Syracuse and which was Ephesus. Better still, few cared.

In 2007 Stephen Wright, who played one of the Dromios, discovered in his attic forty-five minutes of 16 mm film which he had not remembered he had shot on the tour. Taken aback, he invited the cast and crew who had worked on the play to his house in Ealing for a warm evening of wine and abundant buffet, in which we were given an unlooked-for opportunity to examine our young selves. We sat on the floor to watch the black-and-white film which, hand-held, felt as if it had been shot by Raoul Coutard, the most fashionable cinematographer of the 1960s. Some parts look as if they are being seen through a bush. The emulsion bubbles through endless grainy images of our bus travelling along snowbound roads, and of students sleeping at every improvised opportunity, backstage, on benches, on floors, in gorgeous smoky cafés and on the cross-Channel ferry. The women throughout are serene and beautiful, as if used to staying calm under pressure. But the men of the period are like puppets, dancing around nervously, chain-smoking, mugging, making V-signs, joking in a sort of jerky hyperactivity which would later be familiar as the physical lexicon of Monty Python. I am dressed throughout in white jeans and a polo-neck. How uneasy we were, how insecure.

It was moving for all of us that night in West London to reassemble forty-one years on. My Adriana had spent her life as a psychotherapist at the Tavistock Clinic. The attendant lord who had followed me everywhere on stage had become deputy head of MI6 before losing out on the top job and going into private security. One of the most admirable of our number, Jonathan James-Moore, vivid again as Doctor Pinch, with upstanding hair and perfect comic timing, had only recently died from cancer, aged fifty-nine. But the film also confirmed what I had long known: I couldn't act. I had an unfortunate mix of being self-conscious without being self-aware. On stage as off, I was unable to calculate what impression I was making. If I stretched out an arm, I had no internal monitor to tell me what the gesture looked like from the outside. But it did occur to me some time in my second year at Cambridge that, although I couldn't act myself, I might have some modest gift for helping others. First, I staged a version of much the best dramatic writing T. S. Eliot ever did, a witty, rhythmic fragment called *Sweeney Agonistes*, and, cheered by that, I decided to plunge in headlong and direct a production of *Oh What a Lovely War*.

Joan Littlewood's collage of songs and facts from the First World War had affected me when I'd seen it in her own production in 1963. Its boldness was revolutionary. Charles Chilton, a radio producer, had researched the informal lyrics soldiers had added to familiar Edwardian songs and made a documentary, *The Long, Long Trail*. From this rediscovery of what the war had felt like for the soldiers below ground level, Littlewood had made an original piece of angry agitprop. I couldn't hope to match her ensemble of working-class actors, who brought to the pierrot show their shared history. Their authenticity was not available to me. But instead I could give the evening a kind of garish poetry, a passionate sincerity which was all the more potent for being amateur. We were guileless in a way which was oddly affecting. David Pountney, later director of the English National Opera, conducted the band. Mark Elder, later conductor of the Hallé Orchestra, played in the pit. And in one of those god-sent pieces of casting which make directors look clever, Germaine Greer, the future author of *The Female Eunuch*, played the Sergeant Major. No one who saw and heard Germaine, in black fishnet stockings, striding through the audience and belting out 'I'll make a man of every one of you' has ever forgotten it.

I had enjoyed painting a beach house, because, thanks to Roger, we did it to a reasonable standard. The brushwork was fine. But I enjoyed directing a play even more. However, with the achievement came dissatisfaction. Student theatre groups immediately asked me to direct various classics – I undertook Marlowe's *The Jew of Malta*, and later John Whiting's elegiac *A Penny for a Song* – but *Oh What a Lovely War* had spoilt me. It was my first experience of dealing with hot subject matter, treated boldly. My only true interest thereafter was in making new work. Naturally, I had no idea how to generate it. I rang a telephone number in London to enquire about *Dingo*, a war play by Charles Wood which I'd read in a magazine and admired, and was told by the dismissive voice of someone who would one day become my agent, 'Don't be ridiculous, dear. We're not going to waste a good play on a group of students.' For a while I fiddled around, helping a writer who lived in Cambridge with a story about colonial revolution in the hope that it would be good enough to put on. But I was so far out of my depth that the leading actor, pained, looked at me one day before we ever got to formal rehearsals and said, 'David, we can't do this.' At no point did it occur to me that the answer to my discontent might be to write something myself. That was not on the cards.

As Ted Hughes would later put it, you could only come out of Cambridge University a creative writer by 'scrambling through the barbed wire and the camp searchlights'. I wasn't anywhere near ready to scramble.

Perhaps because I was bumping my head on the ceiling of my abilities, I found myself increasingly drawn to the cinema. I had entered my first long-lasting relationship, with a wonderfully cheerful Girton history undergraduate, Diane Millward. Diane was one of a group of girls from St Paul's School in West London, whose enduring mutual friendship was as important to them as any relationship they happened to be in at the time. Not only was Diane herself spirited and funny, she was also part of a circle who understood much more about the world than I did. I got used to their knowing laughter and came to love it. Diane's uncle Sid had a joke Jewish band called the Nitwits, who enjoyed a small cult following sending up classical music. The warmth and straight talking of Diane's devout Central European family in Kensington gave me a standard of comparison for my own chillier upbringing, even though they clearly doubted my credentials to be walking out with their Jewish daughter. My enthusiasm for film had led me to become secretary of the Film Society, which had two regular showings a week of films to packed-out audiences of seven hundred. The movies of the recent past and most especially their heroines – Melina Mercouri in *Stella*, Anna Karina in *Vivre sa vie*, Anna Magnani in *Mamma Roma* and Jeanne Moreau in everything – offered us all an intense sense of possibility, an opening out, an airing which seemed all the more moving for being glimpsed from the Fens. So I was more than ready to collaborate with the society's president, Dick Arnall, who had the ambitious idea of inviting Alfred Hitchcock to Cambridge.

Much to our surprise, Hitchcock came. I read later in a biography that he regarded 1966 as a career low, halfway between the heady days of *Psycho* and the misery of *Family Plot*. But if his spirits were poor, he gave no sense of it. Alfred Hitchcock was the first great artist with whom I ever got to spend any length of time. He arrived for lunch at 1 p.m., but wasn't due to speak until 5.30 p.m. Three or four of us went to the Garden House Hotel, where we fed him slices of cold rare roast beef and baked potatoes and spent the long afternoon listening to everything he could tell us. In 1962, he said, he had sat down with François Truffaut and done twelve hours of interviews about his life's work, so that perhaps accounted for the fact that his thoughts were in such perfect order. Recent film portrayals have made Hitchcock out to be creepy, but in person he was the very opposite. The impression he gave was of being all-seeing. You could put nothing past him. His flow of courteous good sense resonated particularly with me when he said that likeability was a quality which could not be faked. The public had taken Grace Kelly to their hearts because she was indeed likeable. For all Hitchcock's efforts, they had rejected Tippi Hedren because she was not. There was, Hitchcock said, only one actor in the world who was so formidably skilled that he could fake on screen a charm he didn't have in real life. Could any of us guess who it was? Fearing the answer, I replied, 'Cary Grant.' Hitchcock smiled, satisfied. 'Correct.'

The following year, as a deliberate provocation, I invited Michael Winner to show his new film, *I'll Never Forget What's'is-name*. A Cambridge graduate himself, he walked furious into an empty hall and muttered to me, 'I've had more at the Hendon Jewish Fraternity.' I programmed Jack Smith's *Flaming Creatures* with Kenneth Anger's *Scorpio Rising*, for which the society was banned in perpetuity from the science department's Cavendish Laboratories – not exactly the reaction expected from the most rational faculty in the university of reason. But I was also able to invite the Russian director Grigori Kozintsev, who, to a cheering crowd, showed his version of *Hamlet* with Innokenty Smoktunovsky. Kozintsev's elaborately phrased answers to the very simplest questions gave everyone present a chilling sense of the verbal tightrope still walked by Soviet artists. His film also reinforced my growing conviction that the greatest feats of literary criticism were performed by actors and directors, whether on stage or on screen. Never had my formal studies seemed less important. Seasons of René Clair and Kurosawa had so much more to offer.

Problems with our official education had come to a head at the beginning of our final year. When Raymond Williams gathered us together in Samuel Taylor Coleridge's old college rooms to parcel us out for the third time – he intended that I should be taught by a leading campaigner against pornography, who spent his time counting the number of four-letter words in modern novels – we all refused. By pre-arrangement, we staged what amounted to a strike. We told him that we had come to Cambridge to be taught by him, and we were not leaving until it happened. Raymond, I think, was bewildered. He had far more important fish to fry. He was more used to writing about rebellion than to being rebelled against. Since the publication of *Border Country*, an autobiographical novel which reads today as one of the greatest of the period, his creative work had been his most pressing priority. He was planning a sequence of novels, which he would never live to finish, about the people of Wales, going back to prehistoric times. But he was also under sustained pressure from other socialists to prepare what in 1968 would become the May Day Manifesto, a detailed British call to revolution which Raymond co-wrote and for which he was the chosen figurehead. It would be published, with much to-do, on International Labour Day as a Penguin Special, in red covers. As the historian Eric Hobsbawm later observed, not without a trace of jealousy, it was only in England that you might find the militant left demanding to take leadership from a literary critic.

There was clearly a significant difference of temperament between Raymond's generation and my own. Although nearly everyone I knew was taking enthusiastic part in the broad student movements of the time – with Diane, I attended the anti-Vietnam demonstration in Grosvenor Square on 17 March 1968 and witnessed the terrifying behaviour of the police – nevertheless we regarded the drawing-up of revolutionary manifestos as a notably unrealistic activity. The Labour Club had renamed itself the Socialist Society, but even so most of us were all too aware – who could not be? – that we were living through a time more marked by the blood of conquest than by the blood of liberation. We all still agreed with E. P. Thompson that Raymond was 'our best man', blessed with 'a stubborn unfashionable integrity'. But we had a more sceptical view towards inflated rhetoric, from whichever direction it came. We thought that our teachers understood little about power and the tenacity of those who have it. Raymond's dreams of capital overthrown drew strength from his roots in the working class, which most of us lacked. We were one satirical step back from believing that any violent overturning in Britain was likely to be benign. We were also far more roused by the daring and openness of the music, plays, poems and paintings of our time than we were by the deliberations of academics. Raymond lectured on theatre without ever going. He preached revolution as a tenured Fellow at one of the most privileged institutions in the country. Self-aware, Raymond knew more woundingly than we ever could the contradictions of his position. He lived them every day. But he didn't necessarily enjoy being reminded of those contradictions by a new aggrieved generation of bolshie and, as he saw us, middle-class students, intent on righting a professorial wrong.

The result was an embarrassing stand-off from which perhaps neither side came out very well. Years later, the Senior Tutor of the college admitted to me that our experience of finding Raymond elusive had been replicated many times over with succeeding intakes. He went on to defend our educational neglect by saying that perhaps a college like Jesus should be magnanimous enough to let a great intellectual do what he or she must without insisting on the fulfilment of their formal teaching obligations. 'Besides,' he added, 'we didn't have his phone number.'

Eventually, Raymond did concede and take me in for a few spotty supervisions, mostly about D. H. Lawrence, towards whom he seemed to feel an identification which bordered on pity. 'Lawrence, poor bugger, poor poor bugger,' he kept saying, before turning the conversation to last night's Dennis Potter play on the BBC. I loved his calming presence, the essential kindness behind everything he thought and said. But I never got close to him. For a second time in my life, the father was absent. The bulk of my final year's teaching was done instead by Raymond's intellectual godson, Terry Eagleton, who at the time was sunk in tortured Catholic introspection, usually involving young women, and all the more moving for being so helpless and sincere. He had recently published articles in *Stand* magazine arguing that you could not properly be a Christian without being a revolutionary socialist: they were both about transformation, complete and utter. In the mornings, as you arrived, Terry would open the curtains onto a room in which a sense of the night's long agony palpably lingered. For Terry, the ready Marxist aggro came later. To his credit, at this point he did his best to engage with his students' common disillusion. He was not much older than us. When I wanted to do a third-year dissertation on Oscar Wilde, it was Terry who warned me that no examiner would take me seriously if I offered a paper on a playwright whom they regarded as frivolous – this in spite of the fact that Terry would in 1989 himself write a play, *Saint Oscar*, inspired by Wilde's Irish radicalism. And it was Terry who also tried to untangle the youthful foolishness of my anger. When I was inveighing tediously against Cambridge's insistence that everything had to be serious to be meaningful, he looked at me kindly and said, 'David, it's not seriousness you hate. It's solemnity. They're different.'

Tony Bicât, lucky fellow, had been a year above me, so he had already left town in the company of a group of friends who were enraptured by intellectual movements on the Continent. Their talk was of Derrida and Marcuse. Tony was getting by, gigging as a drummer. When student/worker demonstrations broke out in May 1968, the Jesus undergraduates who had left the previous year were free to tear up the cobblestones and throw them at the CRS in Paris while I, still frightened to strike out, was enough of my mother's son to feel I must fulfil my obligation to sit in a stuffy exam room in East Anglia. Underneath all the impetuosity and scorn, I was still a timid boy, fearful of disapproval, fearful of failure. During the holidays, however, I would spend as much time as I could staying with Tony's grandmother, who lived in Earls Court Square in a manner, and with furniture, which any pre-revolutionary Russian would have recognised. Unfortunately, robbed of servants in 1917, Babushka had only ever learned to cook one dish, so every night Tony and I would sit down to eat the same meal of Wiener schnitzel, accompanied by an astonishingly pungent onion and tomato salad, and to discuss what on earth we might do with our lives. The options were many. At one point we considered mimicking a French publisher and issuing what were called *boîtes* – boxes containing objects, drawings, texts and photographs relating to important thinkers of the time. Inevitably, the first one would have been about Godard. We never got as far as the second. But we also talked longingly of working in cinema, without having any practical idea of how we might start. At the Film Society I had invited the head of the BFI production board, the Australian Bruce Beresford, to show us some of his output. But his favoured black-and-white accounts of purposeless folk mooning about in parks did little to make you feel that the UK had such a thing as a vital experimental film culture. Beresford later directed *Driving Miss Daisy*.

In the hope of employment, I had already fired off a series of letters to British film-makers like Clive Donner and Tony Richardson, who had all been kind enough to meet me. Richardson alarmed me in the Woodfall offices in Curzon Street by offering me a glass of the champagne he was already drinking at 10.30 a.m. His producer wore a figure-hugging Jermyn Street suit with a red paisley pattern on the lining. They offered me a job as fourth assistant on their forthcoming film with Albert Finney playing Che Guevara. But it was never made. The charming Clive Donner was planning a film about Alfred the Great with David Hemmings, which even an impressionable twenty-year-old could see had dog written all over it. By a process of recommendation, I got passed down the line to Associated British Pathé, who accepted me for eight weeks of well-paid employment the moment I left university. I couldn't believe my luck. Possessing a fabulous library of accumulated footage, a tiny fraction of which, naturally, I had already seen in newsreel theatres on Waterloo and Victoria stations, Pathé were looking for a way of using their languishing archive to make documentaries for schools. In charge of the project was the personable Richard Dunn. In 1988, as Chair of Thames Television, Richard would become the target of Margaret Thatcher and Rupert Murdoch's co-ordinated fury when, with unruffled eloquence, he defended the airing of the exemplary documentary *Death on the Rock*, which corrected government misinformation about the way in which three IRA terrorists had been shot by the SAS in Gibraltar. Thatcher, never more dangerous than when proved to be in the wrong, punished Richard two years later by making sure that Thames TV's franchise was not renewed.

Tony believed that I had hated Cambridge because I thought it resembled the real world – i.e. a series of uptight English institutions – whereas Tony hated it because he knew it didn't. Why, then, did I make a slapstick attempt to join ITV's rival, the BBC, as a general trainee? Invited before a kidney-shaped board of dark-suited men and women for one of their coveted fast-track entry positions, I was presented with a series of moral dilemmas which apparently exercised the minds of the Corporation's finest. I was asked to imagine a situation in which I was directing a broadcast at Heathrow airport for the arrival of the Queen's plane, when out of the corner of my eye I saw a full jet-load of passengers crash-landing and being incinerated on the opposite runway. What would be my priority be? To turn the cameras and get exclusive, live pictures of a news story? Or to self-censor, in order to spare the audience the sight of living people being burnt to a crisp? I replied that there would be no question. I would cover the news. There was a rustle of shock and discontent. The Chair, who was looking like a snail which had just been salted, asked me whether, in that case, there was anything at all which I would not consider showing on television. Too readily, I replied that of course there was. I hoped to leave it at that. But the Chair persisted, asking to say what that thing would be. I hesitated and said that surely he didn't want me to say. Oh, but he did. 'Very well,' I said. 'Cripples making love.'

If only I had known it, I had begun what would become an unappealing habit of leaving things before it was time. Because I could see a way out, I took it. As far as Cambridge was concerned, I had, in T. S. Eliot's phrase, 'had the experience but missed the meaning'. My restlessness in my last year meant that I spent more and more time jumping onto trains to London, even if the BBC, aghast at the summoning of a physical image they had clearly never before contemplated, were unlikely ever to consider me as suitable officer material. I had put on my beige elephant cord suit from John Stephen in Carnaby Street in April 1967 to go to the *14 Hour Technicolor Dream* at Alexandra Palace and had stood disbelieving as Yoko Ono climbed a pair of steps and stood on top, cutting up pieces of paper which covered a naked model. The event, attended by ten thousand entranced young people and featuring as many happenings as bands, was the first swallow of a spring whose weekly rites would be held in clubs like Middle Earth at Covent Garden and the UFO in the Tottenham Court Road. I went many times, often more like an anthropologist than a person. People of my age were beginning to divide, with overlaps naturally, between those who wanted to change the world and those who wanted to have a good time. The interactions between the two tendencies would eventually create all sorts of interesting frictions, as the claim that by doing the second you might thereby do the first grew less plausible with time. But there were also those like me who stood at the side, watching both groups and liking both, and yet not having that necessary sense of utter belonging that I saw on the abandoned faces of the stoned dancers and in the deep convictions of the revolutionaries.

I did join in a few times, particularly when called back to Cambridge to graduate. The Master of the college, a classicist called Denys Page, made a dreadful speech in which he said 1968 had been a year of militant student protest, but that mercifully such protest had not lapped onto the shores of Jesus College. I was among a small but noisy group who booed him heartily. He had the grace to look surprised.

6

Don't Come

A new phase of my life began in Earlham Street, just off Cambridge Circus, in the summer of 1968. For £15 a week, split three ways, Christopher Hudson, a medical student at St Bart's called Richard Gillette and I found a room each and a shared kitchen in a tiny apartment on the second floor of Nos 5–7, in a lively market street that ran down to Seven Dials. The Australian owners were going to Ibiza. Inside, you could barely turn round. But the moment you stepped out the door, you had the advantage that you were in the centre of the West End. Soho, still filthy dirty, belonged to the alcoholics and the prostitutes. Men in heavy overcoats swilled Pernod with shaky hands in the French pub, while milk-white girls in slacks, heels and improvised turbans rushed busily from club to club. A filling lunch at Jimmy's, the Greek basement, was chicken livers and chips. On Sunday mornings, apart from the odd milk-cart, you had the place to yourself. When Tony Elliot visited, notebook and pen in hand, to collect details of the events he was listing in the first ever edition of his new pocket-sized magazine *Time Out*, he perched on the edge of my bed. There was nowhere else to sit. As the last great smog turned the air thick and wet at the end of the year, I was still sucking down God knows how many cigarettes a day. One morning I woke up with bronchitis, as if a damp cloth were being held over my nose and mouth, and was grateful that the Charing Cross Hospital, housed in the pepper-pot building just off Trafalgar Square, was not far down the road. It was scarcely visible as I approached. A man in the next bed with a collapsed lung was still allowed to smoke a pipe in the designated lung ward, as we all watched *Elmer Gantry* on one bright colour television shared between thirty. When I woke at 3 a.m. from my opiate sleep to find nurses putting screens round the bed of another man in the very last moments of choking to death, I resolved to give up the cancer-sticks. And did.

Recreations of the period mislead by their lack of diversity. In musicians' memoirs, descriptions of outrageous behaviour are justified with the formula 'Hey, it was the sixties.' But for every person who loved drugs there was another, like me, who distrusted them. Yes, the party – often beginning on Saturday night at 10 p.m. and ending on Sunday long after dawn – was always the unit of currency, the common building block of the period. But even before becoming a dramatist, I had the instincts of a voyeur, and still do. I'm always happiest at the side of the room, watching. I didn't respond well to drugs. Their effect mainly was to make me paranoid and to stoke my insecurity. They sent me the message that everything was not all right. When I took them, the universe never seemed to cohere, nor to impart meaning. So I seemed condemned to spend a certain number of evenings per week watching other people drift away peaceably. To me, it seemed axiomatic that one person was going to be more interesting than many. I preferred to go deep than wide. The image of those first London years would always be of closing the door and slipping away early before the dope, already a fog, became a blanket. I was invariably more interested in who I might leave the party with than with anything that happened during it.

The work at Pathé was fun. The office was at 142 Wardour Street, so I could walk there in five minutes. Richard Dunn was an ideal boss, and my fellow researcher was Charlie Gillett, who knew everything about rock and roll. In the early 1960s, Charlie had suggested to the *Observer* that he might write a column for them about popular music. They had replied by saying that not only did they not want his column, but that they found it unimaginable that the *Observer* would ever run any column about pop music, because pop wasn't, and never could be, art. Charlie, with his defiantly short haircut, was indifferent to the fashion of the times. A keen sprinter, he was as lean as James Dean and dressed like him in jeans and plimsolls. Later, it was Charlie who wrote rock's first and best history, *The Sound of the City*. He also discovered Ian Dury and managed him in the early days when, before the Blockheads, he led a pub band called Kilburn and the High Roads. It was typical of Charlie that when Dury was approached by another manager, Charlie let him go, telling him to do whatever was best for the music.

There were to be two sets of films, supposedly pilots for an intended series, one on War and Society, and the other on Sex and Society. Charlie had arrived before me. He had shrewdly calculated that there would, in a newsreel archive, be a great deal more footage of the first than of the second. He had bagged War. I was left with Sex. My search for any usable Dionysian material became so desperate that I ended up making *Sex and Society Part One: The Duke of Windsor*, on the unlikely grounds that at least there was film of *him*. I watched it so often that from memory I can still do a passable imitation of Edward VIII's resignation speech. But much as I was relishing the chance to sit at a Steenbeck and learn how to cut film, I suffered from a bothering sense of urgency. At last I was free. It had taken long enough. But what was the point of freedom if you didn't use it? Both Tony and I had perfected our contempt for the English theatre as we believed it to be. Without having seen it, we thought everything was rubbish. We had both wanted to go into film because film was modern and theatre wasn't. But one afternoon, having a cup of tea in Earlham Street, I asked him why we couldn't start a new company from scratch. How about a different kind of theatre that didn't play to the old audience? Tony looked at my small wireless in the kitchen and said, 'Why shouldn't theatre be portable? Like that radio?'

Seeking a blessing from the country's leading stage director appeared to be a necessary rite of passage for anyone with new ideas. So we wrote to Peter Brook, who invited us to his luxurious, rather formal house in Kensington. It was that easy. We sat down next to the grand piano. Six years previously Brook had directed an unforgettable *King Lear* with Paul Scofield at the Royal Shakespeare Company, which we'd all visited from school, but lately he was moving into a more experimental period, growing closer, in spirit at least, to a nascent alternative theatre than he was to the mainstream. Forced out of his Paris quarters in Les Gobelins by the *événements* of May '68, he had come to the Roundhouse with an international company and staged some beautiful fragments from *The Tempest*. In their jazzy and carefully improvised feeling these scenes very much chimed with the kind of theatre Tony and I aspired to. The afternoon we visited him, Brook took us to a local comprehensive to see a school play which had been written by his friends Albert Hunt and Adrian Mitchell. And then when we sat down to talk, he asked why we were even beginning to think about finding a base. What was the point? Brook said he had just spent ten years on the National Theatre's building committee, helping to plan what would become Denys Lasdun's brutalist fortress on the South Bank. He had become convinced that they were going about things the wrong way round. All the energy was going into bricks and mortar. How much better to stick to our original idea, a theatre called Portable. Why not do the work first, then find out later what sort of building might one day accommodate it? Further, he added, the only way of discovering your identity was by starting. Young directors, he said, always had a list of plays they imagined they wanted to do. They planned something by Kleist or Schiller, and to stage, as they believed, what would be a revelatory production of a Webster, inevitably *The Duchess of Malfi* or, even worse, *The White Devil*. But soon enough, he said, if a theatre company were remotely original, it would find its own direction. At that point, Webster and Kleist could go hang.

This was perfect advice from someone we admired. It was also yet more high-octane fuel for a process which was already moving at the speed of a good idea. Tony handed me a copy of Kafka's diaries and suggested we dramatise them. A cheerful friend from Warwick University, Gus Hope, joined us and laughed when we gave her the title of administrator. The three of us worked out a simple system. We foresaw employing five actors, each of whom would get one tenth of the take. We three would get a further tenth each, and the remaining two tenths would go to the expenses of running the company. It was socialist and it was fair, even if it would turn out to be incompatible with making a living. Gus wrote to Olympia, who responded by giving us a free electric typewriter, and the three of us signed a letter of appeal to Volkswagen, who responded by giving us one of their classic nine-seater camper

vans. Young people trying the same route today are disbelieving when told how simple we found it in 1968. The main reason? So few others had thought to do it.

Asked why she went on the stage, Tallulah Bankhead replied,
'To get out of the audience.' In the following twenty years,
more than seven hundred theatre companies were formed all
over the UK, as if small-scale plays – confrontational, angry,
direct – might somehow reach a gap in an audience's concerns
that nothing else was filling. For popularity drama could never
compete with music. But it could articulate a timely kind of
discontent, and thereby release discontent's paradoxical energy.
By a freak of timing, Portable Theatre was there almost at the
start. We went first to Jim Haynes at the Arts Laboratory in
Drury Lane. Tony and I told him we wanted to put on a show
we were writing together, drawn from Kafka and entitled
Inside Out. Jim said, 'Sure. When do you want to do it?' Jim,
an American ex-serviceman who had founded the Traverse
Theatre in Edinburgh in 1963, was one of the two inspirational
theatre leaders in London who were happiest saying yes. The
other was Peter Oliver, who was the warden of Oval House in
Kennington, a boys' club set up by Christ Church, Oxford, to
welcome local youths. It had originally been skewed towards
sport, but Peter had turned it into a rough performance space
which was open to anyone who felt they had something to contribute. From the start, Portable Theatre relied on the patron-
age of these two extraordinary men, even though we hoped our
long-term future might involve taking theatre where it had
never been before. Our thinking was simple: only by changing
the places of performance could we also change the audience.
Change the audience and you will change the character of the
theatre experience.

Such ambitions are common in the twenty-first century. Plays presented outside playhouses today have to groan under the ugly name of 'site-specific'. It's become a genre, and, like all genres, constrained. But in those days, when Jerzy Grotowski invited us all to trek out to a disused film studio in southwest London to see *Akropolis*, it was just something he wanted to do. In the years of its existence, Portable Theatre would eventually play in army camps, in village halls, in libraries, on canteen floors, in churches and chapels, and even in people's front rooms. A repertory which was uncompromising, at first in the height of its brow but later in the extremity of its analysis, made for some uncomfortable evenings. We walked a fine and occasionally smug line between affront and cackhandedness. We were happy to judge our impact not by the length of the applause – sometimes there wasn't any – but by the level of shock we achieved. A night in Workington when we had packed the van and driven away beyond the city limits before the audience even got up from its seats came to represent the epitome of everything we were trying to achieve. Go in, shake them up and get out. Occasionally, driving home on the empty motorways there would be magical incidents. At two o'clock one morning on the M1 we drew out to overtake a black stretch limo with Count Basie, also returning from a gig, in the back. We travelled alongside him long enough to scrawl a message on a piece of card which we held up to the window. 'You're great'. The Count smiled and toasted us with his glass of whisky. Then we sped on. In our first year of work we would drive our Volkswagen more than fifteen thousand miles.

In 1997, a year before his death, Ted Hughes astonished me at dinner in the open air one summer evening in Malvern by saying how much he envied me my life. 'You chose the theatre.

I wish I had.' Perhaps he was right. Theatre's highs may be infrequent, but they are peculiarly pure. In those first weeks, it didn't take Tony and me long to find a few brave actors willing to risk a punt. Hilary Charlton, William Hoyland, Neil Johnston, Maurice Colbourne and Nicholas Nacht became a company which would stay together on short rations for several months. In no time at all Tony and I were rehearsing in the living room of an unoccupied house, sharing the direction as we had shared the writing. By October, we had begun performing in the Arts Lab where J. G. Ballard had hung the walls with pictures of car crashes. Not long after, we were touring. Tony was all the time on the lookout for playwrights who might give us something unexpected. He had a left-field idea to premiere Lawrence Durrell's unperformed play *An Irish Faustus*. But when we went to meet the author at eleven o'clock one morning in a Covent Garden pub, we were more put off by Durrell's pervasive melancholy than we were by his already having drunk a Pernod with a Fernet Branca chaser before we arrived. His own gloomy view of the play coloured ours. Tony seemed on a safer track with John Grillo, a droll actor, and with Snoo Wilson, an eccentric and highly charged student who was still at the University of East Anglia. Snoo had a shock of unruly brown hair, as if someone had just given him fifty volts. He also had an uncontrollable laugh, in-turned, most often at his own jokes, and an ability to make sentences which came out like pearled, intricate cadenzas. Tony and I had gone to Norwich earlier in the year to see his dramatisation of Virginia Woolf's last novel, *Between the Acts*. Tony was a much more far-seeing producer than me, with an uncanny nose for potential, so when he insisted the play was talented, I believed him, although I had not understood large swathes of it. But when, not far into 1969,

Snoo calculated that the completion of his degree course was more important to him than delivering a ramshackle touring company the new play he had promised, I realised there was only one thing to do. Tony and I were already drivers, stage managers, lighting designers and sound operators. I decided I might as well hyphenate into playwriting too.

Tony insists that I was encouraged in this decision by the fact that I had at the end of 1968 become literary manager of the Royal Court Theatre. This had happened largely by accident. My old friend Christopher Hampton had written an adolescent play about the confusion of a young man who desires his best friend but ends up in a relationship with his best friend's mother. It was first performed at Oxford University, then later for a couple of Sunday nights at the Court. In 1966 *When Did You Last See My Mother?* transferred to the Comedy Theatre for a three-week season, and Christopher, aged twenty, became the youngest dramatist in modern times to be performed in the West End. The music of the dialogue was derived from John Osborne, but the power of the feeling was Christopher's own. On leaving university, he had become the Court's literary manager, in charge of dealing with submitted scripts and advising on the repertory. Fairly soon he had found he had no time to write plays. So he had suggested to the artistic director, William Gaskill, that I take over the reading in order to free him up for the writing. Becoming the Royal Court's literary manager at the age of twenty-one did not seem in any way remarkable or precocious. No one else wanted the job. My office, the size of a broom cupboard, also served as a corridor to the lavatories. For a three-day week, the wage was £7.50.

In Tony's preferred version of events, I spent a lot of my time in the Portable van, as we cruised along the motorway from one far-flung engagement to the next, with my head in my hands, groaning. According to him, I would sit there flipping the pages of one of the thousand new plays the Court received every year, occasionally looking up to say, 'I can do better than this.' But my own recollection is much more stark and practical. It was only on a Wednesday that Tony and I reluctantly accepted that Snoo's repeated postponements did indeed mean he was not going to deliver. We had a gaping hole in our touring programme which had to be filled in time for rehearsals the following Monday. We couldn't afford to renege. And so I was forced to write my first play in just four days by perching a small typewriter on my knee as we sped from gig to gig. I tried it out, line by line, on Tony. The result, a one-act satire on the way left-wing politics were feeding off media celebrity, was unfeeling and obvious. But when I put the Roneoed typescript in the actors' hands, they didn't look unhappy. At some basic level, the page looked right. There was a rhythm. It turned out I could write dialogue before I could write plays.

By now the company itself had changed. Neil and Maurice had left us to go and join the Freehold, a physical theatre group which, like us, was performing at the Arts Lab. One of the noticeable things about histories of the fringe is how completely the women get written out. But they were just as formative as the men, and sometimes more so. Beth Porter, an American actress, had arrived in London inspired by the example of Ellen Stewart's La Mama Theatre in New York, and formed a company called the Wherehouse. It was Nancy Meckler who transformed Beth's Wherehouse group into the Freehold, which, alongside the wildly musical Pip Simmons Group and the People Show, two other fringe favourites, eventually toured to some of the same venues as us, including the ever reliable

Mickery Theatre which, in the early days, was in the middle of Amsterdam. Portable was already unusual – some would say obstinate – in those experimental times for never losing its faith in the power of the word. At first, we presented a repertory in which Strindberg, Kafka and Genet were strongly featured. We were still in love with the European avant-garde. See the work which had seemed to us contemporary, the *nouvelle vague* cinema of Malle, of Truffaut, of Godard, of Varda and of Resnais, and you will be amazed at how literary it is, how steeped in great writing. But among companies closer to America, language was commonly said to be dead, a hopelessly corrupt form of communication which could no longer convey essentials. The future of performance lay in rock music, in video, in mime and in puppetry. The dominant mode was a sort of galleried performance art which relied more on multimedia than it did on any ancestry in literature. If Portable still walked round muttering neurotic European texts, the majority of our fringe contemporaries preferred to stand in vests sweating on one another's shoulders to the sound of rock.

The word 'influential' is today invariably attached to the name of Portable Theatre. Tony Bicât and I both realised quickly that a theatre's influence may well be directly disproportionate to the size of its audience. Influence may be spread as much by firing up the distant imaginations of people who never see the work as it is by inspiring those who do. Nothing wrong with that. But if Portable Theatre was influential, it was also unrepresentative. *How Brophy Made Good* opened at Oval House in March 1969 to no particular acclaim. Why should it? It wasn't very good. When we went to the Traverse Theatre in Edinburgh, I got my first professional review as a dramatist: 'The most pointless evening I have ever spent in the theatre.'

Things could only go up from there. Tony had begun directing my sixty-minute effort with a cast made up from two of our original company, joined by Ian McCulloch and Moris Farhi, a young Turkish actor who was also a novelist, poet and aspiring television writer. His six episodes of *Doctor Who* in which the Doctor would have met Alexander the Great had just been rejected. The cast unsurprisingly tended to turn towards me to ask questions of a highly unorthodox choral text. 'What on earth did you mean by this?' 'Why do you put it like that?' So after a couple of weeks, Tony had taken me out for a drink and said, 'You're obviously itching to direct it yourself. Why don't you?' Although Tony had sky-high ambitions for Portable Theatre, he had few for himself, and they weren't conventional. As he said, we were working towards a kind of theatre which didn't exist, or rather which existed only in his mind. He defined it as rough theatre with fine detail. He would make it happen any way he could. So I largely took over directing my own play. When it opened, my primary feeling was one of relief.

One of the most intriguing things about any artwork is how its destiny is only slowly revealed. Up an alley at the end of West Street, just a hundred yards from the Brighton seafront, lay the Combination, a sixty-seat Victorian schoolhouse. It had a cafe serving the characteristic food of the period, carrot cake, muesli and bread pudding with raisins. The coffee came in those little rounded Perspex cups which had been all the rage in Soho in the days of Tommy Steele. For me, the Combination was the most heady of all sixties theatres, the nearest place in Britain, as one founder said, to San Francisco. If there ever was an acid dream that wasn't a nightmare, it was here. The theatre had been started by a group of friends, Ruth Marks, Jenny Harris and Noel Greig, who had all been at London University together and all of whom were to die too young. It was fiercely collective. Whenever Portable visited we were invariably made welcome and regarded as friendly neutrals in long-running disputes. However, we were aware that our week-long visits provided the resident company with a welcome break to redouble the vigour of its own internal arguments. There was absolutely no assumption, be it theatrical or political, which went unchallenged at the Combination. It was typical of the place that one of their most successful productions was played under the memorable title *Don't Come*. It was an injunction which the loyal audience of strays and hippies was more than happy to disobey. It was packed. It involved, in my memory, a group of naked actors walking around clucking like chickens and reading the Communist Manifesto. The British theatre, or at least our part of it, was already prone to these agonised crises of conscience which were to become so common in the next ten years. Artists were finding art inadequate. Only direct action would do.

Those of us still wanting to persist with putting on plays recognised that the Combination was one of those accidental, magical spaces, like Peter Brook's later Bouffes du Nord in Paris, which make everything seem better. I was learning that one of the most surprising rewards of theatre is to marvel at how a play may gleam at a different angle according to where and when it's presented. The thoughts and feelings with which the audience arrive are half the story. On the road, bruised by travel and slapped down in hostile environments, my writing had seemed, at best, knowing and pretentious. The play came across as a sort of metropolitan sneer which didn't bother to explain what it was sneering about. The author seemed to live in a cocoon of superior attitudes which, without reason, he assumed the audience shared. But the moment *How Brophy Made Good* arrived in Brighton, it unexpectedly began to cohere. As Tony put it, the pervading smell of cold newspaper and wet pizza somehow oozed creativity. What, on the road, had spluttered like damp timber responded to friendly winds and caught fire. In Brighton an audience were waiting who were already steeped in the generous anarchy of the Combination, and who warmed to the inchoate anger of the young man who had written this week's unexceptional show. Under their gaze, the play acquired a purpose and depth which not even the most partial spectator would have been able to detect during its tour. They roared with friendly laughter at the ridiculous insanity of left-wing self-regard in screwed-up right-wing Britain.

It was into this invigorated atmosphere that Margaret Matheson stepped on a Sunday night. It was our last performance in Brighton and as we were packing up the stage to go home, a very conspicuous young woman, with a boyish haircut, tall and beautiful in a long tweed coat, with a thick Scottish scarf and gloves, stayed on when everyone else had gone to tell me how much she had enjoyed the performance. It was a change to see something which made you laugh. She had come down specially from London by train, because she had liked the sound of the play when she had read about it in an obscure professional newspaper. It had never occurred to her that the trip might actually be worthwhile. She worked as a secretary, she said, for the well-known socialist agent Clive Goodwin, who besides representing some of the most political dramatists of the day was also one of the founders of the revolutionary newspaper *The Black Dwarf*. In late afternoons, she told me, sometimes while smoking a companionable joint, they would discuss expanding the client list which already included Fay Weldon, Dennis Potter and Simon Gray. Clive had encouraged

Margaret to establish a list of her own. Trevor Griffiths had been her first signing. I was to be her second.

Her boss took to me as fast as Margaret had done, and claimed me as his own. For some reason, at that moment in his life, which at that point was as thoroughly tragic as it would continue to be, Clive was tickled pink by the idea of me. He had a spacious flat on the Cromwell Road where he both worked and lived and where the offices of the *Black Dwarf* had originally been. It was hung with sumptuous canvases by his wife, 'the Wimbledon Bardot', Pauline Boty. She was already something of a legend, both as a beauty and as an artist, and was believed to be the model for Liz, the liberated woman played in suede coat and with swinging handbag by Julie Christie in *Billy Liar*. Boty, who coined the best ever definition of pop art – she called it 'nostalgia for now' – was the only radical feminist in that movement and, as such, way before her time. She and Clive had been married for only three years when she died of cancer in 1966, at the age of twenty-eight, having refused the chemotherapy that would have had the side-effect of killing her unborn child. Dressed in expensive velvet trousers by Yves St Laurent, I guess, the still-grieving widower Clive was in his mid-thirties, laid-back and lugubrious, dark circles bringing out the light of his Lothario eyes. He was a working-class boy from Kensal Rise who had already been repertory actor, television presenter, magazine editor and newspaper proprietor. On first encounter Clive told me that it was a small miracle that somebody had arrived on the left with a sense of humour. How rare was that? He had, he said, sent my modest jape to Michael Codron, the West End's most prominent straight-play producer. It was Michael who had staged Harold Pinter's first work, *The Birthday Party*, in its famous five-day outing at the

Lyric Hammersmith. By return of post, Michael had written back to say he liked my writing as much as Clive did. He would like to commission a full-length comedy from me. Did I have a subject? Clive asked. I certainly did, I replied. What was it? Feminism. Perfect, said Clive, rubbing his hands.

It would be fair to say that my life was heading fast in a direction for which I was not at any level prepared. Sure, I had been swimming in the waters of contemporary theatre, but my private self-esteem was no higher than when my mother had questioned me about an old man in an overcoat accosting me on the Downs. I was a novice director. I did not consider myself a writer, let alone a potentially commercial one. My literary job for three days a week at the Royal Court had inculcated in me the belief that being a dramatist was a serious calling. The house playwright was John Osborne, but the house god was Samuel Beckett. The image of Beckett's admonishing high-mindedness as an artist was in striking contrast to his gentleness as a man. I always found him easier in the pub than on a plinth. At the time when I'd arrived at the end of 1968, the old Sloane Square powerhouse which had given the world John Arden, Ann Jellicoe and Arnold Wesker had hit a particularly low moment in its fortunes. A stranger to today's vogue for programming subsidised theatres with an emollient eye on the box office, the artistic director, Bill Gaskill, had characteristically scheduled three plays in a row about child murder. The last of them, *Life Price*, had emptied the theatre more completely than the others. So, not above risking a PR wheeze when it presented itself, the formidably ascetic Gaskill had inaugurated something to which he gave the high-flown name of Free Theatre. Because nobody was volunteering to pay money to see this particular play, Gaskill had resolved to give the seats away for nothing.

Needless to say, this innovative policy had attracted a large, grateful and broad-based audience, and brought welcome life into the auditorium. But it had also sent the Arts Council of Great Britain into a full-blown existential breakdown. If a flop wasn't a flop, what was it? They were furious, feeling that their bluff was being called. If the Court got away with it, so would everyone. The arts bureaucrats certainly did not share the high artistic belief which was current at the Royal Court, best put by the pianist Charles Rosen: 'From our artists and entertainers we expect originality, and then resent it when we get it.'

The immediate response of the board of the Royal Court to this funding crisis had been to insist that Gaskill, hitherto the lone artistic director, whose widdershins championship of the plays of Edward Bond had already taken the theatre to the edge of survival, in future be shored up by the company of two old colleagues. From 1969, the theatre was to be run by three people, each of whom was variously formidable and cantankerous – though, to be fair, they argued as ferociously with each other as they did with anyone else. Their savage disapproval of each other's work was something to behold, as they swanned round telling everyone within earshot not to attend each other's productions. One new arrival was Anthony Page, by far and away the most congenial of the three, who had briefly assumed the horrible task of succeeding George Devine when the theatre's founder, after declaring that 'the weight of this edifice has driven me into the ground up to my neck', had died aged fifty-five from overwork in 1966. And the other was Lindsay Anderson, an abrasive iconoclast with the profile of a Roman emperor, whose feature films *This Sporting Life* and *If . . .* had a political bite and confidence more or less unique in British cinema.

I had joined the Royal Court Theatre happy with my place
way down the food chain and knowing in advance that I was
out of synch with some of its aims and ideals. My short theatrical experience was of a free fringe movement in which what
mattered most was what you were saying. There was a directness about it which to us signified urgency. The Royal Court,
with its close ties to a more mainstream aesthetic – Peggy
Ashcroft and Laurence Olivier had both acted there – was far
more concerned with the beauty of the saying. In particular,
the theatre was proud of a hallowed form of social realism
about which not a bad word might ever be said. So it would
never have occurred to me to mention to anyone at my place
of legitimate employment that I had, on the sly, written a short
play, which had even been staged. Lindsay, much loved by his
intimates such as the actresses Rachel Roberts and Jill Bennett,
was, to those of us who loved him less, the very definition of
the man Oscar Wilde was referring to when he remarked, 'He
is so loud that one cannot hear what he says.' He spent the day
standing in corridors, usually in beige socks, rapping out orders
like a sergeant major happiest when dressing down recruits. He
had such definite opinions on everything that you longed occasionally to be refreshed with the soothing words 'I don't know'.
Lindsay did briefly seem human one evening when he came
to a Christmas Eve script meeting – his idea, not ours – with a
frozen chicken from Mac Fisheries in the King's Road, which,
he said, he intended to thaw overnight and share for Christmas lunch round his place with Rachel Roberts next day. He
also carried a small, un-Christmassy packet of Birds Eye frozen
peas. Gaskill, on the other hand, had fought bloody battles for
the abolition of theatre censorship and had, thanks to a defiant
court appearance, contributed to ending the 230-year reign of

the Lord Chamberlain. Bill, often from behind his desk in a biker's studded black leather jacket and jeans, could chill you in a far deeper way. He was given to long staring silences, in which he seemed to be considering, in great visceral depth, whether what you had just suggested was the stupidest thing he had ever heard in his life.

My lack of confidence about becoming a dramatist, engorged in the sweltering hothouse of defensiveness and paranoia which was the Royal Court, was reinforced in a much more positive way by meeting Howard Brenton. Of all the successive strokes of luck which make up the history of Portable Theatre, Howard was the most timely. Tony had known him as a friend for a while after talent-spotting him for the very first play he wrote. That was why Tony invited him to an Arts Lab performance of *Inside Out*. There was believed to be a long-standing Equity rule that if there were more people on the stage than in the audience, the performance should be cancelled. So the three of us had repaired to a Drury Lane pub, where I was charmed by a large man who, in his conversation and in his benign, looming presence, had a distinctive mix of sweetness and intensity. I noticed on first meeting that his conversation, punctuated by tremendous emphases, as if the sustain pedal on the piano were being repeatedly banged down, nevertheless always headed towards a point. It made him rewarding to talk to. Howard was working at the Royal Mint by day in order to make a living, and firing off plays from his basement in Notting Hill through the night. Tony or I had come up with some stupid idea that Portable should in its second season present a history of evil, which, we suggested, should take us from Judas Iscariot to the present day. At our suggestion Howard set off on writing some kind of Chamber of Horrors pageant play, but quickly decided that his real interest lay in only one evil person, a wartime Special Police Constable, also from Notting Hill, who had killed at least eight women before being hanged for murder in 1953. The moment Howard delivered the script of his seventy-minute shocker, Tony and I knew that we had reached that moment which Peter Brook had predicted. We had been handed something so good that from this point on, we would know what Portable was for.

If you read it today, *Christie in Love* remains a brilliant play. Set in a pen made of chicken wire and filled with old newspaper, it dramatises the police's exhumation of the corpses of John Reginald Christie's victims from their burial places in his house and back garden. It plays with the controversial notion that when Christie practised necrophilia, assaulting his dead women, he was, in his own eyes, expressing a kind of love. With torches used for lighting, and with Christie rising from his own grave with a huge papier-mâché head, it was a stunning kind of punk theatre before the word was invented. At the time it was presented, Richard Fleischer had not yet made his dutiful film with Richard Attenborough muttering his way through the part, so the case was mainly remembered by lawyers and campaigners against the death penalty for the fact that Christie had first succeeded in helping to get the wrong man, Timothy Evans, executed for at least one of his murders. But rather than write a simple miscarriage-of-justice play, Howard had burrowed deep into the character of Christie himself, contrasting the strangeness of his deeds with the shocked incomprehension of the police. Howard's own father had been a policeman before moving on to serve as a Methodist minister. As the play's chosen director, I felt an unmistakeable anticipation. This was going to be good. If we had started out close to Godard, now, had we but known it, we were closer in spirit to Fassbinder, who, for his own very similar Munich theatre group, was at the same moment writing a play on the Moors Murders. From now on, there was no question of Portable doing old plays.

On 4 July 1969 Tony and a few others of us set off together in high spirits driving the Portable van to Greece, which when I had gone there two years earlier represented a special kind of freedom. In the restaurants, you went straight into the kitchen to look at what was cooking. It summed the country up. There was no such thing as a menu. Leaving central London at 3 a.m. we bought an early copy of the *Daily Mirror* and saw, from the vivid photograph on the front page, that Brian Jones of the Rolling Stones had been found dead at the bottom of a swimming pool. The Stones' concert in Hyde Park planned for the Saturday would now be dedicated to Jones' memory. Tony and I briefly debated whether this was an important enough event to detain us, then sped down all the way to the deserted island of Skiathos, where a friend was lending us a cottage on an isolated hill, normally shared between a farmer and his pigs. We had a full month off, a lot of it spent poking our donkey with a sharp stick to get it to move. Rather like dealing with the Arts Council, Tony said. Since I had broken up in mutually disreputable circumstances with Diane, my private life had been rackety, to say the least. There had been a cluster of sometimes concurrent relationships which had flashed on and off like ill-phased Christmas lights. A lively companion had joined me in Greece, setting the hills and tavernas alight with her indifference to custom and costume. But when we returned from Greece, tired of being cramped off Cambridge Circus, I had moved with her into new quarters below Portable's offices in Colville Place, just off Charlotte Street. So when it became clear to her as much as to me that we were not going to survive as a couple back in London for many more hours, it was I who, in a gentlemanly way, offered to move out.

It was, once more, pure chance that I was due to have lunch with Margaret Matheson on the morning that the abrupt ending of a liaison had rendered me homeless. I had only seen Margaret in passing a couple of times since the agency had put me on its books, and she had called to say it was time we caught up. We had lunch in Au Fin Bec, just behind Sloane Avenue, and by the time lunch was threatening to merge into tea, we agreed it would be a good idea if instead I moved in with her. The complete change in my way of life was as fulfilling as it was sudden. That night I took my things down to the far end of Battersea Park Road, where Margaret had an astonishingly cheap and spacious flat above a draper's shop. There was plenty of room for both of us, though when, for my convenience in running a theatre group, we tried to get the telephone moved from the far corner of the living room, we were told by the telephone company that the only person in Britain who was allowed a telephone cord more than six foot long was Princess Margaret.

Howard's play went as well as expected, thanks in good part to the detailed and disturbing performance of William Hoyland in the central role. Snoo had joined us from university as a roadie and was preparing a production of his own play *Pignight*, a prophetically environmental attack on the practices of factory farming. Years before its time, it was set on a pig farm and involved a certain amount of offal being fried on stage. We all relished a performance of the play in a school chapel which was interrupted by a Basil Fawlty of a headmaster getting up, appalled, to say, 'Right. All forms below the Sixth to leave at once.' Because we were getting on so well, Margaret was beginning to regret her plan to join her friends Sonny and Gita Mehta in Delhi at Christmas. I couldn't join her, first because I had many Portable miles to cover, but also because I had to work on my promised comedy. But I persuaded Margaret she shouldn't pull out. How often would she get the chance to go to India? In those days people rarely made transcontinental calls, so that during her absence in December her news came only occasionally and on the same blue airmail paper my father had always used. She had left her Indian friends, she said, to travel across to Benares. She had been accompanied by another friend of Sonny's who was also visiting from England, or rather from Scotland where apparently he worked as a theatre director. His name was Richard Eyre, and he was director of productions, though not artistic director, at the Lyceum Theatre in Edinburgh. At first she had found the trip hard going, because her companion, although eupeptic and well-meaning, was far too shy to speak. But once Margaret had settled into the idea, she had found it comfortable for them to stand in silence together watching the burning of the bodies on the ghats.

I spent the time before Christmas on my own settling down to write the play for Michael Codron, whom, superbly tanned and coiffed like an old-fashioned impresario, I had met in his eyrie high above Aquascutum in Regent Street, a stone's throw from another of my father's London haunts, the Indian restaurant, Veeraswamy. I had written *How Brophy Made Good* in such a ridiculous ninety-six-hour dash that you couldn't even dignify what I did with the name of a process. This time I intended to do things properly. I knew that for those of us working at below genius level, a routine would be not just essential but positively welcome. Even Mozart's days had a regular pattern. For the following forty years I would aim to sit down at my desk every weekday at 9 a.m. At the time I had been reading some of the literature coming out of America and been both amused and heartened by it. There was a crazy spirit here which I loved. Novel theories about men being nothing more than a deformation of the female chromosome were beginning to take hold on the wilder shores of the movement, though they had not yet reached the public at large. The popularising book *The Female Eunuch* by my old recruiting sergeant Germaine Greer would not be published until six months after the premiere of my play. I had begun to conceive the idea of a comedy in which a feminist schoolteacher is trying to create a self-sustaining all-female community – a community that's all XX – while at the same time losing the pupils. There would be jokes about schools, jokes about feminism and, best of all, running jokes about cineastes. Essentially what I would be doing was satirising separatism. I had experienced enough leftist movements to know that their self-defining notions of purity always led to disaster. This was what I aimed to point out.

I am not sure how quickly I apprehended what would turn out to be my most important discovery about playwriting: fundamentally, I had no control. Whatever the clarity of my intentions, the actual writing of the play *Slag* only glancingly resembled my original conception. It's a cliché to say that while you're writing a play the characters take over. They appropriate the action and head off in unforeseen directions. However, what would be both truer and more interesting to say is that it's not only the characters. Every line of dialogue, every exit and entry, every development of the story, every deliberate change of mood on the stage pleases or displeases the author for reasons they would be at a loss to explain. The mystery of style is exactly that: a mystery. Yes of course, I could clean the play up. I could redraft. I could look intelligent when people asked me questions. I could, if necessary, make the action more deft. I was perfectly capable of saying, 'That scene's working, but that one isn't. That joke's working, but that one isn't.' But to the basic question 'Why is the play the way it is?' I had no answer at all.

In all my years of supposedly studying literature, this most basic fact about fiction had never occurred to me. I had assumed writers wrote what they wanted. Realising the untruth of this, as I did in Battersea in the deep winter of 1969, was a moment of complete liberation. At last I had discovered an activity in which, refreshingly, the will was subservient. The most significant thing about Milton suddenly seemed to be his blindness. Remember, I had been a teacher and disliked myself when I was. I had not much cared for myself when I was a young theatre director either. Only when I became a creative writer could I rid myself of self-consciousness, and of worldly ambition. No writer can sit down and say, 'I'm going to write a world-beating masterpiece,' because the question of whether you will be able to is not in your hands. You may make all the plans you like, but ultimately you are at the mercy of your imagination – whatever that might be. The page fills or it doesn't. You're powerless. Once I began to write in anything like calm, I noticed very soon that you couldn't force it. If you did try to force it, if you wrote words which did not convince you, a strange feeling, rather like an elephant sitting on your chest, would begin to oppress you. Far from frightening me, this revelation of powerlessness set me free. Because I was no longer in command, I was able to stop worrying about the effect of what I was doing. The inhibiting question 'What will people think of my play?' which might have bothered me had I become a writer as an adolescent, now as an adult became wonderfully unimportant. I had no idea. The play was writing itself. I would have no more influence over what people made of it than I had over writing it.

I was, in short, discovering my subconscious, and acceding to it. For the rest of my life I would superstitiously refuse to answer the inevitable question 'What are you writing?' I have believed from that very first winter of 1969 that if you talk about it, it goes away. How, anyway, can you say, 'I plan to march on Moscow,' when your imagination, unknown to you, is planning to make Berlin submit? I know one thing. If anything has been my salvation as a human being it is this choice of an activity which is, at the deepest level, out of my hands. What a relief! What a blessing! Better still, it had always been a drawback to see life differently from other people. In childhood, it had brought me little but heartache. Now I had stumbled on a profession in which it was an asset.

7

Five Good Scenes

At the Royal Court, at any one moment, we had stacks of plays being considered. For many years the Court was the only substantial-sized theatre in London dedicated to doing new plays, and with the opening of a ninety-seat Theatre Upstairs to replace a restaurant and cabaret club we were still expanding. From the start in 1956, the theatre had attracted manuscripts from writers as diverse as Sartre, Henry Miller and Wyndham Lewis. There were none of today's probationary antics with writers being expected to waste their time rewriting at directors' whim in the slender hope of production. The artistic directors liked you or they didn't. Nearly every play around was submitted – I even received one from Agatha Christie, one of her archaeological ones, not a mystery, but still – and because of the fierce distinctiveness of the theatre's ideology, British dramatists could be relied on to feel strongly about whether they were in or out of favour in Sloane Square. Everyone had a Royal Court radar. In a single week, the artistic directors rejected plays by Alan Bennett, Simon Gray and Peter Nichols, all on the grounds that they were not the sort of thing the Royal Court should be doing. Inevitably with supply and demand so out of balance, there were many dashed hopes. But in those times of messy manuscripts, carbon paper and handwritten emendations, the one certain sign that your play was being fast-tracked for the stage was when Bill Gaskill licensed the expense of sending the original copy off to a firm of professional typists. It was when the theatre piled up thirty spanking new scripts in coloured covers on the casting director's shelves that you knew you were in business.

It was uplifting therefore, when in the new year Clive Goodwin had forwarded *Slag* to Michael Codron, to hear back within a couple of days not from the producer himself but from the swanky offices of Scripts Limited in Beak Street, with some minor enquiry about spacing. When Michael rang in person, he was soft-spoken to a point where I could not quite hear him. He displayed a canny mix of courage and caution which I would come to know as characteristic. He thought that *Slag* was a little too bold to go directly into the West End. Would I like to try it out at the Royal Court first? When I said that sending the play to my withering bosses would be a waste of time and a humiliation – feminist comedy was probably not ideal for a theatre which was neither feminist nor comic – Michael changed tack. For some time he had served on the board of the Hampstead Theatre Club, and he knew for a fact that it was going through one of those gruelling periods of bad luck all theatres are prone to. Why didn't we do it there? It would have the added advantage that we could go into rehearsal almost immediately and open in a recently vacated spot in April.

At this point I was given a little rope and proceeded to hang myself. When Hampstead's founder and artistic director, James Roose-Evans, a rather schoolmasterly gentleman who was all eyebrows and brown herringbone and who would later be consecrated as an Anglican priest, asked me whom I would like to direct the play, I said there was a young American, not long out of Yale Rep, who had enviable resources of self-confidence. I had found myself talking to Roger Hendricks Simon a lot after his production in the Theatre Upstairs of Sam Shepard's *La Turista*.

I liked him. Both Michael and James Roose-Evans pointed out to me that my suggestion was perverse. I had written an original and rather surreal English comedy, what's more, one of the very first plays in the modern theatre to feature an all-female cast – they both said they had never read anything like it – and, for some reason, I was proposing to have it directed by an American man who knew nothing of the culture it sprang from. I said something beguilingly idiotic, like how I thought that was exactly why Roger might be an interesting choice.

From the first week of rehearsals near Swiss Cottage, the scale of my misjudgement was revealed. Indeed, it became apparent during the morning of Day One. Sure, I enjoyed ball games as much as the next person, but I could see that Rosemary McHale, Marty Cruickshank and Diane Fletcher, who made up the outstandingly talented cast, did not want to long postpone their approach to a demanding text by putting on baseball caps or doing improvisations. When on the tenth day the ball games were still continuing, I knew that the situation was serious. Did this director ever intend to get down to work? At nights, I would get phone calls at home from the three of them asking me why I wasn't coming in to rehearsals and what I could do to help. By the third week, aching to get on with the play, they deputed one of their number to call me and say that they no longer had confidence in Roger Hendricks Simon. Would I go to the management and get him replaced? Of course, when I went to James Roose-Evans and told him that rehearsals couldn't go on as they were, he was justifiably annoyed. Who wouldn't be? After all, it was I who had insisted on this outlandish choice of director. But Roose-Evans was even more annoyed when, encouraged by me, he approached the actresses in person. They understandably did not wish to be marked out as troublemakers. They felt that for working actresses to unseat a director would have endangered their futures in their clubby, man-run milieu. So, confronted by Roose-Evans, they backed down, denying that they had ever issued any kind of ultimatum. Yes, it was true they did ring me in the evening to sound off, and no, they didn't find the director easy. But if Hampstead preferred him to continue, far be it from them to suggest otherwise.

My reputation in the British theatre for being ruthless and arrogant may not have originated in these events, but they cemented it. For better or worse, at this point I decided after a sleepless night in Battersea that somebody had to take charge of a deteriorating situation and it had better be me. Margaret encouraged me in this, telling me that it was my play and I had to do something about it. Just over a week from opening, with several of the play's six scenes unrehearsed, I travelled up the Bakerloo line to strike a deal with Roger. He could remain as director in name, and indeed he could also continue in charge of the technical side of putting the play into the theatre, if, in return, he allowed the actresses to answer only to me. To my astonishment, far from being unhappy with this arrangement, he seemed rather to welcome it. He thought my help would be useful. He looked forward to hearing my ideas. He gave me exactly the same blithe grin of contentment which had irradiated his face during ball games. Within an hour or two of this new dispensation, the play began to unlock itself and to find its rhythm, not through any contribution of mine but because the actresses themselves had so long dreamed of being allowed to work. By removing the obstacle to that work, I had done all that was needed. I had let them out of the cage. From now on, my most important contribution was to sit in the rehearsal room every day watching everything get better.

Nevertheless, we were in a high state of nerves at the first preview. As Anthony Page later observed, *Slag* is rather like a marijuana dream. If you abandon yourself to it, you will have a good time. The audience did fortunately roar with laughter, happy to have their socks charmed off by three talented players. We all reached the end feeling pleased with ourselves. So I was puzzled when James Roose-Evans, who was for good reason sick to death of me, insisted on leading me backstage to an unoccupied dressing room. There he sat down with a walking stick between his hands and began an excruciating pedagogic discourse setting out what he considered to be the play's strengths and failings. All my Cambridge hackles rose at having my homework marked. I was back in the Leavisite interrogation cell. I had not the slightest idea why Roose-Evans thought any correctional procedure necessary, since in accepting to produce the play he had presumably discerned some virtue in it. The last couple of hours had represented the first zephyrs of energy to blow through his theatre for months. His spidery dissertation continued endlessly, scene by scene. By the time he had reached halfway, I was dangerously angry in a white-hot, rumbly sort of way, and broke in very quietly to inform him that of all the things I imagined a producer to be, drama critic was not one of them. Further, I said, I had never seen anything in Roose-Evans's own achievements as a director which even marginally qualified him to lecture others. Needless to say, the session then ended abruptly and in disarray, and I found myself for the rest of previews on non-speaking terms with the management, while also assiduously avoiding the beaming director. As I came out, shaking, into the bar to join the cast I was amazed, and secretly rather touched, to find Bill Gaskill standing waiting. He had never in the preceding months given even the slightest indication that he was aware of the play, let alone interested in attending. I asked him why on earth he had come to the first preview. It was far too early, we weren't ready. 'Don't worry,' Bill said. 'It never gets any better.'

In spite of Bill's resounding aphorism, *Slag* turned out a copper-bottomed success. Having first of all pronounced *Slag* too bold, Michael Codron now pronounced it too short, and said it could only transfer to the West End if it were paired with a short sex farce which was running at the Yvonne Arnaud Theatre, Guildford. He took me and Margaret to watch some big-chested girls running round with their tops off, then drove us in his gold Mercedes to eat in silence at the Esher Steak House on the way home. I couldn't take any of it seriously. As far as I was concerned, whatever happened, everything was gain. In those days, success was tangible. You could eat it. The major Hollywood studios all had script editors in London, so I got taken out to seven expensive lunches at seven expensive restaurants by middle-aged Americans who just loved my play. They'd be interested in anything I wanted to do. They outdid each other in the magnificence of the settings in which they told me this. I even went to the Connaught twice, without ever intending to write any of their rotten films. The European head of United Artists told me that he was ashamed of the James Bond films for which he was responsible, and asked if I could come up with one which was less 'fascist'? Hollywood, indeed! Clive, as usual, was keen to make some money so he persuaded me to sell the film rights to *Slag* in perpetuity for £4000. Since the perfect three-storey Victorian terraced house Margaret and I had seen at the top of the Chase, next to Clapham Common, was on the market for £8000, this seemed an auspicious sum.

Early that summer, Margaret and I decided to get married.

Because he couldn't bear to keep it, Clive had given Margaret the chaise longue on which Pauline Boty spent her last days. We were sitting on it one evening when I suggested marriage, and Margaret agreed. Next day we both woke up independently thinking, 'We don't believe in marriage.' But we'd already told our families, and it seemed embarrassing to ring and say, 'We've changed our minds.' More to the point, we were incredibly happy living together. Why on earth did we want to endanger that happiness? Margaret was a Matheson from Jardine Matheson, a firm who in the nineteenth century were partly responsible for the opium wars in China. But Margaret's grandfather had frittered away the family fortunes because all he wanted was to play the violin. Margaret's parents had ended up with nothing but a small farm in tussocky countryside near Hawick in the Scottish borders, where they managed to keep warm drinking Scotch diluted by huge amounts of water. Margaret's father, Commander Matheson, was the second of two brothers to whom her mother had been married successively, following the death of the first in battle. Since the Bible expressly forbids such a thing, the Archbishop of Canterbury, in the best Anglican tradition, had had to sign a special form saying that in the circumstances of the Second World War it was fine. Go ahead. A tall sandy-haired Scot whose everyday mildness sometimes erupted into inarticulate rages all the more ferocious for their rarity, Pat had run the farm at a consistent loss since he had returned from the war. For a couple of years, he and Jean had been retired.

Margaret herself had been too posh to be ambitiously educated. She had been sent to the kind of school where there was more Greek dancing than physics. Full of initiative, she had briefly been a debutante, then gone on a secretarial course and

put herself into the BBC typing pool. From there she had transferred to work for one of the very best drama producers, Ken
Trodd. Throughout the 1970s Margaret would have a zigzag
career, choosing to leave when an employer refused to offer
her new opportunities. Because she had been a secretary she
had a revealing and sometimes caustic view of the people she
later dealt with as equals. She'd seen them from the bottom,
looking up, and often not much liked what she'd seen. There
was a splendid abandon about her behaviour, or there would
have been had she given the smallest damn about ensuring her
own future in show business. But she didn't. She was already
chafing at Clive's employment, and was about to head back
to be a story editor at the BBC in the very department which,
only a few years previously, had refused to promote her. After
a brief diversion to Manchester to be a reporter on Granada
TV's evening news programme, Margaret would soon be helping to plan a series in which Glenda Jackson played Elizabeth I.
Her parents were clearly a little bit surprised by her impetuous
decision to marry someone from so different a background, but
they were never less than warm and welcoming. Hardened to
the unexpected, they took everything in their stride. For my
wedding present they gave me the writing desk on which I still
work. My mother took to Margaret too, though she told me I
was far too young to get married. She feared for me. She was
right. I was twenty-three.

In the 1969 film of Bill Naughton's play *Spring and Port Wine*,
Hannah Gordon is finally willing to give in and surrender her
body to Keith Buckley for the first time when she is shown
that he has painted the walls of their future apartment white.
No dramatic scene so perfectly evokes the period. Margaret
and I prepared our new house in Clapham and, like so many

of our generation all over the western world, sought to wipe out the past by whitening the walls and laying down hessian. It was only hippies who adorned and complicated, everyone else stripped. The floor sander became the totem object, often handed on between neighbours, just like the airing cupboard-warmed yoghurt cultures couples regularly shared. To 10 The Chase, revealed thus from top to toe, Margaret added a sapling magnolia tree which is still there today, glorious. Margaret and I had made a pact that if I failed my driving test for the third time on the day before, we would take it as an omen and cancel our wedding. But I passed, so at the beginning of August we went to a seafood lunch for family only and on to the Wandsworth Registry Office. Lastly we held a wedding party in the Parsons Green house of Caroline Younger, Margaret's best and oldest friend. Caroline was something of a minor heiress, the daughter of an Edinburgh beer magnate, and loved by all for her instinctive gift of hospitality. The Hares and Mathesons mingled among our contemporaries, who were mostly in floral shirts or blouses and sporting Victorian amounts of hair. The bride wore Laura Ashley and the groom had sideburns which reached down to his jaw.

As we left to go on our honeymoon weekend, the sky darkened to blackness and there was an apocalyptic thunderstorm. For weeks afterwards, guests would ring us, ostensibly to tell us how nice the wedding had been, but more urgently to ask where the dope had come from, and where might they buy some more? We made a few calls but never found out. After we went to sleep in the Metropole Hotel in Brighton, I woke in the night to find my face blown up like a football to around twice its regular size. I had forgotten to mention to my bride that I suffered from asthma. In the nine months I had lived with her, the subject had never come up. Margaret assumed that I was dying on our wedding night. Had she but known, all I needed was to work off my reaction to the lobster lunch by going to Brighton Hospital to have my veins opened. Next day, while playing clock golf on the seafront, I was stung on the end of my finger by a bee.

The reason we could only take a single weekend was because I had to hurry back to London for rehearsals of the two plays which Portable was due to stage next. I had rushed off a ragged one-act play about William Blake, which took me some steps backwards towards my student enthusiasms, while Howard had pressed in the opposite direction with a coruscating play called *Fruit*, about a disabled osteopath who sees right the way through the politicians he manipulates. He was performed with infectious abandon by Paul Brooke. Tony directed my play, I directed Howard's. If *Christie in Love* was Portable's most far-reaching achievement, *Fruit* was in some ways its most emblematic. Howard had fallen in love with a French intellectual movement called situationism. Its adherents argued that although capitalist society seems solid, it is in fact only a spectacle. Direct action can disrupt that spectacle, just as when a bottle is thrown through a cinema screen. The film continues, but the tear in the fabric is a permanent reminder to the audience that the picture is not real. Howard's resulting play managed in the space of an hour to generate anger, mirth, bewilderment and outrage in equal parts.

When we took *Fruit* and *What Happened to Blake* to the Theatre Upstairs, the press was lying in wait for us, desperate to choke off any source of artistic vitality which they had not sanctioned. But, in this matter as in others, Bill Gaskill had taught us too well. As its original director, Bill had eventually managed to get Edward Bond's play *Saved* accepted as a classic in the face of what had been determined and often hysterical opposition. But *Saved* was only the fourth of the defining post-war works which had been abused on their first outing with only a few distinguished dissenters. It had joined *Waiting for Godot*, *Look Back in Anger* and *The Birthday Party* in a dismal line of incomprehension. Who, asked Bill, could possibly take critics seriously? How could a group with such an impeccable record of being wrong in the past have the immodesty not to imagine they were going to be just as fallible now? Bill, to the predictable outrage of the newspapers, had even stopped giving free tickets for the Theatre Upstairs to the *Spectator*'s critic, Hilary Spurling, pointing out that since she never enjoyed anything she saw there, she might as well not bother to come. It had led to a glorious public dogfight about free speech with all parties stretched right up onto their hind legs.

True, when Lindsay Anderson had arrived at the Royal Court, his highly tuned fascination with reputation meant that a more propitiative tone had briefly taken hold. The press representative, a beautiful young ex-model called Gloria Taylor, was dispatched to have dinner with one or two of the enemy and to explain to them, preferably by candlelight, why the show they had been watching was not so complete a failure as they seemed to think. At one such dinner, in a restaurant a couple of streets away from the Court and at two o'clock in the morning, Milton Shulman, the enamelled reviewer on London's main paper, the *Evening Standard*, responded to Gloria's entreaties by saying, 'Yes, but you see, I only go to the theatre now in the hope of cunt. If a play doesn't have a cunt in it, I'm not interested.' On Christmas Eve later that same year, I saw Shulman bullying a young shop assistant on the perfume counter in Peter Jones to

the point of tears. At that point my attitude to theatrical criticism, already sceptical, hardened into something steelier. I have
not read much since to change my mind.

The Arts Council, however, was a different matter. From
the outset, they had been far more understanding towards us,
perhaps relieved that at least two of the people working on the
untameable fringe had been educated at a university whose
name they knew. They had funded us show by show, insisting
on reading scripts in advance. We wanted to put things on a
more reliable footing with the award of an annual grant. To this
end, Tony and I had been invited in to see Lord Goodman, who
as well as being Chair of the Arts Council had a certain fame
as Harold Wilson's most formidable fixer. When I started the
meeting with a predictably self-righteous monologue – 'Aren't
you worried that all this important work is going to be lost?'
– Goodman interrupted me with the perfect line for someone
who has seen it all before. 'Let's get this clear before we start.
I'm not worried about *anything*. If I *worried*, I wouldn't sleep at
night.' The encounter thereafter was swift and effective. 'Give
these people what they want,' he said to an official, and it was
done.

Secretly, although we didn't care to say so out loud, daily
touring was beginning to exhaust us. As we moved into our
third year on the road, I found myself in the back of the van
working obsessively on illustrating a nationwide map of service
stations, each neatly marked with names like Forte or Granada.
It was a sign. More seriously, one night in Wales when Tony
was driving five actors home after a show, a Mini pulled out in
front of him. The Volkswagen went into a slide and tumbled
the actors round as though in a spin dryer. Mercifully nobody
was seriously injured, but it marked perhaps the end of the days

when Tony and I thought of running a theatre company as fun, as a lark. As other groups like ours also became better known and stronger, so a familiar circuit of arts centres sprouted up all over the country, ready to take anything recognised names offered. I directed a new play by an unfamiliar author. During rehearsals, the play fell apart in my hands. When we saw the result, then, in Tony's words, 'We both hated to see a play done by Portable where people just got up from desks and put things in filing cabinets: the dull texture of TV naturalism.' We were both becoming discontent with our own creation. We wanted to move onto a larger scale and to make our impact more political, but we had, as yet, no real idea how to do so.

I was in this itchy mood when the Royal Court decided to host some anaesthetic conference on the Future of New Writing in its auditorium. As someone who thought that the future of writing probably lay in writing, not in talking, I impulsively invited anyone who would like to write a new play to join me in the stalls bar, while we left non-joiners to opine. It was not the most inspired action of my life, but it may have been the most typical. About twelve people came to the bar, and I suggested we reassemble the following Wednesday. When seven of the twelve, including Trevor Griffiths, Howard Brenton, Stephen Poliakoff and Snoo Wilson, did indeed turn up, I had found a room which I had hung with wallpaper. To each of the playwrights I issued a different coloured crayon and over a series of lively sessions in the following six weeks, we wrote a whole play on the wall. It was based on a cutting from the previous week's *Sunday Times* about a case of oral rape in a van on the motorway. It featured a cast of characters who belonged in a lost British underbelly which was rarely, if ever, represented in drama. Inevitably, *Lay-By* was heavily male in its point of view.

When it was read thirty-five years later at the Royal Court by a group of women dramatists hoping to emulate our original methods for group writing, most found it repulsive, though some loved its honesty. For better or worse, it had represented the first attempt by anyone in the British theatre seriously to address the subject of pornography.

Nothing in his previous behaviour, or indeed in anything he had ever said, prepared me for the moment early in 1971 when Bill Gaskill, more than normally forbidding, called me into his office and said that the theatre had no suitable new play to put on in a few months' time. There was, he said in a tone which suggested both exhaustion and despair, no alternative but to plug the unfortunate gap in the schedule with a revival of my own play *Slag*. Sad, but there it was. An admission of defeat. Naturally, he said, the Court couldn't contemplate transferring a production from a lesser venue, so there would have to be a new one, to be directed by Max Stafford-Clark, the lively young boss of the Traverse Theatre in Edinburgh, who had never worked at the Court, but whom Bill admired as a free thinker and source of unspoilt energy. Also, he said, since Christopher Hampton was leaving after the deserved transfer to the West End of his play *The Philanthropist*, I might as well take over Chris's position as resident dramatist.

After a couple of frustrating years in the job, I was more than happy to stop being literary manager. I don't think I could have kept my sanity and gone on reading countless plays with titles like *Mend My Shoe*, *Tell It to the Bees* or *Fame Hath No Pity*. Christopher himself had always been needlessly kind to me, going out of his way to act as a loyal and calm intermediary in what were often bruising differences of opinion. I had found myself in the position of a futile lobbyist, trying to get the three artistic directors to stage work by writers for whom they had no sympathy. I had succeeded in getting Howard Barker played at the Court, but to my other suggestions the powers remained stubbornly and often rudely resistant. Their intransigence came to be reflected in my own. When, against my counsel, the three had insisted on mounting an indifferent prison play of Frank Norman's to open their autumn season, I had slipped out of the eventual production at half-time, knowing I didn't need to see any more to feel vindicated. But Lindsay, observing my empty seat for the second half, had next day called me in and, in barking Anglo-Indian tones, given me an imperial dressing down. It climaxed in my sacking. It was, he said, unforgivable disloyalty for a literary manager to walk out of a first night in his own theatre. What sort of behaviour was that? But when at the end of the week I went to collect my little green packet of wages from the huts at the back, the accountant laughed and said no one had mentioned my being terminated to him, so why didn't I just carry on? When I next saw Lindsay, he seemed unsurprised that I was still around.

Now I had no opportunity to respond to my unexpected promotion to resident dramatist with a new play because I was already kicking myself for agreeing to do an English version of Pirandello's *The Rules of the Game*, which Anthony Page had bravely asked me to adapt for the National Theatre. Awed as I was to be allowed into a rehearsal room with Paul Scofield and Joan Plowright, I was aware that my own contribution was downright poor. I had just enough technique to handle my own view of the world, but sorely lacked it when handling someone else's. Scofield, who on his day was as fine an actor as ever lived, was never well cast when jealousy was the motor. It wasn't in his nature. While at university, I had taken a summer job tearing tickets as an usher at the Old Vic, and had watched the National Theatre's embryonic company of actors in productions of *The Recruiting Officer*, *Trelawney of the Wells* and *Love for Love*. Now, only a few years later, here I was with my director in casting sessions with Laurence Olivier, of whom I was frankly terrified. He had recently been very ill so his neck was enclosed in an alarming salmon-pink brace. If you spoke, he would choose to answer by turning his whole body in your direction and fixing you with the famous gimlet stare. I learned to stay silent. Everyone always claims that when he was off stage Olivier looked like a bank manager. But with this apparatus he looked more like a creation of Frankenstein's. He might as well have topped the whole thing off with a bolt through the neck. When Anthony tentatively proposed the name of an actor he was thinking of employing, Olivier, demented, gave the four of us in the tiny room the full back-of-the-circle command performance. 'I will not have that man in my theatre. He is a rank amateur!'

Although youth is much the greatest asset anyone can bring into a theatre, it is not a cure-all. When the pit pianist at the Theatre Royal Newcastle, where we were doing a try-out, asked me what sort of play *The Rules of the Game* was, I stupidly replied, 'Italian'. To his obvious dismay, Paul Scofield walked out at the first performance to the strains of 'Poppa Piccolino'. When we got to London, we were one production in a doomed programme of expansion for the National into the New Theatre in the West End. The season, which saw off both Scofield and Christopher Plummer, was only later redeemed when Olivier was talked into playing James Tyrone in O'Neill's *Long Day's Journey into Night*. There was nothing the old actor-manager liked better than coming to the rescue when others had failed.

Selfless, we paved the way for him. But any disappointment I might have felt was balanced out by events in Sloane Square, where, throughout the run of *Slag*, the sun always seemed to be shining. I loved sitting on the steps and watching the House Full sign being put out. Nothing had ever excited me more than having my photograph taken with John Osborne, whom I regarded as the gatekeeper, the person who had made things possible for so many others. I had been far too nervous to address a word to him. One week after another, I got ravishing glimpses of what the upside of being a playwright might be. As Michael Cunningham would later write in his novel *The Hours*, I thought what I was feeling was the beginning of happiness. In fact, it *was* happiness.

Not only had Max turned up from Edinburgh in his E-type Jag to do a beautifully accomplished production, but the three actresses, Lynn Redgrave, Barbara Ferris and Anna Massey, had an upbeat approach. The play was already proven. Their job, they said, was to make it sparkle. I enjoyed their company as much as I enjoyed their acting, and nothing made me cheerier than stepping out with the three of them for an Italian lunch in the King's Road. They were all as witty off stage as on. Anna became another close friend, someone with whom to be solid in the darkest days, hers or mine. When Noël Coward came to see Anna in the play, we all lined up in the foyer to greet him afterwards, and he shook my hand. 'Ah, the playwright,' Coward said, summing up the evening in a way with which I couldn't disagree: 'Five good scenes and one terrible one.'

Part of the charm of Chelsea was that it was full of unexpected people, especially American actors and directors who had come to escape the pitiful contraction of the Hollywood they had once loved. Sometimes there seemed to be more of

them than us. If it was one of those days when you didn't pass
Ava Gardner coming down Sloane Avenue, then never mind.
You'd still pass Lee Remick. One day, on my way to rehearsal
through Eaton Square, my heart stopped when Henry Fonda
loped by, his walk as distinctive as his radiant blue eyes. James
Baldwin, believing Fonda must be black, had written of him,
'White men don't walk like that.' He was in blue jeans and a
brown fringed suede jacket and clearly lost in thoughts of times
and places miles away from SW3. It stopped again when the
phone rang and it was, of all people, Stanley Donen, asking me
to write his next picture. It turned out that the world's finest
director of musicals lived in Montpelier Square in a private
house with its own lift. After a short upward journey, I met a
man whose dour demeanour did little to evoke the carefree gaiety of Gene Kelly or of Debbie Reynolds. The script he asked
me to reorder was a mournful hand-wringer, derived from
Fellini's *8½*, about an over-privileged director who is having
trouble getting himself together for his next film. It was called
One. It ended with the director spurning his shoot and heading
instead for a desert island. My heart sank. I had been hoping for
Singing in the Rain.

Deep into what was becoming a blissful summer, Margaret and I decided to skip town. We set off for a Greek island.
Because we liked it so much, we stayed. Or rather, we moved to
another. And then to another. I'm not sure we ever knew some
of their names. One was somewhere near Mykonos, where,
with no signs of permanent habitation at all, sculptural young
Scandinavians, French and Germans lay stretched out sleek
like cheetahs, entirely naked on crescent beaches, their skin the
same colour as the sand and the setting sun. It was Arcadia. At
each large island, a telegram would be waiting at the post office

from the Royal Court management, presumably sent scattergun across the Cyclades, pointing out that I was contractually out of my holiday period and ordering me to return immediately. We laughed as we tore them up. Usually, it is only years later that you become aware that you might once have been young and lithe. For a few weeks in 1971, bronzed against the wind and with nowhere particular to go, Margaret and I were aware at the time. And the awareness made us happy.

On my return everything which had been easy suddenly became difficult. I did have a reasonable time at the Edinburgh Festival directing *Blow Job*, a typically provocative play of Snoo's which then set off on a tour. The joke was that it was actually about safe-cracking. However, when Snoo and I went on television to discuss it, Eamonn Andrews, a popular Irish broadcaster who believed himself to be a family favourite, stopped when he saw the title on his idiot boards and said, 'I'm not saying that word.' *Lay-By*, also presented by Portable, was enjoying a gratifying *succès de scandale* at the same Festival in Snoo's louche production, partly because the Traverse cleverly scheduled it at 1.15 a.m. This gave it a special glamour. When the play later had a one-night outing at the Royal Court, with bodies being lowered on winches into vats to make jam, and hardcore pornographic pictures being distributed by actors among the audience, Lindsay Anderson, thunder-faced, whispered theatrically to Christopher Hampton, 'I suppose this is your fault.' Here was the heart of the problem. None of the directors at the Court much liked the direction a lot of new writing was taking. They found any kind of confrontational art childish and immature. We thought Britain couldn't go on as it was. They thought it could. So when I delivered my next play, *The Great Exhibition*, plotted around a Labour MP who takes to flashing on Clapham Common, it was immediately clear they had no wish to present it.

It would become a common stumbling block for resident dramatists at the Royal Court that the one thing they couldn't expect was to get their plays performed. Read, yes. Done, no. The Royal Court was known as a writer's theatre, but there remained a tension in the fact that it was already run, like most British theatres, by a caste of self-interested directors. Like some of my successors in the post, I found I had no advocate within the building. Originally I had been brought in to read, not to write. We had been in a forced marriage and now it was time to divorce. When I decided to resign – how exactly could I be resident dramatist when they wouldn't do my play? – the three directors succeeded manfully in hiding their dismay. After all, by walking out I was solving their problem for them. Michael Codron, who had cannily contracted me for two plays, suggested his homeless comic dramatist go back to Hampstead. The board had in controversial circumstances replaced its founder James Roose-Evans with the more irenic Vivian Matalon, who told me that he had heard from everyone that I was impossible. It didn't matter, he said. He liked impossible. Codron suggested that to direct the play we should get in the silent man from Benares, Richard Eyre. When we had eventually met at the house of our mutual friends, John McGrath and Elizabeth MacLennan, I had warmed to Richard immediately and relished his dry self-deprecation. He, at least, seemed to think the play was funny. The fact that David Warner and Penelope Wilton leapt at the chance to appear in it also encouraged us in this belief. Sara Kestelman always says that her decision to turn down the third of the leading roles was the biggest professional mistake she ever made. She's being kind.

Normally it's when a playwright is sitting in the auditorium that they overhear remarks that pierce them to the heart. At any of my plays, I can guarantee to be placed next to the person who is loudly enjoying things least. But in the case of *The Great Exhibition*, it was after an early preview as a couple were walking away from the theatre that I saw the woman put her arm round her partner's waist and say, 'I'm sorry, darling, that was *my* idea.' That remark summed up my experience too. *The Great Exhibition* did well enough, the audience laughed, and after six weeks it was off. The cast had acquired Carolyn Seymour, the granddaughter of Moura, Baroness Budberg, who, in the late afternoons, ran a literary salon where she would regale you with stories of being the mistress of both Gorky and H. G. Wells. Rehearsals were from time to time disrupted by the blackouts attendant on the latest miners' strike. Richard did a flawless job, and for any lover of first-rate acting, time spent watching David and Penelope is never wasted. But fictions with central metaphors contain their own dangers. The metaphor tends to hang around, somehow squeezing the life out of the play, taking it nowhere. As in a bad production of *The Seagull* or *Rhinoceros* or *The Wild Duck*, my particular metaphor seemed over-obvious and obscure at the same time. The act of exhibitionism was meant to illuminate my view of recent Labour governments, prone to displaying but not doing. I certainly didn't know enough about the Labour Party to write well about it, but, in Pauline Kael's words, 'Such is the treacherous power of an artist, that sometimes even the worst ideas are made to work.' In the bar in the interval on the first night I heard a drunken David Mercer loudly declaring, 'Some of these jokes have very distinguished theatrical ancestry.'

The mention of Chekhov is appropriate. *The Great Exhibition*, if I had but realised, dramatised the same dilemma as Chekhov's young masterpiece, *Ivanov*. At that point I had never heard of it, though before the turn of the century it would provide me with one of my most fulfilling experiences when I adapted it for Ralph Fiennes to play at the Almeida. A man, in my case a Labour MP, in Chekhov's a landowner, is disillusioned before his time. At the age of thirty-five, he's already burnt out and has no idea what to do with the rest of his life. In both plays, he is trying to stop himself becoming a hand-me-down Hamlet. Only one of my friends guessed that I had named my central character Hammett not to evoke Spillane, but to evoke Denmark. Like *Slag*, *The Great Exhibition* came without what Orson Welles called 'the dollar-book Freud', i.e. that moment when you know the author feels obliged to offer some explanation of the work's meaning. In the case of *Citizen Kane*, it was Rosebud. But with these two plays there was none.

In those days, my facile anger was as often burning against distant things as close. The lordly feelings of betrayal which inspired some of the satire in *The Great Exhibition* came from a growing conviction that everything that was collective and worthwhile about Britain was being shipped out to sea. When Raymond Williams had warned us, at the election of Wilson's second administration in 1966, not to believe in Labour governments because they invariably let their supporters down, we students had dismissed him as a despairing old cynic. But now, six years later, watching the hard-won achievements of the immediate post-war period running away into the gutter, and a hapless Edward Heath government struggling to implant a makeshift culture of managerialism, I was faced with a much more difficult question. If social democracy could no longer deliver betterment, and yet revolutionary socialism was a dangerous illusion, then what exactly was it that I did believe in?

In such circumstances there was inevitably an apocalyptic strain in a lot of fringe theatre to which Tony and I were vigorously contributing. But whatever the contradictions of our politics, our artistic belief in the short life of collaboration was genuine and principled. In our view, the chief vice of the British theatre was its continuing insistence on clinging to institutions which had long outgrown their purpose. Any company which was vital didn't last long. Nevertheless we were reluctant to throw away an admittedly small Arts Council grant which had taken so much determination to get. So we handed Portable Theatre to a new artistic director and told him to get on and do whatever he wanted, with the sole condition that it be different from what we had done. Tony and I went back to the Arts Council and asked them to fund a new company which we had decided to call Shoot. The time had come, we said, for something much bigger and much more ambitious: a large-scale touring company dedicated to the production of new and topical plays. The Arts Council, not exactly fine-tuned to the notion of permanent revolution, refused us at first sight, but did say they would return to helping us project by project. The desperation of our politics surely underlay some of our recklessness. Steadier hands would have held course. But we were also moved by a proper and admirable impulse which said that if we didn't move on, we would get stuck. We had done nearly four years with Portable and that was enough.

We decided to devote Shoot's first, and, it turned out, only show to what was happening in Ireland. From 1967 onwards, the Troubles, always rumbling, had flared with renewed vigour, first through a campaign of civil disobedience against injustices suffered by the Catholic minority at the hands of the Unionists in the North, then more directly through paramilitary confrontation on both sides. Reginald Maudling, my fellow Harewood old boy, when appointed home secretary in 1970, had got on the plane to return to London after his first visit to Northern Ireland and said, 'For God's sake bring me a large Scotch. What a bloody awful country.' The killing of fourteen unarmed civil rights protestors by the British Army on Bloody Sunday, 30 January 1972, had brought things to a head. Direct rule from Westminster was soon to follow. Yet about these events, the British theatre had kept a cowardly and shameful silence. What more important task could there be for any new theatre company than to tackle this subject of which everyone else appeared to be frightened?

It was obvious that no single writer could fulfil this commission. So we asked the original *Lay-By* writers to forge another joint-authored play, though this time not to be written on a wall. Most were up for it. Why not? It was time someone did it. And what was the worst that could happen? We could only fail. The core group was this time strengthened by the addition of Tony himself and of David Edgar, who had been working as a journalist in Bradford, and who brought some reportorial vim to the group. We rented a sodden pebbledash bungalow in south Wales for a week. One of our number arrived, put some beer-laden Sainsbury's bags down on the kitchen table and loudly started the proceedings by demanding, 'Now there's not going to be any nonsense, is there? We are pro-IRA, aren't we? No messing about?' Understandably, in a week of hectic dispute, interrupted by muddy, rain-lashed walks across stumpy hillsides, things never really calmed down from there. There were a couple of Marxists among us, but my own state of political turmoil slowly percolated into the finished play. Probably I was representative. Most of us didn't believe violence was going to deliver justice for the Catholics. We thought, rightly, that once mayhem had started it would gain a criminal momentum which would make it almost impossible to stop. But on the other hand we didn't believe that things could have remained as they were. If there was any viewpoint uniting the seven of us, it was the feeling that what was going on in Ireland was a deeply *English* problem. That was the reason we called the play *England's Ireland*. Mainland Britain's claim to be acting as some sort of impartial referee between two warring tribes was risible, and, more importantly, destined to end in tears. How could any British government expect to have its claims to neutrality taken seriously when it had itself been implicated in so many crimes in the territory?

All of us went over for some barricaded weeks in Belfast, which we found to be in an improvised state of civil siege, half town, half army camp. Some of us stayed longer than others, and some got further into the opposing camps. But none of us pretended to be experts. Nor did the play make us out to be. Indeed, if the evening had certain strengths at that time very unusual for a British play, they came from the refreshing honesty of its viewpoint. But as we started pulling the text together, it became clear that it was going to be difficult to find anywhere to put the play on. We wrote fifty-four letters to theatres up and down the country and got three replies. We were being frozen out. To its credit, the Arts Council were as annoyed as we were. When pressed for a reason, various venues produced the usual excuse that they were not – perish the thought! – fearful for themselves, but they could not responsibly put their audiences in danger with such incendiary material. One particular scene, the strongest in the play, had everyone worried. An IRA man appears and talks to the audience in direct address while holding the bloody limbs of one of his victims in a plastic bag. Well, asked the theatres, with such provocation, how did they know they wouldn't get bombed?

Snoo and I decided to co-direct. Since the writing had been shared, why not the direction too? It was an arrangement which worked surprisingly well, although when we started rehearsals with a cast of twelve and a terrifying weekly wage bill of £600, we had almost nowhere in prospect to present the play in the UK at all. Ritsaert ten Cate, the Dutch hero of the British fringe, had invited us to play a few introductory weeks in his new Mickery Theatre. It was typical of his courage, but his wooden playhouse, set among misty, silent canals in the Utrecht village of Loenersloot, twenty minutes outside Amsterdam, was hardly at the epicentre of the Irish problem. Up till the last day the text was still being rewritten. Some of our seven writers saw it through, some didn't, but Tony and his brother Nick were always there, taking advantage of the presence of exceptional singers like Tim Curry and Dennis Lawson to contribute songs which were often inspired by the tattered book of ballads they had found in a Belfast second-hand bookshop. The cast was equally divided between Irish and English actors. The cultural differences were apparent in rehearsal and beyond. Often, giving notes at the end of a run-through, you would find the two nationalities had arranged themselves silently on opposite sides of the rehearsal room. When socialising, the Irish would drink themselves into passionate arguments at daybreak, usually revolving round what someone had or hadn't said in Dublin fifteen years earlier. The Brits, on the other hand, preferred to stay serene and drift away on dope. When Sunday evening came and we were left out among the overflowing ditches of the Low Countries with nothing to do until Tuesday, some of the company would drop acid to help pass the time. I do remember thinking, as I spent too many medical Mondays talking actors down from bad trips, that I had not gone into the theatre to become a nurse.

When in 2013 Snoo died from a heart attack, aged sixty-four, running for a train after tending to his beloved bees in Dungeness, his obituarists were right to play up the fertile anarchy of his comedy. His dramatic voice was his and his alone. But they underplayed the fact that in his private dealings with his colleagues he was an unfailing gentleman. Considering the ferocity of his imagination, Snoo was, like Howard Brenton, as courteous a person as you could hope to meet. How else could we two directors, both with strong views, have worked without acrimony? How else could we have smoothly delivered a living play by Caesarean operation? When, for my own part, I too had to find ways of passing the actors' empty hours, I continued working on a stubborn and intractable new idea of my own. When I had reached page 25, I absent-mindedly left the manuscript in the theatre overnight. When I came back next morning, it was gone. It had been cleared away as rubbish and already mulched at ten o'clock by the local garbage men. In panic, I started retyping as best I could, from memory. This gave the opening scenes of the new play a flow and potency they had never possessed in the original. From the beginning, I knew I had a great title. *Knuckle*.

One night, well into the run of *England's Ireland*, Margaret and I took a train from Amsterdam and arrived in Paris in time, we hoped, to see Brigitte Fossey in a dress rehearsal of the French premiere of *Slag*. It had sets by René Allio, and such was the general classiness that even the poster was by Lila de Nobili. Behind me in the otherwise empty stalls at the Théâtre Michel, as we waited past midnight for the run-through to begin, were two men I recognised as Louis Malle and Costa-Gavras. I asked them what on earth they were doing. Oh, they said, they had dropped by because they had heard the play was going to be interesting. I nearly passed out. I had queued at the Arts Cinema in Cambridge to be transported by *L'Ascenseur pour l'échafaud* and *Le Feu follet*, by *The Sleeping Car Murders* and by *Z*. Significantly, the fact that these two foreign film-makers were waiting to see my play meant more to me than any recognition that might come my way back home.

We followed our rural Dutch season with two Sunday nights at the Royal Court. The first was attended by some representatives of the IRA, who childishly drew attention to themselves by talking throughout and trying to put their legs over the seats in front of them. Partly as a result of a hellacious review in the *Observer* by the American critic Robert Brustein, which accused us of lacking the humanity to keep the ideological animal at bay – 'I find it virtually impossible to exercise the task of dramatic criticism in regard to such a work . . . If the Irish question had never existed, certain English writers would have felt compelled to invent it. They . . . help the bloody butchers at their work' – the subsequent few weeks of Roundhouse performances filled up with a large public eager to know what the fuss was about. Not many seemed to come out sharing Brustein's view that our endeavour could be justly compared with that of Goebbels. We could have stayed at the Roundhouse much longer and indeed were asked to. But with Portable's usual disregard for the main chance, we resolved instead to fulfil a promise to the Glasgow Citizens to do two nights there, because they had been decent enough to ask us in the days when nobody had wanted us. We were all on fire. During these weeks, a political play was put where it belonged, in large public spaces, with all doors open, all comers welcome. *England's Ireland* was a seed box. In my own mind, it was a bell which couldn't be unrung. Sure, its craft fell short. No wonder. It was our first attempt.

As far as our company was concerned, it was also the last. Experimental theatre companies, like literary magazines, need patrons. It had become clear that Tony and I would never have the resources, and perhaps lacked the resolve, to do the kind of work we wanted on our own terms. So henceforth it looked as if we would have to do such work on other people's, or not at all. What lay ahead was some sort of accommodation with the existing British theatre, for which I was ready but Tony wasn't. During our absence the original Portable Theatre, whose name had been pointlessly changed to Paradise Foundry, had not prospered in the hands of our appointed successor. The Arts Council had insisted on putting in a professional administrator to take over from Gus Hope. The outcome, for whatever reason, was insolvency. Although we were no longer running the company, Tony and I were still responsible for it. We had not had the sense to take our names off the notepaper.

The result, as the writer Rob Richie all too fairly observed, was that 'the company that often seemed to have a bizarre fixation with the English police force found itself in court'. Tony and I were both telephoned early one morning and ordered to appear that same afternoon in Westminster Magistrates' Court, which was then in Mortimer Street, by chance a stone's throw from the old Portable offices. After a fortifying German lunch at Schmidt's on the corner, we were both put in the dock and offered no defence on the charge of failing to pay National

Insurance contributions. Having been charged with a crime I did not know I had committed, and with no idea of the appropriate punishment, I felt a satisfying identification with Kafka, whose diaries had first got us into all this. The magistrate announced that we were going to be fined. Later, Tony paid off the company's lawyers and I paid off the National Insurance. The accountants waived their fees. The two of us soon tried to calculate whether we had, overall, put more money into Portable Theatre than we had taken out.

The outstanding personal benefit of our years on the road came from the necessity to sit through our own work. There was no way out. Because we were, in the early days, operating the lights or the sound, sometimes stage-managing and even acting, so night after night I would have to watch and listen as speeches, passages, scenes and, on occasions, whole plays lost the battle for attention. Every cough, misplaced laugh and heavy eyelid would strike me to the heart. I would go cold, feeling the audience's collective attention wander off my inventions and onto their dinner. Samuel Beckett never had the courage to attend a performance, regarding the play's public exposure as an irrelevance. Even when he was directing the production he left town after the dress rehearsal, abandoning the actors he had helped lead. But as a dramatist who, to the contrary, was committed to believing that the audience's response might well be as significant as the play, I was given a brutal education. It has never left me. Ever since, on any individual evening, in any country in the world, whatever the language, I am reluctant to deceive myself about the evening's progress. I know from bitter experience how porous audiences are.

Unexpectedly, within some months, a couple of talented new producers with fresh energy would be trying, without any luck, to get Portable going again. But by then we had largely lost Tony to film and television. Henceforth I would much miss his salty commentary on the crushing failures of hope which give theatrical life its distinctive flavour. When in September 2001 Al-Qaeda flew planes into the World Trade Center, I rang Howard Brenton to say, 'Look what they're doing. They're tearing a hole in the fabric. They want capitalism never to look the same again.' Howard replied, 'Yes, but somehow I don't think those young men had read the situationists.'

8

I Saw Her Today at the Reception

Margaret and I had begun to live like young bourgeois. If we had known of Flaubert's injunction to be regular and orderly in your life so that you may be violent and original in your work, we would have said we were obeying it. We had dinner parties with three courses, all of them cooked, nothing bought in, and afterwards we played bridge. In 1973 our part of Clapham was still a lower-middle-class dormitory. Only one house in ten had been gentrified. We would go out in the evening, sometimes with friends, to restaurants like the Great American Disaster for what was London's only halfway edible hamburger, or to the Horse's Head in the Fulham Road for meat pies. We would think nothing of driving all the way to Limehouse to go to the Young Friends because, again, a decent Chinese was almost impossible to come by. The Ganges in Gerrard Street was the best place for Indian, its excellence chiming with its politics. The Bengali owner ran it as a co-operative with the staff. We even drove to Eastbourne one night for what we realised would be one of the historic last chances to catch music hall: the great male impersonator Hetty King, then aged eighty-eight, captivating as she did her rolling walk, smoked her pipe and sang 'All the Nice Girls Love a Sailor'.

Admittedly, there were occasional unexpected incidents. The schizophrenic girlfriend of a Portable actor climbed the drainpipe of our house, got in through a window and started a squat. Another actor, a lodger, fell asleep under a sun-lamp and woke up with her skin coming off in strips and as blind as Tiresias, before we took her to hospital. When Billie Whitelaw needed, for the storyline's sake, to be painted topless for a television play Margaret was script-editing in the series *Sextet*, she would only agree if the painting was done in our front room, so that we would be close by in the case of any advantage being taken. And when a play of Snoo's needed a goat, the animal lived in our back garden all day, before we pushed her at six o'clock every evening into the back of a Citroën 2CV to go to the Royal Court, where she climbed the seventy stairs to the Theatre Upstairs, leaving behind her a trail of pungent small raisins. Our next-door neighbours, the Hollands at No. 12, introduced us to a charming Bulgarian friend called Georgi Markov, with whom we had an enjoyable dinner, shortly before he was assassinated on Waterloo Bridge with the tip of a poisoned umbrella. But these were small bohemian detours along a smooth domestic track. At twenty-five, Margaret and I were living lives of premature calm. Yes, like so many people we knew, we had wanted to get away from our homes at the first possible opportunity. But in no time at all we had built homes of our own.

By bad luck, our friend Richard Eyre had for the second time got himself into a slightly ambiguous pickle. For someone who was so charming and diffident, Richard had developed an annoying habit of being appointed, but not quite. It was to happen to him for a third and final time at the National Theatre in the 1980s, when after his acclaimed production of *Guys and Dolls* he was the most plausible successor to Peter Hall as artistic director. On that occasion, he was made to act as a sort of theatrical Prince Charles for five years, during which he became understandably shirty. But in 1973, something sim-

ilar happened with the Nottingham Playhouse. This theatre
had originally been one of the jewels of the post-war repertory movement. John Neville, who still radiated the glamour
of his partnership with Richard Burton at the Old Vic in the
mid-1950s, had forsaken his screaming stage-door admirers in
1963 to go instead and join Frank Dunlop and Peter Ustinov
running the snazzy new building in Wellington Circus. More
recently it had been in the hands of Stuart Burge, a director at
that point well into his fifties, who was telling Richard that he
wanted to leave. Or did he? At the same time, he was warning
that the theatre's board, under the chairmanship of the formidable local councillor Cyril Forsyth, was not yet ready to take
on a younger artistic director, even if anointed by Stuart himself. Better, he was saying, for Richard to behave as if he were
artistic director in all but name, but to leave the breaking of the
formal news to a moment of Stuart's choosing. He promised to
hang around for a while to give Richard cover.

This was a highly unusual arrangement, and one calculated
to make everyone jittery. So when Richard came and asked me
to be the provisional literary manager at the Nottingham Playhouse – to be the provisional artistic second-in-command to his
own provisional directorship – he also explained that, should
I accept, I would not actually be able to tell anyone. Further,
Richard added, it would be wiser if for some time I didn't visit
the city of Nottingham, since my physical presence in the building and my assumption that I had a job there would only create
confusion among the staff. But in the same degree that Richard's status was bizarre, so were his plans blazingly exciting. He
was planning a repertory in which new plays would predom-
inate over old. A natural fan of a whole batch of writers who
had found current managements arduous and hostile, Rich-

ard planned to blow open the doors. He believed that if newer names were given the opportunity to write for Nottingham's epic stage and large auditorium, they would rise to the occasion.

Needless to say, I loved the prospect. It was tailor-made for the change in my thinking. Sure, I had yet to confirm to myself that I was a professional playwright. I was envious of the vocational certainty that, working closely with them, I had felt emanating from Howard Brenton and Trevor Griffiths. As far as I was concerned, I was a director who occasionally wrote, often with the aim of filling in the obvious lacunae in subject matter which distinguished an inward-looking theatre culture. But I had at least grasped something important about my character. For better or worse, I was always happiest when I had a cause. From daily contact with so many, I had come to realise that, because of the nature of public performance, being a dramatist took a toll. It was in the nature of the job. You were telling several hundred people every night that you were worth listening to. 'In the theatre,' wrote Iris Murdoch, 'the audience is a court against which there is no appeal.' I could see from the often grouchy public characters of older warriors like John Osborne and Harold Pinter that this struggle on your own behalf could be conducted at huge expense to your peace of mind. Playwriting is combative: for every one yes in Shakespeare there are seventeen nos. So, for me, it had been a source of considerable comfort to be part of a company, as I had been at Portable. That way I would find myself fighting not just for my own writing but for others' as well. It was something more than safety in numbers. It was a group. A movement. An idea.

Richard's phantom status in Nottingham seemed symbolic of what was happening more generally in the theatre at large. A new crowd was taking over in all but name, providing most

of the energy and the ideas. And yet the old folk were clinging on, unwilling to admit publicly to the scale of the change.
My sense of generational grievance had been reinforced by the
bumpy reception afforded to the manuscript of my latest play,
which I had finished in the first week of the new year. Against
my wishes Michael Codron had been rash enough to offer the
finished draft of *Knuckle* to Oscar Lewenstein. Oscar was a
sometime communist who had hit gold producing the Woodfall film of Fielding's *Tom Jones*. It had made millionaires of
everyone involved. Oscar had recently surrendered the chairmanship of the Royal Court board in order to step in as stopgap
artistic director to replace the exhausted triumvirate, who some
time in 1972 had disappeared quarrelling into the distance. On
first reading, Michael was reluctant to put what he said was a
challenging play straight into the West End. Oscar, predictably,
gave him a dusty answer. This sort of thing was not what he
was looking for at all. As the son of immigrants whose lives had
been saved by their acceptance into Britain, he disapproved of
this new fashion for anti-British drama. Although Oscar had
claimed on his appointment that he saw Royal Court writers as
being like his own children, I was one offspring he was more
than happy to leave out on the pavement. But with my own
agent I had a far more delicate problem. In the first week of
January I had handed the play over to Clive Goodwin. Light
the blue touch paper and retire. Clive was deeply unimpressed.
'David, I took you on as a comic writer. That's what you are.
Now you're trying to be serious. It's not going to work.'

We had met together to have a lunch at which Clive had
not pulled his punches. *Knuckle* was, among other things, a
loving pastiche of an American thriller. A tough-guy style, in
conscious tribute to Ross Macdonald, the author of *The Moving*

Target, was used to tell a story set, with deliberate inappropri-
ateness, in the British home counties. To help make a living
during the Portable years, I had agreed to write a column in
the *Spectator*, a monthly review of crime novels of all sorts –
police, detective, spy – and had come to appreciate how supple
the form could be. Because of his feel for the abandoned prov-
inces and for the overlooked, Georges Simenon had long been
one of my favourite writers. W. H. Auden's recommendation
that Raymond Chandler's books 'should be read and judged,
not as escape literature, but as works of art' made no sense to
me. Thrillers *were* works of art. But although the top layer of
style in my play was satirical, the content was very far from it.
I was transposing film noir to the stage in order to tell an intimate story about an arms dealer who comes home from travelling abroad to search for his sister who has disappeared. In
doing so, he falls for his sister's best friend. The play had, in
the manner of these things, a hugely complicated plot, most of
it off stage. But ultimately it was about who ends up deserving
approval and who doesn't. The play was moral. Clive, sitting
back and getting into his stride, told me repeatedly that this was
not the sort of thing I was good at. Why on earth had I written
it? The joy of my stuff, he said, was that it didn't buy into anything. That was why it was funny. It was refreshing. But if I
abandoned satire, he insisted, I would become one more dreary
playwright lecturing the world on how to behave. Surely I, of
all people, should know there were enough of those already?
Although Clive's indictment became tougher as he built his
case, his tone remained airy and nonchalant throughout. He
shrugged a lot, as though there were not much anyone could
do faced with such an obvious misdirection. By the time coffee
came, he suggested, much more in sorrow than in anger, that I

Mum and Dad, Abbey Close Church, Paisley, just having married,
22 October 1941

My sister Margaret and DH,
St Leonard's, 1951

DH with Roger Dancey, cataloguing
the primal scream, California, 1965

The Fields House prefects at Lancing College, 1964: first L, James Watson;
third from L, DH; centre, Patrick Halsey, who took me to Dachau

Portable Theatre: watching from the stalls, Snoo Wilson, DH and Tony Bicât

Cambridge: DH pen and ink drawing by Richard Cork, 1966

Howard Brenton, photographed by Snoo

Royal Court: the playwrights of the 1971 season, L to R DH, Ted White-head, David Storey. Front and centre, the gatekeeper, John Osborne

DH with Tennessee Williams, Manhattan, 1978

Andrew Dickson, Rene Augustus, Helen Mirren, Hugh Fraser,
Mick Ford, band and vocals for *Teeth 'n' Smiles*, 1975

Fanshen, the first production

Bill Paterson, in charge of black propaganda in *Licking Hitler*, 1977

Kate Nelligan, the bona fide great actress in *Plenty*

From L to R, Darcy, Margaret, Joe, DH and Lewis, in our loft in SoHo, Christmas, 1978

DH with Kate Nelligan, preparing the dance scenes for
Dreams of Leaving, 1979

should face up to the fact that I'd taken a wrong turn. Best put
Knuckle back in a drawer.

I think I had already decided long before the lunch that
Knuckle was the best thing I'd ever written. No, more than that:
I felt it was the *first* thing I'd ever written. But even if I didn't
believe it before lunch, I certainly believed it after. Here was
something which, on first reading, one of my most committed
supporters was telling me to tear up. As I left the restaurant, I
knew I'd reached a fork in the road. I was no less insecure than
I had ever been. But on this occasion I was determined to be
more resolute. I had already stumbled across Cocteau's timeless artistic advice: 'Whatever they criticise you for, intensify it.'
And I was finally ready to take it to heart. I went home, stewed
for a while and then rang Clive and asked if he would mind
if I showed the play to another agent. Just to check. After all,
there might be more than one possible opinion about it. Clive
said he could hardly stop me. Why, though, did it have to be
another agent? He sounded alarmed. Surely I wasn't thinking
of leaving? I rang Christopher Hampton, who was represented
by Peggy Ramsay, at that time by far the most celebrated and
formidable play agent in London. Christopher arranged for the
manuscript to be sent over that afternoon. At six the next morning, fast asleep next to Margaret, I got a loud call.

Bill Gaskill was once asked how he defined a great actor.
He mischievously replied, 'One who knows their lines on the
first day of rehearsal.' But if you asked me today how I defined
a great agent or a great producer, I would still say, 'One who
reads the script overnight.' As I stirred before daybreak on the
pillow, I recognised the voice of the woman who, when I was a
student, had told me not to be stupid when I asked to be allowed
to produce one of her client's plays. This time, a different tone.

'I haven't woken you, have I? I'm so excited, I've been up all night and I just had to ring.' 'How did you get my number?' 'Oh, I just rang Christopher.' 'Did you?' I thought immediately of a playwright in another part of London also being woken at six and, what's worse, for another playwright's number. 'I couldn't wait to speak to you.'

By the time I was having a second lunch with a second successive agent in two days, I was feeling that my feet were never again going to touch the ground. Peggy was in her early sixties, a mutable woman, the very opposite of Clive, usually dressed in expensive clothes of an indefinable but definitely bygone era. Where she found them I don't know, but on one occasion, years later, she admitted she was wearing an original by Leon Bakst, who had designed for Diaghilev's Ballets Russes. It came complete with diamanté skull cap. She was at all times given to hugely theatrical gestures with fluttering hands, and startling swoops of volume and pitch in her voice, like a wonky radio. Not someone to whom you would ever knowingly confide a secret, unless you wanted it bruited around, she could electrify the ears of everyone in a large restaurant while supposedly being discreet. But she could also go from nine-words-a-second to total silence at the blink of an eye. She repeatedly crossed and uncrossed her legs for emphasis, often while recounting intimate personalia. Clear evidence remained of her early career as a singer in the Carl Rosa Opera Company, and also, in her reddenings and distant stares, of a romantic history which she herself used to label 'indiscreet'. Among her lovers had been not only the Romanian dramatist Eugène Ionesco but also the virtuoso violinist Jascha Heifetz, who, she claimed, could not play unless she was in the hall. 'And let me tell you, when you hear it repeatedly, the violin makes a remarkably *ugly* noise.'

Underneath the extravagance of her manner, Peggy was fierce, shrewd and unsentimental. Not long after the war she had discovered a talent for imagining the impact of a play in production merely by looking at it on the page. Because this gift for reading drama like a musical score was so rare, Peggy had been set up in business by a couple of managers called Dorothy and Campbell Christie, who did not, however, share her enthusiasm for what they called 'the new intellectual drama'. But her agency had grown strong thanks to a binding mix of the artistic and the commercial. Muriel Spark and David Mercer may have provided fibre, but Robert Bolt, with what she called his chocolate-box David Lean pictures such as *Lawrence of Arabia* and *Doctor Zhivago*, was there to balance things out with soothing applications of cash. It was Bolt who said of Peggy that although she despised success, she was deeply suspicious of failure.

That day we fell to talking about her one-time client Joe Orton, whose plays she had championed from the outset. An original comic dramatist, beholden to no one, he had been murdered by his professionally jealous boyfriend, Kenneth Halliwell, who had hammered Orton's skull, then killed himself. Peggy had been one of the first people to go round after the discovery. At lunch she stressed to me how quickly you become used to horror. Initially she had entered the room backwards, but in no time at all, she said, she had forgotten that the scene around her was meant to be ghastly and was simply finding it a little bit inconvenient to have to step round Halliwell's body to answer the door. She told me, in a comparison that brought me up short, that I reminded her of Joe, because, as with him, there weren't any precedents. With tremendous emphasis, she said, 'Thank God. You haven't been *influenced*.' When I started explaining that I didn't understand the idea of influence, because surely if another writer was really good and you admired them, you would obviously do everything you could to get out of their shadow, not shelter under it, she just looked bored and said that was obvious.

Peggy's attention was prone to wandering, especially when someone told her something she already knew. Or something she thought limp. Or simply not daring enough. Repeatedly she would tell you, 'Talent is a matter of courage,' and for her the two things were more or less interchangeable. She held in vivid contempt certain well-known dramatists who in her view lacked the guts to look deep inside themselves and tell the truth. But that day she was extraordinarily focused. She voiced not a word of reservation. *Knuckle* was one of the most important plays she'd ever read. It was at once romantic and anti-romantic in a way which she would never have thought possible. 'And that ending!' she kept saying. 'The ending! The boy doesn't get the girl! I love it!' She had already reread the play several times, and could command every detail of the complicated plot. She even had strong ideas about what colour the set should be and drew something on a paper napkin to show me. At first light, she had rung Michael Codron, who had long been her closest friend and colleague, and told him that for the first time in her professional life she was planning personally to invest in a play. There was no question, she said, of this play being tucked away in the subsidised theatre, a sector of which, by and large, she was thoroughly contemptuous. It was full, she said, of people who were spoilt and took no risks. No, *Knuckle* must go straight into the West End in a proper commercial production.

No sooner had she proposed this than she flirtatiously retreated. 'Of course it's not up to me. That's a decision you must make with your agent.' She said the word 'agent' as though it were dirty, like 'condom'. I told her that my present agent did not care for the play, and I was wondering whether she would agree to represent me. At this, Peggy simulated outrage. 'Please. I have never in my life *stolen* a client from another agent. I would never do that. I never *poach*.' I made my own retreat, saying, of course, no, that was not what I was suggesting. But on the other hand, if I found myself without an agent, would she take me on as a client? 'Ah well,' she said, as if fluttering a fan beneath her chin, 'in those circumstances . . .'

In no time at all I was off like a rabbit down the Piccadilly Line. In Clive's office in South Kensington I explained to him that I could tell from the reaction thus far that *Knuckle* was going to be a deeply divisive play. It was going to make any battles my work had so far engendered seem tame. It would be unbearable for me to be defended by someone who was not in good faith. Clive rallied at a flattering level of hurt. As an agent, it was inevitable that you didn't like all your clients' work, he said, but he intended to represent this play professionally like any other. He felt that he was being punished for being honest. What was he meant to do? Pretend? I said there was no blame or punishment. Again, how could there be? You can blame people for what they do, but you can't blame them for what they are. Clive was a person who disliked *Knuckle*. More seriously, he had spoken to me of the play as an aberration, a mistake, something I'd come to regret. I didn't see it that way. I saw it as the direction I wanted to take in future. I was onto something. With any luck, there'd be more like this.

For the next twenty years, admittedly, the full flush of Peggy's passionate representation would not be an unmixed blessing. When she took to waking me regularly between six and seven with a mixture of scandal, gossip and hard theatrical news, I found myself one morning putting the phone down and saying, puzzled, to Margaret, 'It's as if she's in love with me.' This was met with a derisive response. 'As if? *As if?* And what exactly is the difference between "as if" and "being"? Do you really think a forty-year age gap means anything to Peggy?' Understandably my new status went down no better with Peggy's existing clientele than it did with my wife. Other authors took to crossing the room specially to tell me how tired they were of hearing my name. 'Why can't you be more like Hare?' 'Hare doesn't write like this.' Whatever the ostensible subject of a conversation, they reported, Peggy would drag it round to the qualities of her new enthusiasm. As in the days of Mr G——, I was back to being teacher's pet, with all the hostility that role attracts. Some of my peers couldn't wait for me to fail. But although Peggy's powers of persuasion had stiffened Michael Codron's resolve to present *Knuckle* straight off in the West End, they were ineffective in persuading the most fashionable leading actors of the day, some of whom lost no time at all in refusing the central role. We did at least acquire a director, the laconic Australian Michael Blakemore, who had spent the previous few years basking in the sun as Laurence Olivier's loyal lieutenant at the Old Vic. The play's sixteen scenes, switching between locations, presented exactly the kind of complex technical challenge to which Michael invariably rose. But it had also become clear that, absent a star, it would be some time before anyone could mount a production. It would turn out to be a full year of waiting.

Luckily, I had plenty to get on with. Howard Brenton and I were both intrigued by an overripe local government scandal which was fighting Watergate for newspaper space as the leading story of the day. It was known as the Poulson affair. John

Poulson, soon to be taken to trial, was a corrupt civic architect who in the previous fifteen years had developed a nationwide network of compliant civil servants. In return for cash in hand, they had been willing to look favourably on his applications for lavish development contracts, such as the Aviemore ski centre. Poulson operated closely with the Newcastle city boss T. Dan Smith, who had tried to create what he called the Brasilia of the North. From his initial eagerness to remove the genuine social evils of slum housing, Poulson had grown, step by step, into a full-scale criminal. He was proud of it: 'I took on the world on its own terms and no one can deny I once had it in my fist.' But what struck Howard and me was how extraordinarily small that world was. There was something pathetically British, and therefore rather moving, about how local councillors, local authority officials, civil servants and even Westminster politicians were eager to sell out for so little. Some surrendered their independence and their futures for a weekend for two at the Grosvenor House Hotel on Park Lane. For others, it was £50.

When he was released from prison in 1985, T. Dan Smith was ready to draw a political moral which resonated with me at least: 'Thatcherism . . . could reasonably be described as legalised Poulsonism. Contributions to Tory funds will be repaid by the handing over of public assets for private gain.' From the 1980s onwards, notions of public and private, kept separate for so many years after the war, would become disastrously intertwined. Politicians of both leading parties would be seen as people with no other function but self-interestedly to hand what belonged to the taxpayer over to private profiteers, always at way less than market value. They were facilitators, nothing else, for people who grabbed more money than they did. The reputation of electoral politics would thereby nosedive. It was hardly surprising. If democracy didn't care to defend what was owned in common, what was it for? With foreign policy meanwhile outsourced to Washington, the profession of politics in Britain would soon have a catastrophic identity crisis of its own making.

Even in the 1970s, the notion of writing a play about collusion between developers and local government held particular appeal in Nottingham, precisely because it was one of many big British cities to have been threatened post-war by a noxious combination of local business interests and lousy architecture. But the subject also had dangers, most of which we ignored. Now that I have had a lifetime's experience of handling topical material, it seems extraordinary that Howard and I ripped so gaily into our parody without pausing to consider the legal implications. All right, we gave our central characters a light fictional covering. The events which had inspired the play were strategically disguised. We invented the setting, a nonexistent Midland city called Stanton, to which our hero Alfred Bagley, posing as a witless old tramp, arrives in 1945. Like aniseed across the trail we threw in some casual mockery of Harold Wilson's poetry-writing wife Mary, with her character reciting a terrible poem which begins: 'Stanton wakes. The milkman calls.' But even so, by the time we sent the play out to actors, Poulson hadn't even been formally arrested. And by the time he was sentenced, our play was done and dusted. We did at one point make a light-hearted visit to get the text approved by a notably relaxed lawyer in London, but by and large Richard encouraged us to get on and write what we wanted. This was like *England's Ireland*, only better.

To make quicker headway, Howard and I retreated for a month to Hawick. Margaret's parents had gone off to Italy for the spring of 1973, so we decided to lock ourselves away in the deep Scottish countryside and write. Since marrying Margaret, I had rather taken to gumboot life. She had a large horse-loving family, including a likeable elder sister, Sarah, who had been a friend in need to many grateful students at the Royal College of Art. They found in her a good sense and human practicality which their tutors often lacked. Early on in the process of getting-to-know-you, Margaret's father, Pat, had asked me casually, as some sort of initiation rite, if I could possibly do him a favour and kill eleven chickens. I was determined not to be fazed, so I had gone out in the driving rain and wrung their necks, one by one, with the Matheson dogs all barking excitedly at the sight. When Howard arrived in the Borders, he too responded to the blossoming surroundings which alternate the barren and the lush in a way which is quickly addictive. Unsurprisingly, animal imagery began to infiltrate the dialogue. When, at the end of the first act, Bagley gives the mad wedding speech during which he has a heart attack and dies, he alarms the guests by beginning to caw like a crow. We took inspiration from the big black fellows on the lawn outside our writing room in Hawick.

At various points, Margaret came to check that we were all right. The sound of our laughter was so raucous that she had become alarmed, thinking we must be ill. Howard was a pleasure to write with, mainly because he woke up cheerful every morning. Unusually, he explained to me, he had never known depression. He simply didn't know what it was. Howard and I had both recently read Angus Calder's important work of history *The People's War* and been inspired by its analysis. Calder proved that the rejection of Churchill by the British electorate immediately after the end of the Second World War had not been an inexplicable act of ingratitude towards a victorious war

leader. Rather, it had been the popular expression of a growing nationwide sentiment, both in the army and at home, that
in no circumstances must Britain go back to how it had been
before the war. Howard and I rooted our dynastic satire deep
in that post-war idealism. As we worked, we swapped control
of the typewriter, sticking to an early rule that a line of dialogue
would only go in if we both approved. But as the play gathered
pace, we noticed that it seemed to be in a style which neither
of us recognized as our own. A mysterious third person had
entered the room, whom we nicknamed Howard Hare, and
who, very definitely, was the owner of a fuck-it, scabrous kind
of voice which was new and weirdly independent, wilful even.

Richard, still serving lengthy probation, had asked me to
join him for auditions back in the White House Hotel in Earls
Court Square to help form the new Nottingham company for
the coming autumn. Howard and I had revelled in our freedom to write something as large-scale and panoramic as we
wished, so we needed an astonishing twenty-four actors, plus a
live horse, to play the result in repertory with *The Taming of the
Shrew*. The young Jonathan Pryce, who had already electrified
the stage of the Liverpool Everyman, was committed, and we
built around him. Richard and I held open house together until
the final day of meetings, when a young drama-school graduate
came in and did a Charles Wood monologue, cutting the air
occasionally with his hand. He took our breath away. It was the
best general audition I'd ever seen. We were forced to explain
to him that all the proper parts had gone, but that if he cared to
join us and play as cast in little one-line roles as they arose we
would be very happy. He said he'd love to. His name was Geoff
Wilkinson, but later he changed it to Tom. Tom Wilkinson,
like Jonathan Pryce and Zoë Wanamaker, became a stalwart of

the company, one of those people it was always a pleasure to see walk onto the stage.

Not long after, I joined Richard in Nottingham, just as the dexterous Stuart Burge finally disclosed to the board that they had unknowingly acquired a new director. Since the news had been equally received, it was my firm intention to stay and help carry on building the repertory. Richard, in preparation, was moving into a Georgian house in the Park, in the very centre of Nottingham, accompanied by Sue Birtwistle, whom he had just married. Sue, tall and confident, was going to run the Theatre in Education company, which in the 1970s was such an important feature of any rep. I went to live as a lodger in their house. They were so generous that it was impossible to be anything but amused when Richard, running back in for something he'd forgotten, left Margaret's Renault 8 on the top of a hill with the handbrake off, with the inevitable consequences. Together Sue and Richard became the most hospitable couple in the East Midlands, handing out huge quantities of food and drink nightly to a shifting cast of guests – actors, writers, directors, designers and musicians – who would gather, usually after a show, to laugh and make music long into the night. Not even my transient obsession with Carly Simon, which was driving everyone else in the house nuts – I played the same tracks twenty times a day – could prevent this from feeling like lift-off. Richard was about to do something new and revolutionary. He was about to transform a regional theatre given over to high art to one which did eleven new plays in his first season. It was unheard of.

John McGrath had suggested the name *Brassneck* for our tale of civic greed. Whether as one word or two, it meant 'effrontery'. Howard and I had seized it eagerly. Richard, as producer, had never made any secret of his jealousy that I was getting to direct. He fancied the play for himself. He astonished me on the first day of rehearsal when he introduced me to the company by saying, 'David's going to be directing the play, but it's his first production in a big theatre, so don't worry, I shan't be far away.' The company looked as stunned as I did. One of the actors said to me later, 'It was my first job, so I assumed that's how everyone behaved in the professional theatre.' In the previous few months I had come to think Richard was my friend – after all, we'd done everything together – and now here he was, cutting my legs off at the knees by publicly telling everyone I might be incompetent. Once I got to know Richard better, I began to recognise this kind of change in temperature as part of his make-up. He had a gift which made him an outstanding producer. He would always take one step back to get a better view of the scrum. Artistically, I had to be right in the middle.

In the event, Richard's white charger stayed safely locked up in the stable. *Brassneck* could hardly have gone better. The board of the theatre weren't too keen on an early scene which, thanks to a smuggled document we had obtained, accurately recreated the secret rituals of Freemasonry, with everyone rolling up their trousers and talking gibberish about the Great Architect. They didn't like it when the audience laughed. There were more than a few walk-outs. And not everyone was convinced by a third act in which the Bagleys, the prototypical entrepreneurial family, move from construction into the ultimate capitalist product, heroin. In the days before whole western economies came to depend on black markets in the stuff, it was all thought to be a little far-fetched. There was a disapproving air of 'Come on, boys, a joke's a joke.' Capitalists dealing in drugs, indeed! But you would have needed to be a very cold fish indeed to resist the fizz of the play, its zest. It was brazen. *Brassneck* had an infectious, strongly narrative drive as it set about portraying a family who crashed straight through the pieties of respectable British life. For once, public corruption was ripped into in public and with a will. From where I sat in the first row of the balcony, you could watch the smiles spread through the auditorium. Paul Dawkins, as Alfred Bagley, the conniving patriarch of the dynasty, gave the performance of his life. The third act began with a recording of the Rolling Stones singing 'You Can't Always Get What You Want', and I've rarely known a song create such a thrill of expectation. To this day, every time I hear that perfect opening couplet, 'I saw her today at the reception/A glass of wine in her hand', I have memories of the heady oxygenated kind of theatrical happiness which comes only when you know that a nail is being hit bang on the head.

Having planned to stay on at Nottingham, I then didn't. In an ungainly panic that I was about to commit myself to something I would do very badly, I changed my mind. I was aware that in walking away so soon I was letting Richard down. It was unforgivable. In what prospered over the subsequent thirty years as a close theatrical partnership, in which Richard went on to direct six of my plays, I had occasionally to remind myself that retreats happened once or twice on both sides, but they were from thoughtlessness, nothing more. By achieving a play which got Richard's regime off to such a popular start, I had served him far better than I ever would have done by hanging around. I hadn't guessed that I would be so uncomfortable running a large theatre. I took it too personally. When one of the stage carpenters impregnated an usherette, I went running across to Richard in his office to ask, 'What are we going to do?' He very reasonably looked at me and replied, 'Nothing.' He looked even more bewildered when I said, 'But she's terribly upset.' I wasn't cut out for the regular institutional mish-mash of unexpected events and hurt feelings, whereas Richard was. He was able to sail above it. When he saw the usherette later that day, he knew exactly the right thing to say to her and I didn't. After Nottingham, in particular when Richard went on to run the National Theatre throughout the 1990s, I felt I was able to be more practical use to him by not being a brochured part of his team. I got used to the phone ringing on my work desk every morning at 9 a.m. It was always Richard, calling for fifteen minutes' perspective from a different angle of view. I was more than happy to act as his confidential *consigliere*. It meant that we would discuss whatever was most annoying him without it going any further. I would never claim to have contributed to any of the innovative and bold decisions, not least to premiere *Angels in America* and to introduce multiracial casting, which made the period of his artistic directorship a benchmark. But I did stop him doing the odd stupider thing.

Some time during the summer, while I had been away in Nottingham, Edward Fox had been cast in the leading role of Curly Delafield in *Knuckle*. Edward was showbiz aristocracy, without yet having a name that promised to fill theatres. He was the eldest son of the exceptionally handsome agent Robin Fox, who had done so much to help ensure the survival of the Royal Court in its early days. Edward was also the brother of James, who had contrived to star in at least two of the best British films of the previous decade. And his younger brother, Robert, would one day in the 1990s take over as my trusted producer. Edward himself was enjoying a period of fame and prosperity, thanks to an implacable performance in Fred Zinnemann's expert film of *The Day of the Jackal*. To my excitement, the great cinema actor

James Mason, long a favourite of mine, was offering to play the role of Curly's stockbroker father. But Mason's insistence that, for tax reasons, he could not leave Switzerland for more than two months meant that Michael Codron would not even consider him. What were we meant to do? Rehearse in Lausanne? At the time, when theatre was less conciliatory than it is today, short seasons were frowned upon by powerful managements. It was a decision I would come bitterly to regret, because Mason's presence would have got the play off to the charged start it turned out to require. Instead, after being turned down by Donald Sinden, who preferred to do a shaky Rattigan play at the Duchess – he said to a disbelieving Codron, 'Yes, I know it's shit, but at least it's shit about me' – the part was to be taken by Douglas Wilmer, who, while dealing in antiques, at the same time had a solid reputation as television's own Sherlock Holmes.

The most urgent question waiting on my return, however, was who should play Jenny. Although the arms dealer, Curly, is the play's protagonist, its moral pivot is the young woman who has been best friend to Curly's sister, and who works in the Guildford club which I had copied closely from my Cranleigh outings. In thriller terms, she's Barbara Stanwyck, smarter than anyone else in the town and more desirable. I had not been available when a young actress from the Bristol Old Vic had auditioned. In that theatre town, the purity of her ambition had attracted the resentment of other actors, who were accustomed to more English strategies of disguise. But now in audition she had managed to bowl over both the Michaels, Codron and Blakemore. They were insisting that I meet her as fast as possible, before anyone else whisked her away. It would be her first appearance in London. So on the day after *Brassneck* opened in

September, I got off the train at St Pancras and went straight with my luggage to what looked like an upmarket call girl's apartment on Curzon Street, just yards away from Shepherd Market. The flat next door even had a red neon sign. Kate Nelligan lived in a tiny, thickly carpeted space with her older boyfriend, the television director Mark Cullingham. It turned out she was a working-class Irish Canadian from London, Ontario. Her real name was Patricia. She had suffered polio as a child. She had played Gertrude at university, liked the feeling, and decided to come to England because acting was better understood in London, Eng., than London, Ont. Her father was an ice-rink attendant and some of her family were priests. Meeting her for the first time, I was struck by how Kate seemed in some way not contemporary. There was nothing of the hippy about her. She was dressed stylishly in clothes from somewhere solid, like Jaeger. The effect was of timeless elegance, unexpected in somebody so young. She already seemed like one of those mature French women who know what to put together in a perfect picnic, how to sail a boat, how to make an omelette that's brown on the outside but runny in the middle, and where to buy the best binoculars for a day at the races. With perfect maquillage and a chic coif, if she reminded me of anyone, it was Stéphane Audran. Since the principal quality any actress had to bring to the role was poise, the casting seemed to me within minutes of my arrival open and shut. At twenty-three, Kate Nelligan had as much composure as anyone I'd ever met.

The hour we spent together did not seem life-changing. When I caught sight of her looking shifty on TV in a naval bodice-ripper called *The Onedin Line*, I simply thought she belonged to that group of actors who don't prosper in rubbish. Margaret and I were off to Vietnam in a couple of months, both of us certain that it was time to break the regular rhythm of our lives before it strangled us. We saw the opportunity and we were going to take it. But first Tony Bicât and I had to deal with an approach from Max Stafford-Clark and David Aukin, who, much to our surprise, wanted to take over the remains of Portable Theatre. We imagined they wanted to pick up a shell company which already existed because it was less effort than creating a new one. Max, who had just given up running a workshop company at the Traverse Theatre, probably wanted to get his hands on our grant. But no, when we met up at David's house in St John's Wood they told us that they had heard we were fed up. They really did want to inherit what they saw as Portable's permanently inspiring mission to get radical theatre out and about. Our initial surprise had been because David was already married to Nancy Meckler and administering her company. The Freehold's strict belief in the physical and the non-verbal had been employed by hardline fringe fans as a strong rebuke to Portable's vestigial loyalty to the word. When I put this to David, he just laughed. 'Oh no,' he said. 'It's been like a holiday. But everyone knows, to get anything changed we have to go back to language.'

At the meeting, Tony said lightly, 'I never want anything to do with the theatre again.' It was not what he meant. Court appearances and lawyers had worn him down, and he was being flippant. But not knowing Tony as well as I did, David and Max made the mistake of taking him at his word. When they later discovered that because of Portable's maladministration in our absence it was easier to start a new company than rejig a troubled old one, they asked me to join them. The founding idea was that we should all have a ready facility for any of the three of us to use as we wished. After my discomfort at Nottingham, I said I would only join on the condition that I wouldn't have any responsibilities for the day-to-day running. Because Max was a railway enthusiast, we discussed whether to call the company Rolling Stock or Joint Stock, without my truthfully understanding the difference. It was something to do with carriages on the old North British line that made us plump for Joint Stock. Max had been impressed by two acts of *The Three Sisters* which the Freehold had presented in various rooms up and down Nancy and David's house. So much so that he wanted to kick things off with a promenade production drawn from a Heathcote Williams book about the men and women who spoke on soapboxes at Hyde Park Corner. The audience would wander from speaker to speaker listening to whomever they fancied. Max had already begun a series of workshops, which, to my amazement, he was co-directing with Bill Gaskill. Bill and Max, priest and hedonist, had fallen in unlikely artistic love. My old boss was now technically my employee.

Before leaving England at the end of 1973, I managed to infiltrate a Snoo Wilson play, *The Pleasure Principle*, into the Theatre Upstairs at the Royal Court. It was the last time Snoo and I would work together. Snoo, like Caryl Churchill around the same time, was feeling that property ownership was defining attitudes in the renascent urban middle class. His madcap assault, complete with fireworks and George Fenton, the future composer of the score for *The Blue Planet*, running around in a gorilla suit, had arrived as a text in Snoo's usual state of uberous disarray, covered with scrawls and crossings-out and extra dialogue bubbles dribbling away down the margins and sometimes even over the page. The manuscript, with a lot of green ink, looked like one of Proust's, only more so.

After fitting the play out with an expert comedic cast which included Dinsdale Landen, Julie Covington and Brenda Fricker, I helped Snoo winnow the action down to a comprehensible point where he enjoyed what was for him an unusually smooth popular and critical success. The theatre was packed for the run and people liked it. The goat was excellent throughout. But although at the end of the process Snoo didn't actually say so, I could tell he thought his director had unintentionally defanged him. He had been tamed, but at a price. As Tony put it, trying to fit Snoo into a category was like trying to stuff a large duvet into a small drawer. By providing his audience with something they could enjoy and understand as a social comedy, I am not sure Snoo felt I had done him a service.

The Pleasure Principle opened on a Monday late in November, and by the Wednesday Margaret and I were on a short hop to Paris, to pick up a much longer UTA flight to Saigon. One of Margaret's sisters, Nina, was married to a diplomat who had just become Australian ambassador to South Vietnam, where, in some luxury but also some isolation, they were beginning to bring up their young family. Living behind high white walls in the Rue Pasteur, surrounded by palm trees and servants, they were more than happy to see us. The Paris Peace Accord had been signed in January of the same year. The old US war criminal Henry Kissinger, who had survived satirical immolation in *Dr Strangelove*, had only five years previously brought about civil war and the rise of the Khmer Rouge by dropping 500,000 tons of bombs on Cambodia illegally. He had represented one of two equally dishonest parties. Unlike his opposite number in the North, Le Duc Tho, who refused the Nobel Peace Prize, Kissinger was now in the process of accepting it, he said, 'with humility'. I should hope. He was the author of a farce. There wasn't a single person in Vietnam, North or South, who didn't know that Kissinger's peace was phoney. Neither side had the slightest intention of sticking to the so-called agreement. But it was, for the Americans, serving its expedient purpose of giving them the excuse they desperately needed to fulfil Richard Nixon's electoral promise to get out of an ever more costly and damaging war. Some 550,000 American troops had been withdrawn, and the South left to its own devices. In a pattern we would see repeated many times, Nixon, lately mired in Watergate, had talked of peace with honour. But, like Bush, like Obama, Nixon was more than happy to settle for peace with shame if it meant he survived.

At the very moment everyone else was fighting to get out of Vietnam, Margaret and I were determined to get in. For the month we spent there, there was an extraordinary atmosphere. Ten years later I would write a television film whose themes were classically Chekhovian. Stephen Frears directed it. It was called *Saigon: Year of the Cat*, and it would detail the story of a middle-aged English woman, played by Judi Dench, who has worked for years in a Vietnamese bank and doesn't want to leave when the end is near. As in a Russian play, a whole society knows that change is inevitable but chooses to pretend it doesn't. Wherever you go, there is a haunting disparity between the official version of the future and what everyone, in their heart, knows the future to be. In Saigon, during the phoney peace, it wasn't just that the whole city was waiting for the day when the Vietcong would inevitably come screaming down the hill. You could also tell from the mysterious explosions in the night – oil dumps going off in another part of the city – that the threat came not just from outside but from inside as well. There were salaried employees setting fire to their own workplaces.

Things had reached a saturation point where you couldn't tell your enemy from your friend. When the end came in 1975, it only needed the lightest of pushes for the whole thing to topple. Saigon was already eaten away.

Against all advice, Margaret and I took the chance to travel. We never felt in any serious danger. We were warned that the roads were not safe by night, because the Vietcong controlled certain routes once darkness fell. But by day the greatest problem was that the cramped and crowded buses were built for Asian frames, not for lanky English playwrights measuring six foot one. Getting all the way up to the hill resort of Dalat was particularly painful. When we got there, we stayed in the Grand Hotel, right by the lake. It was almost completely unoccupied, except by the rats which scurried self-importantly across marbled floors, with free play to hurry on to their pressing business. They might as well have carried briefcases. Our suite, the size of a bowling alley and hung with dusty mosquito nets and crumbling curtains, evoked Miss Havisham's quarters. We went via Da Nang all the way up to Hué, which was eerily quiet, as though the 1968 Tet Offensive had stunned it into silence. Underneath the beautiful city's Swiss calm, with the wide river flowing imperturbably on, you had the sense of people who had endured one unimaginable catastrophe and who knew that the arrival of the next was only a matter of time. Its serenity was charged with fear.

Back in Saigon for Christmas, we enjoyed a life of privilege, with caddies throwing diplomats' golf balls discreetly back onto the fairway should they regrettably land in the rough. The French ambassador, using Vietnamese fighter pilots, flew us all out on a hair-raising journey to an uninhabited island, where, at the third attempt, we made a landing in strong cross-winds.

Waiters in white jackets and white gloves were already attendant behind long trestle tables set out on the beach. The tables
groaned with champagne and fresh seafood. It was like the
scene when the great press baron gives a picnic in *Citizen Kane*.
After lunch, Margaret and I watched as the foreigners laughed,
splashed and flirted, speculating in many languages as to who
had the smallest bikini, the tightest trunks. Oh what larks! We
felt free to mock a whole class who couldn't admit their lives
were about to change. I had no presentiment that my own was
too, and no less radically.

9

Cream and Bastards Rise

We returned to a Britain which was in the middle of a nervous breakdown. Life had already begun to feel different in October 1973 when OPEC, the oil producers' cartel, had used the occasion of the Yom Kippur War to hike up prices by seventy per cent and deliberately to fix the supply. Our plane back from Saigon was three-quarters empty because airline fares had shot through the roof. No one was travelling. We lay out across three seats, and were given complimentary dry Martinis at 7 a.m. in a bid to re-attract our custom. Back home, sensing that the oil shortage would give coal miners a welcome new bargaining power, and with inflation running at twenty per cent, the National Union of Mineworkers had put in for a whacking pay rise for their members. Edward Heath, never even in his more confident moments the most secure or cogent of leaders, was in nervous and sometimes secret negotiation. For one reason or another he had decided that the coal workers' aims were political, not economic. Heath later claimed that he had asked Mick McGahey, the leader of the Scottish miners, 'What is it you want, Mr McGahey?' and that McGahey had replied, 'I want to see the end of your government.' Whatever the truth of this story – and to a dramatist's ear the dialogue rings false – Heath had taken up residence in the bunker, believing he was heading for a definitive showdown with the unions.

Rehearsals for my new play began on 31 December in a

church hall in a basement next to St James's, Piccadilly. The next day, the prime minister announced the three-day week. The purpose, he said, was to avoid power cuts and to ensure continuity of supply. But the effect, unsurprisingly, was to create a superfluous sense of crisis. Blackouts became a regular feature of daily life, and television shut down at 10.30 p.m. The previous summer the director of *Knuckle*, Michael Blakemore, had invited me to his seaside house in Biarritz so that we could put our heads together. In the late afternoons he used to go down to the wide Atlantic beach and show off his native prowess, standing straight as a pencil on a speeding surfboard. Over dinner one evening he had voiced a widespread sentiment which I was to hear many times in different forms. Michael said that when he had arrived in Britain from Sydney in the 1950s the country had admittedly been awful, but basically it had worked. Now, he said, it was less awful but it didn't work. I argued the opposite, paraphrasing Raymond Williams: 'If people cannot have justice officially then they will have it unofficially.' The fact that British citizens had lately become so much more militant was surely to the good. It was a disputatious time, certainly, but that's because there were important things to dispute. If people were today demanding their rights, well, wasn't that a sign of vitality? And if they also chose to question archaic social structures because governments had lost all touch with the electorate, was that not better still? An element of disruption was a small price to pay, even if the direction of change was still not clear. Yes, there was an apocalyptic air in the country these days. Portable Theatre had been predicting social breakdown for years. But to me it was quiescence which was unnatural, not protest. It still is. I find the sullen state of affairs forty years later in which everyone is resigned to put up with social injustice and do nothing about it far more spooky and unnatural than the roller-coaster days of the mid-1970s.

At rehearsals Michael used to start every day by laying out a disorienting assortment of pills on the little table in front of him from which he directed. Since he always seemed to be in pretty robust health, and had cut a more than plausible figure on the rollers in the Bay of Biscay, I had no idea what purpose this neurotic forest of orange tubs served. As a companion, Michael had been so sceptical and caustic that it was a little shocking to see that he appeared to be a willing martyr to hypochondria. Presumably still not adjusted after a mere twenty years to the un-Australian climate, he remained wrapped in his coat and scarf throughout rehearsals, pulling them tighter as the weeks went on. Somehow this added to my feeling that things weren't ever quite going to settle. I quickly appreciated the degree to which subsidised theatre creates a common culture, usually involving at least a few people who've worked together before. Even if they haven't, they've worked with other people who have. But this bunch were liquorice allsorts, with no shared history. For all the nostalgia generated by present-day producers talking of better times when serious plays were supposedly abundant, *Knuckle* was the only new play to originate from a commercial management in the West End in the whole of that year. All the others were transfers, blown in by favourable reviews. With lights and heating going on and off at regular intervals, no wonder everyone felt a little exposed.

Coming from the Old Vic, Michael's approach to directing was initially technical, instructing actors to pick up particular props at particular moments and to put them down again at another moment that pleased him. A lot of the stage picture was already prepared in his head, with moves to a degree predetermined. He allowed freedom, but within limits. Michael began from the outside in, believing that if only he could get the tram in the groove it would begin to speed. Again, this method might have suited a group who were already well known to each other. But with actors from such different traditions, it reinforced the feeling that everyone was in a different play. Malcolm Storry, playing the unpleasant role of Sarah's old boyfriend Max, had come directly from the fringe theatre, so directly that Michael Codron had installed a telephone in his flat because Malcolm had never been able to afford one. With his background as a teacher Malcolm would clearly have been happier with more discussion, while Douglas Wilmer, retreating ever deeper into his script and sighing a lot, seemed happier with none at all. Edward Fox, never a natural fan of directors, had developed a clever strategy of echolalia, always repeating the last two or three words of whatever Michael had just said to him – 'Go downstage, yes. Pick up the bottle, yes. Not too quickly, no' – without ever really intending to do any of it.

I am not quite clear when it was exactly, probably around the third week, that I decided that Kate Nelligan was the greatest actress of our time and that she was fulfilling the needs of my play more completely than I had ever imagined possible. I think it was at the first run-through. Everyone else was stumbling around, forgetting lines and saying 'Sorry' and 'Oh, where am I meant to be now?' And here was this extraordinary actress, sitting in the middle of the rehearsal room, very calm, very still, smoking so gently that little wreaths adorned her, already in total command of my text and of her character. She had a way of floating a line so that it hovered like the smoke, weightless, in the air. I had no clue how she did it. All eyes went to her. But I do very clearly remember the moment when I realised that my feelings of gratitude and admiration were reciprocated. After one such run-through, Kate took my arm as we were all crossing Piccadilly to go for a good French lunch in the upstairs room of Edward's favourite Le Petit Café in Stafford Street. Somehow the gesture said everything, and we both knew it. But just in case I'd missed its meaning, as we went past the Royal Academy, Kate added that she couldn't believe her luck. 'You're a great writer.' We walked on in silence. Since we continued to work together until 1983, this mutual feeling, finally expressed between us, made the pair of us both insufferable for years. But it probably created work of an intensity neither of us would have achieved apart.

When we got to Oxford, where we were due to open a two-week out-of-town run on 29 January, the Playhouse Theatre looked shuttered and dead. Paul Scofield, at lunch during the rehearsals of *The Rules of the Game*, had told me a long story about how he once couldn't find the place when he was acting there during the war because it was so dark, and had been shocked by US servicemen throwing a beaten-up black colleague out of the back of a truck onto the pavement in Beaumont Street. Now I knew how he felt. It turned out we were all staying in the rambling Randolph Hotel just down the road. By an unhappy quirk of design, it had its kitchen grills so placed in the catacombs below that a smell of rank lamb fat hung over the whole place twenty-four hours a day and even crept into the heavy drapery in the bedrooms. Candles placed strategically on the stairs added to the air of nineteenth-century decay. My inept dramaturgy, alternating far too often between short scenes in the same places, like bad television, had lured John Napier, the future designer of *Cats* and *Starlight Express*, into a premature attempt at innovative technology, though sadly on nothing like the budgets with which he would later make his whizz-bang reputation. On either side of the stage were switchback metal arms of the kind you see at fairgrounds, which were used to deliver overcomplicated sets from the wings. Inevitably, most of the three days of technical rehearsal was spent with actors standing watching as the production crew put their hands on their hips or scratched their heads. Once the machines did work, the effect was both unexciting and repetitive.

It was consoling, then, to open on a freezing Tuesday night to a reasonably warm response. Later, when I understood a good deal more about directing, I would come to believe that any director's first and most important responsibility is to explain to the audience what kind of play they are watching. When we see a fresh production of a classical play, *Hamlet*, say, or *Tartuffe*, and we exclaim, 'It's as if I had never seen the play before,' that is because the director has somehow managed to mediate the experience, to relax the audience's understanding to a point where they can open themselves up to everything the actors want them to see and hear. For myself, I was to give up directing plays in the late 1980s precisely because I felt I had failed to do this. Twice in succession, audiences could not feel where exactly a play which I had directed was meant to be pitched. The task for Michael Blakemore on this occasion was almost impossible. There were so many warring plays fighting under the single title *Knuckle* that it would have been hard for any director to know which one to highlight. The text alternated between being violent and political, prosaic and poetic in a way which was both highly original and almost impossible to control. The only fault with Michael's loyal production – if it could be called one – was that it was too true to what he was given. If, as V. S. Naipaul says, 'Plot is for those who already know the world; narrative is for those who want to discover it,' then clearly there was too much of one and too little of the other. In such circumstances it's hard to see how anyone could have done better than Michael, who was by now reacting to the closure of power stations by wearing more coats and scarves than ever. When you chanced upon the posed photos in big frames outside the theatre, *Knuckle* looked like standard boring West End fare. Today I have friends who once walked past it on exactly those grounds. Admirers of the play would say that it was far too complex to be simply conveyed. Its detractors would say it was far too confused.

The unexpected bonus was that the Oxford audience, much of it made up of students, relished the layer of thriller pastiche but also could see through to the underlying subject. In the history books, it is Margaret Thatcher who is credited or blamed with adjusting the country to a new, more ruthless kind of capitalism where no one has any responsibility except to look after themselves and their own families. It was Thatcher, they say, who blew away the claims of a previous generation of Tory grandees who, as a result of wartime experiences fighting side by side with men from working-class backgrounds, still cherished a more socially responsible kind of Conservatism grounded in notions of the common good. She called them 'wets' and never missed an opportunity to say how little their consideration meant to her. But if this version of history is correct, it is very hard to see how by 1974, five years before Thatcher's election to power, a casual dramatist had already written a play which turns on the very argument which would come to transform Conservatism. Thatcher may indeed have overseen the triumph of the unsparing new philosophy, but she was not its author. It had been simmering away among renegades for a long time.

In *Knuckle*, Curly's father, Patrick Delafield, is a stock-broker, whose allegiance is to quiet, calm, respectability and order. Curly himself is an arms dealer, an unabashed market supplier, whose love is for making noise as much as for making money. He sees his father as a hypocrite, while his father sees him as a lout. It was clear at the first performance that the young audience were already primed for this standoff. From their reaction, you knew some of them had lived it and were pleased to see it laid bare. Casting directors would curse me for years to come because they said every second applicant actress used it as her audition speech – it would become a cliché – but when, with side-light hitting her at the front of the stage, Kate first launched into the barbed monologue 'Young women in Guildford must expect to be threatened', you could feel a shiver of excitement throughout the audience. Although there were too few people to create the momentum for anything you could call a hit, there was definitely a thoughtful atmosphere which gave us real grounds for hope. Peggy wrote me a note after the first performance: 'I have never seen a production of a play which so absolutely reproduced the promise of a text. Everything you conceived and Michael and I read is either fulfilled or will be fulfilled.'

Inevitably, during the first week together, Kate and I grew close. Within a day or two Michael Blakemore, as alert in these matters as in all others, found us out in some minor inconsistency. We were meant to be in one place and were obviously in another. Our stories mismatched. We hardly needed discovery to make us cautious. We were cautious enough already because both of us could feel, with our shared feelings of embattlement – Kate against England, where she felt disliked, and me against the English theatre where I felt hugely disliked – how incendiary a mix we would make together. We fired up each other's feelings of anger and isolation in a way which was both heady and dangerous. Having been brought up in Bexhill, I had formed a poor opinion of unfulfilled desire. I had seen its casualties all around me. But I was not blind to the dangers of fulfilled desire either. For both of us, with partners in place, love was a catastrophe. Kate and I were completely obsessed with each other without necessarily being made for each other. She was already rightly enjoying a thrill of discovery around her performance as Jenny. In Oxford, during that fortnight, we both felt we were standing on a little spit of dry land which was unlikely to stay dry much longer.

In the second week of performances we were still rehearsing and even making a few cuts, though not many. The American notion of 'fixing' a play had thankfully yet to cross the Atlantic. Producers trusted their own judgement. A play was what it was. Some people would like it and some wouldn't. There was no proleptic imperative to answer criticism before it was made. Of course you wanted to make sure that everything, including the writing, was as polished as possible, but you would never seek to change the nature of the play itself. Michael Codron had admittedly asked me to stop using the word 'capitalism' in interviews. He said it was uncommercial and off-putting. The word stopped people coming to the box office, because it made the play seem dull. When I asked him what name I was meant to give to the system under which we currently lived, Michael smiled ingenuously and said, 'Call it life.' So it was lucky that he was at rehearsals in person to see the results of some minor tinkering on the final Thursday, when news arrived that Edward Heath had stopped agonising, pulled himself together, looked over the cliff edge and declared a general election. He was, he

said, going to the country with the question 'Who runs Britain?'
We were all thrown for a loop. With the miners out on strike
and power outages a nightly possibility, Codron made the only
decision available to him. It was pointless to try and go ahead
with our scheduled mid-February opening at the Comedy Theatre in London. It would be commercially disastrous because
nobody's mind could fairly be on it. We must hold off, going
into a frustrating kind of standby, idling until early March.

This departure from the prepared schedule unnerved me.
I was in a personal mess but at least we had all been moving
towards some sort of professional resolution. Now everything
was suspended. A yawning gap of time was opening up, in reality only a few weeks but in the circumstances endless. Disori-
ented, I was overwhelmed by a feeling that my life was about to
fall apart like pick-up sticks. Years later, I would read Lucien
Freud: 'There is no such thing as free will. People just have
to do what they have to do.' Kate and I returned home to our
partners, both of us enchanted prisoners of the other. I tried
to pretend to Margaret that nothing was happening. So Kate
did to Mark. Peggy, who, like a nurse watching over a dangerously injured patient, had attended many of the Oxford performances, sensed a disturbing change in my mood and, fearful,
packed me off to a tiny little vertical one-up one-down which
she kept for writers near her home in the back streets close to
Brighton station. When I got there she took to lecturing me by
post, addressing me in Thomas Mann's phrase as 'Life's Delicate Child':

Yes, failure is POSSIBLE – so what? J Joyce failed, Beckett
starved, Carmen flopped, Proust was turned down by Gide.
Dostoevsky starved; all the early Tchechovs and Ibsens failed

ignominiously. Just pin your ears back and let Michael Cod operate . . . Your work is far more important than you are, because it is what everybody can actually hear and see. The only way you will get failure is to deliberately <u>bring it on yourself</u>.

But I still paced the promenade every night, the wind and rain lashing my face, feeling a riptide had picked me up and was carrying me, powerless, towards disaster. Suddenly I had turned into one of those explosive, mystifying adults who used to bewilder me when I was a child.

We started previewing *Knuckle* two days before the election. The Comedy Theatre, since renamed the Pinter, is a gloomy playhouse at the best of times, placed as it then was along from London's most depressing vegan restaurant in a meaningless street off Leicester Square. On the Tuesday, it was immediately apparent that the warmth extended to us by Oxford students would not reach down to the traditional West End audience. In the first week, with the election campaign bubbling along, there was scarcely any audience at all. Inside the auditorium a chill wind whipped round the ankles of the few spectators, while in the foyers the bar staff, theatre haters to a man, did their best to make sure that any concentration the actors might be able to generate would be ruined by clattering crates and shattered mixer bottles. We were losing an uneven war against Schweppes. In the pub opposite I first met the film director Stephen Frears, who in a year or two would become one of my closest friends and among my most valued. He was coming to the play but his pre-theatre conversation was entirely about an actress, Anne Rothenstein, with whom he was hopelessly in love. I said nothing. On the Thursday, Heath was told by the nation that the answer to his question 'Who runs Britain?' was a resounding 'Not you, sailor.' Labour had 301 seats, the Conservatives had 297. But in a manoeuvre as undignified as it was doomed, a sulky Heath tried desperately to cling on, calling the Liberal leader, Jeremy Thorpe, in to Downing Street to try and persuade him to help fiddle a mandate he had not earned.

While boxing at prep school I had learned to forestall the blow by anticipation. I prided myself on it. But at this crucial moment my footwork had failed and I was taking the blow full in the face. On Monday 4 March Heath conceded, Labour came to power, and *Knuckle* opened. Harold Wilson's third administration would quickly settle with the miners and end the phoney war. But no such settlement was available to me. Over the weekend I had told Margaret what was happening between me and Kate. We decided to sell the house and to separate. Neither of us wanted to continue in a relationship which was insincere. On Monday, going to my first night, I walked down Panton Street to the Comedy alone. At this point as mad as a pork chop, I stuck up a poster backstage on which I had scrawled in black Pentel a quotation from Ross Macdonald, whose books had started me off on the path to *Knuckle*. It read: 'The bottom is littered with good guys/ Only cream and bastards rise.' It wished the company good luck. When I went in to see the actors in their dressing rooms, Douglas Wilmer thanked me for my best wishes. He then summoned up a perfect timing he had not always manifested on stage to look me in the eye and declare, 'If this play runs, I'm leaving show business.' By the time I went on to visit Edward, I had been shocked into realising how selfish I had been. Absorbed in my own problems, I had ignored the toll the mixed reception for the play was taking on everyone else. It was an exposing piece. For Edward in particular, cinema's current golden boy, it was an extraordinary test of nerve to know you would have to walk out every night and give a fine performance in a play which large parts of the audience were determined to make clear they did not want.

I sat in the pub during the performance, getting drunk on a lethal combination of Guinness and champagne. Peggy would always insist that things actually went quite well. 'I wish you'd have heard the hush with which the first-night audience listened to your play. I was swept overboard by it. I shall go and see it continuously,' she wrote to me afterwards. But as I walked back to the stage door to see the actors after the curtain call, I bumped straight into Clive Goodwin coming out of the theatre. From his point of view, he'd had a very good evening. 'I told you it didn't work, and it doesn't.' Next morning, I bought a new notebook and got on a train at St Pancras. I had already made the day's most important decision. I was a playwright. Since I was experiencing all the unhappiness that goes with the calling, why go on denying it? Why had I been so scared? Was it just fear of failure? If so, the tactic was a write-off. Determined that the hysteria of the last few weeks was not going to silence me, I scribbled down the first line for my next play. 'Oh fuck, I forgot the child.' A rock band would play a set, go off to enjoy themselves and then realise they had left their one-year-old baby behind. At once, I loved the idea – the band on stage, the tiny child abandoned. But in the notebook I also wrote down two rules which I intended to follow in this new manifestation. First, I would never write a play if I had nothing to say. And second, I would never write a word for money.

This second prescription turned out less idealistic than it may have seemed. In my own case, it was intensely practical. I would stumble on a paradox: by caring exclusively about vocation, I would find myself free-gifted a career. In the subsequent forty years, I have never had to waste time agonising over what to write. Decisions which bother some of my colleagues about whether to consider this offer or that have never detained me for long, since my criteria for choosing remain so simple. In some way, I envy anyone who writes for different reasons, to feed their family, say, or to blaze their name. For them, writing is a means, not an end, and therefore not so killingly important. If the only thing you care about is what you aim to say, it leaves you especially vulnerable. Even on the train that day, I remembered that Margaret had always said she loved two things about me. I had never claimed the privileges of an artist. I had never said, 'Oh I can't do the washing up, I'm a dramatist.' But secondly, she said, she knew that my self-hatred was so deep that it would act as a kind of regulator, a shut-off device which closed the whole system down whenever I was in danger of believing any praise that came my way. I was aware, as I closed my notebook, that at least the first of these two reasons for loving me would no longer obtain.

I reached Nottingham and told Richard nothing of what was going on. Having abandoned my position formally, I was more than happy to help him as best as I could with some of the first-rate new work he was already planning. For twenty-four hours I pretended to concentrate on what we were doing, reading plays and talking about them, while inwardly seething at my own stupidity. I went into a hopeless slump of self-pity, telephoning Peggy at regular intervals to blame everyone in sight, but most of all myself, for leading my play into such a perfect ambush. How could I have been so stupid?

Back in London a day later, I moved into the empty basement of Tony Bicât's new house in a crescent in Chalk Farm. He and a young theatre designer, Jenny Gaskin, who had trained with Howard Hodgkin and then done a couple of Portable's best stage sets, had recently married and had their first child. I found on my return a letter waiting for me, typed, but covered in scrawls from a familiar hand.

I would remain grateful for this letter for the rest of my life.

Dear David,

This is written from home at 6 am on Wednesday the 6th – a time of day when truth stares one in the face.

Now, you either believe that the theatre is important or you don't. If you do, then you tell the truth on the stage and <u>expect to be listened to</u>. Your play attacks capitalism and says that the City is corrupt. You say that England is a place of dishonour. You say this in the heart of the West End, to people who have all had to compromise or sell out to get where they are – the rich first-nighters and the British <u>press</u>.

When you find that these people <u>don't</u> want to let other people hear what you are saying, you and the rest of us say it's because the play isn't 'commercial' and should have been tucked away in a small out-of-the-way hall. Hampstead! Royal Court!! It's like a revolutionary who has the opportunity of blowing up Parliament saying <u>if only</u> he'd blown up Dewsbury Town Hall he'd have got away with it.

YOU ARE RESPONSIBLE for what you write and you must take the consequences. You have said things in the West End which have never been said and you expect to have notices which greet a well-made play with French windows. Of course the men who are hired by our National Press are going to consider their own jobs. They are hired helps of perhaps the most disgusting Press we have ever had.

You are writing a play attacking what that audience and that Press <u>live by</u>. They do their best to get the play removed by typical means – they ignore the message and savage the package. The attack you make <u>is total</u>. Then you disappear to Nottingham having refused to sit through the first night. David, you have to face the firing squad if you want to change the world.

. . . Max [Stafford-] Clark is, of course, right when he says 'Why didn't you attack in Dewsbury? or in the <u>permitted</u> area of Hyde Park where orators are allowed to speak revolution.' The capitalist system of the theatre paid for your attack. The only person who is running away <u>is the author</u>. But you can't run away, because you have <u>written the words</u> which can be heard <u>8 times a week</u>.

Let's all be calm and try and keep the play going. You have to live <u>through</u> the pain, David, and you'll come out on the other side. So Gide tells one.

Peggy

In fact, although the play had been devoured and expelled by most of the critics, it had also become clear that Kate, in contrast, had enjoyed a triumph in the role of Jenny. Various experts with long memories had lost no time in acclaiming her performance the most impressive West End debut since the war. She and I laughed together at what we called 'if only' reviews. Those who were prepared to countenance the play at all had said it was worth seeing 'if only' for Kate Nelligan. Not long after the opening, Peggy surprised me by ringing to say that one particular critic, Harold Hobson from the *Sunday Times*, felt that a historic wrong had been done to the play itself. He would very much like to have lunch with its author. Hobson had already written one supportive review, swimming proudly against the tide, in the same direction he had swum before for Beckett and Pinter. Peggy reported that Hobson was 'distressed' – Hobson's word, I have it in a letter – by his colleagues' reaction and he might be willing to follow up with a second review the following Sunday when he had been freshly briefed. Oh, and one suggestion. Was there any chance? Mr Hobson would very much like to meet Miss Nelligan too.

Hobson was one of the longest-serving and at that time best-known of the British drama critics. He enjoyed an influence which today would be unimaginable, not solely because of his position but also because of the unpredictability of his views. He had been born severely disabled and felt his life transformed at the age of ten by sight of a Bible in the illuminated window of a Christian Science church. At a time when playhouses made no special arrangements, Hobson had to be carried like a baby from his wheelchair and put in the seat he demanded on the far right side of the front row. At dress rehearsals before London openings the most junior assistant was deputed to sit in that seat throughout to see 'what the play was going to be like for Harold'. When Edward Fox, Kate and I assembled with Peggy and Michael Codron at Prunier to meet him we were anticipating an ordeal. But Hobson's pleasure in spending time with Kate was so obvious, and in some strange way so entirely innocent, that the exquisite meal passed like a flash. He just liked being with actresses. Kate dealt with him sublimely, like a practised sales assistant able to reassure the customer that they had made a perfect purchase. For once in my life, my A level in Divinity proved to be of some practical use as, over the lustrous sole, Harold and I traded quotations from the Thoughts of St Ignatius, traces of which Hobson believed he had detected in

Knuckle. I was more than happy to let him entertain the idea. But there was no doubt about his more urgent field of interest. Edward beamed throughout, like a proud father. Sure enough, the following Sunday a second lengthy encomium to *Knuckle*'s unique theatrical power struck another blow against the common wisdom.

After Oxford, it was hardly surprising that I had entered a period of free fall, with no sense of my mood from one moment to the next. Kate at least had the theatre to go to every night. I'd meet her afterwards and we'd go to Manzi's to eat spanking fresh halibut and chips off red-squared tablecloths. But in all the important ways I had simply surrendered to circumstance. Peggy wrote to me, 'Both you and Margaret have a group of people who would do anything to help you and encourage you both – if you stay together, or if you decide to stay apart. We liked it when you were together, but that's up to you both.' Anyone who has been through such an experience tends to say that it is the only time they have felt they were alive. But they often also say that they have no wish ever to go through it again. Both things may well be true at the same time. Everything that I discovered about Kate in the following six weeks was delightful. In private, she was good-natured, relaxed and sharp as a knife. She had come to Britain with no idea of what to expect, and had been bewildered by the natives' reserve, their recessive refusal to say what they meant. Life, first at Central School, then at Bristol, for someone unused to English guile, had been tough and damaging. Her inability to hide her intelligence had not helped. She had begun to feel that she would never survive. The script of *Knuckle* had arrived through the post as a sort of tourist guide-book to the emotional topography of the district. The moment she read it, something had clicked. She felt less alone. She wasn't mad, someone else understood, someone else treated England as a foreign country. When she met the author, the feeling had been confirmed.

It would be wrong to say we were happy together. How could we be? In a play, *Skylight*, which I wrote twenty years later, I coined the phrase 'Happy like murderers, perhaps'. There was a level of excitation and of volatility at which I'm not sure I could ever have lived. Some time in early April Kate turned to me and said the only possible thing either of us could do at this point was to go home. The prospect of not going home was too terrible to contemplate. Her boyfriend Mark had been exceptionally kind to her in Bristol when she had believed herself to be having a breakdown. Now Mark was so unhappy that she, in turn, feared for him. Every moment she failed to reconcile, she felt bad. Further, she had no wish to be a home-wrecker, to break up what had been my own hitherto contented and supportive marriage. A bond had been established between her and me, she said. It would always be there. The best thing both of us could do was trust that bond and get on with our lives.

In the circumstances, it was impossible to argue. I was not sure that I had the strength of mind to continue at this level of tension. Peggy loved to repeat her favourite saying that nothing could be achieved by will alone. It turned out to be as true in matters of the heart as I knew it to be in matters of the pen. The speed with which Margaret and I realigned ourselves suggested a return to normality, as though what had happened was a disruption, nothing more, like a wind that had blown through our lives and then passed. The threat of chaos had gone. Margaret had kept faith and as a result our love, though not unaffected, had held strong. It was too late to save our house, which had already been sold to somebody unable to believe their luck.

Clapham was a coming area, and it had been snapped up. But we could easily enough buy another, this time in a handier but shabbier quarter, Richborne Terrace, near the Oval, where prices were low because of a torture chamber recently discovered in the basement of a neighbouring house. We were moving eastwards like crabs across South London. Impatient, Margaret had yet again left the BBC, where she'd ended up story editing some prominent series, and gone to work as a talent scout for David Susskind, the American chat-show host, whose hunched back and albino hair gave him a mildly satanic air which wasn't misleading. He had a production company which was planning to make television drama and films in the United Kingdom. At the theatre, my play, if not prosperous, was at least still playing. We were all happy to operate on the Weightwatchers principle that maintaining is gaining. For as long as we were on at least we weren't off.

Thanks to Codron's loyal management, *Knuckle* was eventually to last for four months, a perfectly respectable run, though usually to tiny houses, and with Edward a lasting hero in my eyes, not just for the growing subtlety of his performance but also for the stoic tenacity of his character. He never faltered. To thank him, I would take him for suppers after the show down his natural beat, the King's Road – him dapper in his cavalry twills, radiating charm, and every waitress's eye shining at his heartfelt compliments. Kate, too, was astonishingly good every night, becoming, like Claridge's, one of the London sights every American producer had to visit. The play's commercial survival was down to an unlikely intervention. John Sutro, a longstanding theatre angel of impeccable right-wing pedigree who still wore evening dress and a white silk scarf to first nights, had rung Michael Codron to tell him he was willing to go on putting money in because he thought it so important that *Knuckle* continue to be available. As far as he was concerned, the West End would be a lesser place without it. He didn't mind how much he lost. I believe there were others. For those who cared, *Knuckle* became that kind of cause.

Having heard such violent arguments about the play, all sorts of interesting people were turning up in Panton Street to see it. One of them was John Boorman, who had already directed Lee Marvin in *Point Blank* and had made the cornpoke classic *Deliverance* just two years earlier. Now, it turned out, he wanted to make a film of *Knuckle* with a screenplay by his old friend from Bristol, Tom Stoppard. They had been looking for something to do together and here it was. I thought the whole thing an improbable prospect. After all, *Knuckle* was a stage parody of film noir. Were they going to take out the parody or go with it? The play's techniques were already cinematic. What would cinema add? However, if two such gifted people wanted to have a go, it was up to them.

At the Royal Court, we had been taught that a condition of club membership was equal disapproval of Tom Stoppard and of Harold Pinter. Perhaps that's why I never joined. In person, whenever I had bumped into Tom I had found him good company, a fountain of fresh jokes and common sense. Uniquely among domestic intellectuals, he disdained to deploy his principled anti-communism as a surrogate means of pursuing a more spiteful, more personal animus against the British left. He had integrity. But Tom was, we were told, the embodiment of everything to which the Court was opposed. Lindsay, who spat bullets irregularly from his teeth all day, emptied a whole magazine whenever Tom's name was mentioned. He called him a university wit: this despite the fact Tom had never been to university and Lindsay had. From the perspective of today's doggedly careerist theatre in which it's a breach of *omertà* for any theatre practitioner publicly to speak ill of another, it's interesting to notice that just as the country was fiercely disputatious in the 1970s, so too was the culture. Never for a moment did anyone make the mistake of even pretending that we were all in this together. Directors and writers thought nothing of swinging an axe and hacking bits off their enemies. And, make no mistake, they really were enemies. Psychologically, the game was being played for keeps. Theatre was pitched against theatre, with none of today's ecumenical mumbling. As a communist Joan Littlewood despised the CND liberals at the Court for being 'middle-class and proper'. Without evidence, she accused George Devine of being an anti-Semite. As literary manager at the Court, it had been my job to visit every theatre in the country to find new plays. My bills for travel and for my tickets were paid uncomplainingly. But when I put in a chitty for seeing a new play at the Royal Shakespeare Company, payment was firmly refused. Bill Gaskill relished telling me that the Royal Court was never going to pay for anyone to visit the work of that appalling company. If I wanted to go, that was my business. But I must pay for myself.

Violence of speech was so common that nobody was exempt. Of one playwright whose plays I recommended, Bill responded, 'He should be buried in a hole in a field.' I had even jumped back in the *Knuckle* rehearsals when I had felt that Malcolm Storry was feeling unhappy and had suggested to the mild-mannered Michael Blakemore that he might like to take him out for a drink and a chat. 'I'm not doing any of that Royal Court rubbish of interfering in actors' lives,' he had responded with a sharpness that betrayed unexpected rancour. So perhaps it was not unusual that when Tom sent me his finished script I turned the rhetorical ratchet up way too high. In my own defence, it was a difficult script to get through. Tom told me to my satisfaction that search as he might – and he was a student of thrillers, like me – he had not been able to find any flaws in my complicated plot. It was watertight, he said. So it puzzled me why on earth he had chosen to overcomplicate matters still further. What was already a long play with masses of irritating offstage action had been turned into a film twice the length. The whole thing even ended with an animated sign-off, 'That's All Folks', in imitation of the old Warner Brothers cartoons like Bugs Bunny, Daffy Duck and Porky Pig. I sent off a letter to Peggy telling her I thought the script was terrible and that I didn't think it would ever get made. Understandably, since Boorman never rang again, I thought no more about it.

Nothing had prepared me, therefore, thirty-six years later in August 2010, for the unannounced publication of the text of my letter. Unsurprisingly, I had forgotten that I had written such a thing. After her death in 1991, Peggy Ramsay's estate had bequeathed all her correspondence to the British Library with a standard embargo on sensitive material. But a curator had sought publicity by tweeting that she had in her possession a sensationally rude letter by one British playwright about another. She strayed further by releasing it to the *Sunday Times*, who gobbled it up and inflated it across a whole page. I felt compelled to write to Tom, apologising for the behaviour of my younger self. I was ashamed. I explained that over the years I had come to find a dramatist's obligation to crusade on his or her own behalf embarrassing and demeaning, and that I admired Tom for his contrasting equanimity. I mentioned that fond as I was of our mutual friend Harold Pinter, I found his hair-trigger touchiness increasingly ridiculous. Harold was, with justice, numbered among the most famous and praised dramatists on the planet. He'd hardly been dealt a bad hand and yet he insisted, right until the end, on pretending that he was the victim of some organised conspiracy to do him down. Nothing, I said, could excuse my own youthful combativeness, which was as jejune as Harold's. But at least Tom might understand that because of the rough water my early plays had been through, I had at times found it difficult to accommodate. For a long time, I'd turned into a pretty unpleasant person.

Tom wrote back as follows:

Dear David,

The one thing in your letter I couldn't let go by was 'I think this made me a pretty unpleasant person.' I hated the thought of you settling on such an idea of yourself. We're all being continuously 'described' by a nexus of people's angled view of us. If you say so, you, for whatever reasons at whichever occasions, wouldn't accommodate. Pretty unpleasant! But that's not a truth about you in isolation; there's always an axis. The work is a child who never becomes self-reliant. The parent has to look out for it. I accommodate too much. I don't think you do . . . About the axis: I had a nightmare actor in rehearsal and flagged him up as selfish, arrogant etc. When I called him on it, nervously, he said 'Don't you realise I'm terrified?' I hadn't.

You know who you are. If you were different the plays would be different. Actually they simply wouldn't be . . . In the end, it doesn't matter what one thought about Harold's uncomfortable anger. It was himself saying 'This is what matters, it's fucking serious!' And he wrote what he wrote.

I think you both made your rough weather by it mattering
to you. As a spectator, I don't regret it of either of you . . . It
sometimes got combative, which I can understand. I can't
regret your reluctance to accommodate, your crusading if you
want to call it that. We write what we are.

Any play which occasioned two such beautiful letters, even
separated by such a long time-span, cannot, I believe, have
been wholly worthless. But I knew that my writing was, at a
technical level, incompetent. Too much speech, reported and
otherwise. It could never quite pass Valéry's test of 'giving the
sensation without the boredom of its conveyance'. As a matter of principle I have refused all subsequent offers of stage
revival, even though, or perhaps because, the memory of what
we all went through on the first production is indelible. In a
way, some of us who climbed on that particular boat at that
particular time have never quite climbed off. Now, whenever
someone comes along with a gleam in their eye thinking they
alone have worked out how to release the fish from under the
ice, I always say no. A British television version with Emma
Thompson and Tim Roth did nothing to persuade me I was
wrong about my own incompetence. Nor did an American
television version, reimagined in Los Angeles, with Gretchen
Corbett and Michael Cristofer.

Some time later, Irving Wardle of *The Times* sought nobly
to perform the trickiest of all Olympic fixtures for the critic:
the retrospective volte-face, the hands-up hands-down, I-got-
it-wrong *mea culpa*, the swallow dive into the empty pool of
error. He admitted that he had not been able to take in *Knuckle*,
the play, because he had been so angered by *Knuckle*, the event.
It had infuriated him and his fury had blinded him. Wardle

had admired Portable because it played at what he called 'virgin addresses'. But the subsequent appearance of a play by someone of my age – just twenty-six – and my political views in the West End had brought back to him all the primal sense of betrayal he had felt as a young man when John Osborne first of all inveighed against the Establishment, then, in Wardle's view, was seen to join it. Wardle said he had attacked my play so strongly not as a work but as a foreshadowing of what he expected to be a pattern. A rebellious dramatist would eventually stop rebelling and move to embrace the very things he or she had rebelled against. Wardle wasn't going to fall for it. He was not willing to be pulled round that same track twice. But if that was indeed the grounds of his hostility, Wardle was right to recant. It would soon become clear how wrong he had been.

A certain theme had been introduced into my life in the last three months, played at first quietly, on the piccolos perhaps. But soon, as in a symphony, the violins would come in, and then, unmistakably, the whole string section would take up the tune.

10

Spilling the Sacrament

It wasn't long before Margaret discovered that she was pregnant. The rightness of having returned to her was reinforced. Usually, the less you notice happiness, the greater it is. This was the best thing that could have happened. In the summer of 1974, the prospect of a child brought us both a redeeming sense of purpose. I was able to settle back down to work and find a rhythm. And so was she.

Looking back, it would seem bittersweet that although Michael Blakemore and I remained firm friends the most lasting effect he would have on me professionally was to bring me together with Peter Hall. Two years later, after Michael had presented a paper criticising the way Hall ran the National Theatre – Michael claimed less as a public service, more for his own benefit – these two men were to have a public falling-out which would rankle with them both for the rest of their lives. But in the days when they were getting along, Michael had mentioned to Peter that he was collaborating with a playwright he might like. Peter summoned me to lunch in one of those crepuscular restaurants which were just beginning to siphon up the new middle class's new wealth. He was bursting out of one of what I would come to recognise as a series of tailored velvet suits, always buttoned under impossible pressure at the waist, and all in the strange half-colours which would one day soon provide the queasy palette for the carpets and seats at the new

National Theatre on the South Bank. Peter understood that I was interested in touring. In the process of taking over from Olivier at the Old Vic, he felt that the moment for the National to have its own small-scale touring programme was long overdue. A proper National Theatre should be on the road, and not just in traditional venues. He would be very pleased if I would direct one of its first productions.

In later years, I would find that face to face almost nobody resembles their reputation. Whatever you have gleaned from gossip is generally wrong. The *on dit* turns out to be the *on ne sait rien*. Over and again, on meeting someone I have only heard about, I have been confounded. To Peter's name the word 'Machiavellian' was stubbornly attached, perhaps because of his lynx eyes and papal looks. At that first encounter I was peering round corners to see from what crooked angle of approach he could possibly be coming. But, face to face, on that afternoon in Covent Garden, Peter and I had the first of countless conversations in which he was honest, direct and to the point. I had been warned by others mentally to ask of Peter the question 'What does he really mean?' but I stopped asking it as soon as I realised that the answer was invariably 'Exactly what he says.' On occasions, as in the 1980s when he chose to shut down the Cottesloe, the smallest of the three auditoria on the South Bank, in order, he said, to shame the government into funding it properly – as though shame were a unit of currency in which Margaret Thatcher ever dealt – then, yes, I did find him overly political, and oddly naive. Peter, like Harold Pinter, had been foolish enough to vote for Thatcher in the first place. He could hardly complain about the outcome. But in his individual dealings he was beyond reproach. When he said to me that Trevor Griffiths' play *The Party*, about the British left's response to the

revolutionary demonstrations in Paris in May '68, had not ben-
efited from a souped-up production at the Old Vic, and might
be seen to better advantage on a smaller scale and in places
where it would find an audience more attuned to its politics, he
was speaking nothing other than the truth. It had played only
thirty-six times. Laurence Olivier had given his last stage performance as John Tagg, the Glaswegian Trotskyite, who was
modelled on Gerry Healy, a notoriously unbending leader of
the Socialist Workers Party. On the night I had seen the play,
the actor had seemed distracted and ill at ease, like a lifelong
gambler who'd been thrown off his game by knowing he was
likely playing his final hand. He had stumbled badly at various
places in the first act. But Olivier would not be small-scale touring. I was free to restart with a fresh slate.

Before we got up from the table Peter told me he was also
interested in me as a dramatist. When it opened in a year's
time, he was very keen to attract people like me and Howard
Brenton into the new National Theatre. It was important, he
said, to open the doors to the young. What was I planning to
do with my next play? Thinking nothing of it, I told Peter that
he was too late because I was already committed to my own
touring company, Joint Stock. Had he heard of it? He had.
Had he seen Max and Bill's adaptation of Heathcote Williams'
The Speakers when it had played a short season at the Institute of Contemporary Arts earlier this year? He had indeed
and it was wonderful. Well, I explained, that production had
come out of a new workshop process which Max and Bill were
pioneering. Over a long period of time, they had explored the
material at leisure, allowing the actors a significant amount of
input. This rare openness meant that the actors were seen to
have much more invested both in their characters and in the

event. To prepare for *The Speakers*, they had even been sent out to beg on the streets of London. Only in the last few weeks had the whole thing been pulled together with conventional rehearsal. The directors had created Hyde Park Corner by upturning a few boxes and letting the audience wander from speaker to speaker. Because the result had a spellbinding mixture of surface and depth, I had decided that I wanted to find out more.

By chance, they had approached me first. Pauline Melville, who had done assorted jobs including, in the early days of the National Theatre, working as casting director at the Old Vic, would later be known as the author of a collection of short stories about her native Guyana, *Shape-shifter*. Recently she had returned to college, and found that a book called *Fanshen* was being passed from hand to hand among her fellow students. It was written by a Pennsylvania farmer, William Hinton, who had been in China for six years as a tractor technician. He had been sent out by the US government after the Second World War to help supervise agricultural innovation in backward rural areas. There he had witnessed the land reform programmes which Mao's revolution instituted in the 1940s. Pauline had given the book to Bill, telling him it was a promising subject for a play. When I read it I found that it began with vivid descriptions of the terrifying feudal conditions which Chinese peasants, particularly the women with their bound feet, had endured well into the first half of the twentieth century. Within that first 150 pages were countless possible stories of cruelty and exploitation. They detailed the violence both of the landlords' regime and of its overthrow. But as a playwright I was already as resistant to dystopias as I was to utopias. They had no appeal for me. I found myself much more excited by the post-revolutionary parts of the book, in which the peasants, in imposed collectives, were encouraged by their political masters to adopt a system of control called 'Self-Report, Public Appraisal'. At ceaseless meetings, peasants were expected to report on their own short-comings and to correct the failings in their behaviour, at work and away, by group discussion. Leaders as much as peasants were intended, in theory, to be held to account. It was when the book turned into a frank questioning of whether there ever can be such a thing as true democracy, or whether all societies main-tain the same hidden systems of control, that the book became much more complicated and knotty. It was in these agonising shades of grey, rather than in the melodrama, that I found the potential for a play a thousand times more stimulating. How interesting to investigate what happens when you claim to involve everybody in society's decision-making processes. How marked a contrast from the society we were living in.

When, recently, I have described to acquaintances how forty years ago a group of white middle-class actors set out on the fringes of Chelsea to play Chinese peasants, they have smiled as though the whole idea were condescending and ridiculous. All I can say is, it did not seem so at the time. Nor did it seem so to the many audiences all over the country who came to be fascinated by it. At that moment in England, what choice did we have? As Pauline remarked, after two successful miners' strikes and the uprising of the shipworkers led by Jimmy Reid on the Upper Clyde, the concerns of the play seemed timely. Workers' control was on the agenda. By doing a play about China, we were opening up a whole area of history of which the British knew little. When *Fanshen* became, as it did, one of the best-remembered fringe productions of the 1970s, it was partly because the subject matter had been so original, but also because the acting and direction had an integrity which carried all before it.

On the first day of the summer workshop, before a word had been written, and when we all just had a daunting seven-hundred-page blue paperback in our hands, there was a certain amount of grumbling. One actor, who had been in the plays of Edward Bond, said, 'Oh my God, it's not one of those plays where you have to hoe, is it?' But once we had all gorged ourselves on Chinese peasant jokes we settled to a fruitful period of experiment, individual actors researching individual areas like eating habits or prostitution. Bill, in particular, focused down, seeking to find a suitable style while often answering actors' reasonable questions with his familiar dead stares. I was almost fond of them by now. 'YP,' he used to say sometimes when an actor asked for help. It turned out to mean 'Your problem.' But it became plain over the weeks why Bill had become known as the outstanding Brechtian director of his day. His defining priority was at all times to do justice to the suffering of the peasants. For him, this was a matter of immense gravity. His criterion for examining any representation was to ask whether it was adequate to the experience the peasant had undergone. Directing became a searching form of moral enquiry which eliminated the irrelevant and the shallow. Combined with Max's extraordinary gift for detail, it made for a formidable combination. Once Bill laughed when he was telling me that he had grown tired of people praising the amazing clarity which marked his productions. 'They say to me, "Oh but it was so clear." I always want to reply, "How would you prefer it? Muddy?"'

The method of work evolved as we did. There was never a conscious moment at which we all decided at the workshop to adopt the discussion methods used by the peasants. It just happened. One of the first things the Chinese had to do when working towards equality was to classify their current status – landlord, rich peasant or poor peasant. One day, as we walked back from lunch to the Pimlico rehearsal room, Bill suggested that it should not be the landlords who got the workshop going that afternoon. We should simply wait until one of the actors suggested we start. I think we sat for about ninety minutes before one of the actors took control. But eventually he did. Once everyone was given the right to run rehearsals, most of them enjoyed it. Pauline was particularly inspiring. Similarly, it was my idea that for once the production team should not talk about the actors behind their backs. On every play I had ever worked on, directors and writers had retired to the bar, or upstairs to theatre offices, to complain about the actors, just as, I am sure, actors sat in pubs complaining about us. On *Fanshen*, I proposed that Max, Bill and I should only ever say to each other what we were willing to say directly to the actors. Abandoning this subtle form of distancing made for a refreshing experience. When, in 1975, the finished play went into rehearsal, the directors no longer gave formal notes. Instead they improved the production by a time-consuming process of letting actors volunteer their own failings.

'*Fanshen*' means 'overturning', but there was one overturning which I, as writer, was not prepared to contemplate. I took part in improvisations, trying self-consciously to be an actor. I was more than happy, in return, to let actors make up scenes as we went along. But never for a moment did I doubt that I had skills distinctive from theirs. Once the workshop was over, I went off like any regular dramatist to sit in my room and write the play. It took me four months of sweat and all the gifts of analysis and précis I had to clear a path through such a massive book. The narrative became my responsibility and so was the thinking. This was a revolution of method, but not of function. Never did I imagine that the writing of a play of *Fanshen* would have been enriched by collective effort. Nor, in their heart, did anyone else. At the cinema, I am bewildered by films in which actors improvise individual lines, as though the first thing that came into an actor's head when he or she turned up on a film set were likely to be somehow more expressive than dialogue a writer had thought about for months. 'Wow,' said an actor at the climax of a recent film in which his character had just been told the boy he believed to be his son was not really his. 'That's a real slap in the face.' Improvisation, when deployed by a master like John Cassavetes, is a revelatory technique. But it's a technique which takes months of care and preparation. Serious improvisers refine their methods, just as a writer does. The current fashion among American actors for putting the script to one side and wandering who cares where off-piste is producing a cinema of approximation, with all television's vices and none of its virtues.

At times while writing *Fanshen* I was forced to break off to prepare my production of *The Party*, which, in recreating the world of the fashionable left in 1968, was taken by those who knew to be set in a fictional version of Clive Goodwin's flat. By coincidence, I was back recreating an environment from which I had exiled myself. But the element of social satire which had made the experience arch and self-conscious in the Old Vic was the aspect of the play which interested me least. What I loved was its rippling rhetoric. For all Trevor's deft handling of socialist ideas, there was also underneath his writing, as underneath that of Raymond Williams, a basic working-class instinct of generosity, common in life, but rare in the theatre, which made the play soar with a music which reached right into the hearts of its audience.

As it happened, *The Party* was the occasion of my growing up as a director. It came about through an actor using a chance phrase. In some of the featured roles I had cast several inexperienced players, so I was getting far too habituated to a process in which I teased out performances conforming to an idea that already existed in my head. In the first weeks, there was an awful lot of the director saying, 'Please do this, please don't do that.' The fact that six of my cast had themselves been directors at one time or another only made things more decisive. But in the two central roles were veterans who both merited a far different approach. Jack Shepherd, a highly nuanced graduate of the Royal Court who had been outstanding in the plays of Edward Bond and David Storey, was playing the drunken writer Malcolm Sloman. His climactic speech in the second act argues that revolution will not happen from the strategies of any political party, but will come about spontaneously from the people themselves. And as John Tagg, whose life's contrasting ambition has been the building of exactly the kind of controlling revolutionary party Sloman loathes, I had cast Fulton Mackay. Fulton would later be hugely popular as the prison officer Mackay in the Ronnie Barker series *Porridge*. But, unknown to the English television audience, he already had a long and treasured place at the heart of Scottish theatre, not least at the Citizens' in Glasgow to which my mother had taken me in the mid-1950s.

There was one afternoon in the rehearsal room when I was chopping but the chips weren't flying. Fulton, ever ingenious, found some crafty new way of beginning the twenty-minute monologue which forms the sinewy centrepiece of the first act.

'I'll, erm . . . take issue with our comrade's, er . . . analysis and model presently.' When Fulton had finished the first fifteen lines, I was thrilled. So I began, like an idiot, to describe what he had just done in words of my own and to comment how expressive it was of his character. But no sooner had I started praising it – 'And what was so good was . . .' – than Fulton shut me up with some words which were eventually to change my whole idea of the job. 'David, whatever you do, don't spill the sacrament.'

I was taken aback. It was the painter Jean Dubuffet who said that art was no use if it was simply the act of declaring ten per cent of things in the world beautiful and ninety per cent ugly. In the same way, I realised that directing was pointless if it was simply the act of deciding that ninety per cent of acting was bad and ten per cent good. It was particularly destructive to summarise to actors in words what they were conveying far more eloquently in spirit. When I had first started writing plays, I had discovered the mystery of writing. Why had I imagined that acting was any less of a mystery? It was not that I had become an overly controlling director. I hope I had always allowed actors freedom to experiment and find their own way. But I had been overly literal and reductive. Fulton, in one resonant metaphor, reminded me of the genius of what good actors do. The most powerful elements of theatre will always be beyond description. They're there in the moment and then they're gone. When Fulton told me not to spill the sacrament, I stopped being a clumsy schoolteacher and became a collaborator. From that day on, I knew that any ability or understanding I had when dealing with actors was firmly rooted in Fulton's rebuke.

When the play went out on tour, in theory we were back to the ideals of Portable Theatre, but with one big difference.

Hayden Griffin had designed a stage which could be put down in any environment. Portable had just blown in to the latest place where it was due to perform, made some obvious decisions, hung up some lights and got on with it. Fassbinder, in his films, believed that weird accidents of light and movement could be far more beautiful than anything that Hollywood expensively calculated. In the theatre, so had Portable. The casualness was the whole point. We had a strong conviction that if we ignored the finer points of presentation the audience would concentrate instead on what we were saying. The work would seem urgent precisely because we couldn't be bothered to normalise it, to smooth it down to conventional expectations. But my mind in these matters was changing. I was beginning to believe that Portable, by nixing aesthetics, had denied itself some of the theatre's full eloquence. Hayden's platform, designed not just for my production but for a whole forthcoming policy of touring, meant a degree of control undreamt of in fringe days. It was an empty square with bare sanded boards, built over a metal-sprung cage. You could then add whatever scenery you liked. Actors reported that it was a pleasure to stand on, and for most actors confidence grows from the feet up. In performance, the stage looked like a big table, tipped towards the audience. The relationship was always just right. You could assemble the whole thing in an hour or two. It had already served for a production of *Romeo and Juliet* and it would serve just as well for *The Party*. On every single touring date, whatever the overall space, you could give things an identical definition which meant that the look and the feel were much more polished. We had lost some of Portable's roughness, but with a cast like this, and with Jack and Fulton blazing on every cylinder, Trevor's lament for the impotence of the

British left struck home all the harder for its precision. The arrow flew true every night.

Hayden himself was an obstreperous South African with a contrary attitude which expressed itself most of the time in a kind of half-audible angry muttering. More or less everything pissed him off, though you couldn't usually quite hear why. The only things he really liked, apart from a well articulated stage, were deep-sea diving and liquor. I took to him at once. He had left his home country and was forbidden by the apartheid regime to go back, for reasons which were not entirely clear but which I gathered from more angry muttering were something to do with active participation in the activities of the ANC. He'd been a courier, I think, though a courier of what exactly I never cared to ask. With the charming and gifted Rory Dempster as lighting designer, we became a natural team whose principles and feelings chimed. We had all entered the theatre at the same time and been exposed to a group of ideas which derived from Brecht, and in particular from his productions for the Berliner Ensemble, which had visited London in 1956. The instinct of directors at the Court, just like those of middle-class home-makers in Clapham, had been to strip everything away. The aim was to refine things down to essentials. Hayden, Rory and I had all approved of the desire to clear the stage of junk. We saw that aim as political. Everything that was on the stage had to be there for a purpose. It had to matter. Light was there for the actors' faces, not to make pretty effects. But, for political reasons again, we had come to feel that black-box austerity had itself become a cliché, a way of avoiding meaning rather than expressing it. In the wrong hands, it seemed to be a way of not taking decisions. Austerity was fine, and nothing was ever going to come between us and our passion for an empty space.

But like fashionistas who had only worn black, we wanted to start risking colour. More than anything, we wanted the freedom to make images again. *The Party*, a naturalistic play set in one room and proceeding in real time, allowed us little of the licence we craved. The question was where and when we were finally going to be allowed to let rip. Having for so long tried either to ignore or to crash the question of style, I felt I was now ready to pioneer it.

By the time the holidays came and the tour was over, Margaret was about to give birth. My parents came to stay with us at the Oval in expectation of becoming grandparents. Dad had retired at sixty and had settled into the unaccustomed business of living with his wife. He had always promised her that on retirement they would take a world cruise together. But soon after they reached Australia Dad had to be taken off the ship and flown home with a clot on his leg. It was yet one more anticlimax on a long list, and a sign of an increasing frailty which would mark out Dad's last twenty years. For Mum, marital proximity, so long delayed, was threatening to turn into a nursing job. The thing to which she'd been most looking forward had been taken away. But I noticed that the impact of at last living with her partner was beginning to change her. Dad's absence had played on her neediness, but his presence had made the playing field much more level. She had become a touch tougher and more self-certain. It was as if for all those years she'd been in need of abrasion, of interaction, and now she had it. The pining cat at last had a scratching post.

Mum's wider attitudes were changing as well. In May 1973 Edward Heath's energy supremo Lord Jellicoe was revealed to have been using the services of call girls from a company with the unimaginative name of Mayfair Escorts. It was, by Conservative standards, a minor sex scandal, a shrivelled squib after the Roman candles of Profumo and Lambton, yet for some reason it was the occasion of my mother making a final decision. It was the last straw. She was sick of them. When she made her ruling it reminded me of the tone she had used to exile Mr G—— from my life. She was never going to vote Tory again.

Mum and Dad had arrived on Christmas Eve. Margaret woke at four the following morning, and I drove her along the deserted streets hanging with river mist to St Thomas's hospital. Nothing moved on the icy landscape except us. There was a bit of a panic at nine thirty when it looked as if the birth might have to be induced, but the very threat of forceps, brandished but never employed, produced our son. Because he was the first child to be born in Lambeth that day, all the nurses from the hospital came to sing carols round his crib. A less level-headed boy than Joe might have his head turned by such a greeting. Margaret went back to the ward, where a group of women had concealed a festive vodka bottle in a waste-paper basket. They all saw the five days you had to stay in hospital as a welcome holiday from family life, so I left the reclining mothers preparing to party. When I got home at lunchtime, I drank a single glass of whisky, a drink I normally can't stand. For the only time in my life, alcohol did what it's advertised to do: it filled me with pure euphoria. I ate Christmas lunch alone with my parents.

Nothing prepared me for my radical change in feeling. I spent the next week in a daze. Perhaps because of my experiences with my own father, I was thrilled to be a father myself and was doubly determined to do better. In the middle of January I had to go off for a week to New York, where Perry King and Kitty Winn, through no fault of their own, were about to star in an inept production of *Knuckle*. My first contact with it was dismaying. The founder of the Phoenix Theatre, T. Edward Hambleton, tamped down his pipe, lit up, then fell fast asleep at the beginning of the rehearsal-room run-through, waking a couple of moments before the end to declare the whole thing first-class. His snores had punctuated the playing throughout. It was my first visit to New York since I'd been there as a student with Roger Dancey. In 1971 the most radical producer in America, Joe Papp, had rung from the Public Theater – 'Hi, it's Joe Papp here' – to tell me he was about to mount the American premiere of *Slag*. He had then rung to tell me it had opened to general praise. And he'd rung for a third time a few weeks later to say it was closing. Each time he was courteous and energetic, telling me how hilarious my play was, and how refreshing it was that at last there was a young writer who wanted to put women on stage. 'Good for you, David.' But at no point had he invited me over.

Now that I had returned after so long, it was predictable that I found myself, with *Knuckle*, in a familiar mess. The pattern had been established in childhood: whatever happened was going to be my fault. Either I could let the production pass, just mark it down as a stinker and take my punishment, or I could make myself unpopular by trying to do something about it. As usual, I chose the latter. By the time I'd given the director a four-hour talk on everything that was wrong with his production, I could see him heating the branding iron in the flames of his resentment to singe the word 'Impossible' on my forehead yet again. Backing off, he asked me to go away for a few days during which, he said, he would put my notes into practice. Fat chance. Digging in deeper, I said I didn't think this would be a practical solution. I'd give him twenty-four hours.

In New York, I was carrying with me some early pages of the new play I'd started on the train the day after *Knuckle* opened in London. It had developed a little from the first idea, but not very far. A rock band would be playing a couple of sets on the lawns at a Cambridge May Ball and you would see both the performances they would give that night and, in between, the wild, shocking disarray they happened to be in offstage. It was a blindingly simple notion. It would not be a musical, but nor on the other hand would it quite be a play. Kicking my heels, I wandered down to SoHo, which was still in the early days of having its industrial premises taken over by painters, film-makers and fashion designers. Something in the atmosphere hit me strongly. I hadn't been in the area since 1965, and clearly everybody thought they were very bohemian, colonising a part of the city which had been written off as unlivable in. But if you listened to what they were talking about, people had moved from hippy to yuppie without passing through action.

I went to the Broome Street Bar to have a beer. In such bars, the talk had once been of civil rights, of Vietnam and of revolution. These days, to judge from what I was overhearing, it seemed to be exclusively about yourself. Here, as everywhere, were hung Andy Warhol's images of boring personalities from the past. America was looking backwards, turning into a place of myth and memory. I sat there for most of an evening listening to people talking ever more loudly about their relationships. A woman on a payphone was screaming at the top of her voice, 'Don't write me, don't phone me, I never want to see you again.' At no point did anyone in the bar seem to discuss anything which was happening in the non-relationship world. It struck me that the rolling stone really had rolled on down the hill and come to a complete stop. Whatever promise of insight had once been held out in the injunction to have a good time had long been snuffed out. The project was no longer to make the finest possible society. It was to gild the finest possible cage. I had given up on bands like the Beatles years previously when they had started wittering 'Let It Be'. But now it was like the weather had changed for good. Publications such as the *Village Voice* and *Oz* had looked outwards. It was only a matter of time till there was a magazine called *Self*.

In the conception of any play or film there is always a moment of blinding excitement, and this was it. The visual image had long been in my head – the contrast between the grungy band and the privileged surroundings, even if the original idea of the abandoned baby had dropped away. But how would it be, I thought that evening, to conceive of a heroine who refused to go down the path my own generation seemed to be taking? What if I created a rock singer who would do anything, literally anything, rather than see her horizons shrink to those of the Broome Street Bar? I started writing with such pleasure that it ceased to matter to me what happened to the errant production of *Knuckle*. I did go back once and found it little improved. My input had been futile. I decided to leave town early before the audience passed judgement. By a blissful coincidence, my plane from JFK to London took off by an unusual flight path, so that we circled midtown Manhattan before heading off over the Atlantic. I could actually look out of the window and see down to the theatre below where at that very moment – 8 p.m. – the curtain was going up on a travesty of my play.

On my return, I persuaded Tony Bicât to write the lyrics for the new play and his younger brother Nick to write the music. Nick, a gentle and soft-spoken man with an effortless access to melody, had often added kick at Portable and at Nottingham by writing incidental music. He was that rare kind of composer, like Alex North, who loves and understands non-lyric theatre. Unleashed to do more, he relished the chance to come up with a proper rock 'n' roll score. Both Nick and Tony thought that my portrait of a humorous, exhausted and drug-taking band on the road was influenced by our own time with Portable. The jokes brought back memories. And fairly soon the three of us were flying, far too preoccupied with our night of stage debauchery and mayhem to take much notice when in February the Conservative Party elected a female leader. It didn't seem an event of much significance. By the middle of April I had a new play which I couldn't wait to put on. Luck was with me, because it was to be speeded into production with almost indecent haste. Early in 1974, the Royal Court had rediscovered its soul and purpose with three Athol Fugard plays, two of them starring John Kani and Winston Ntshona. In their indictment of the way the black population was being treated in South Africa, they took political theatre in London to a superb new level of accomplishment. Nobody could sit in the audience and not be cheered both by Fugard's writing and by Kani's dazzling acting. As a result, the will existed to hand artistic control of the Royal Court over to two younger directors, Nicholas Wright and Robert Kidd, who arrived, refreshingly, with no scores to settle and no grudges held. Nick, in particular, had produced the *Rocky Horror Show* while running the Theatre Upstairs. So now his first priority was to try and win back all the writers the Royal Court had managed to alienate.

The directors had already planned their first season, which was to open in late August and to include new plays by Howard Barker and Edward Bond. But in an uncharacteristic default, Christopher Hampton, Bob Kidd's regular collaborator, had failed to deliver his expected play, *Treats*, on time. There was an ominous gap. One day my rock play *Teeth 'n' Smiles* was finished, next day it was scheduled. I insisted, without too much argument, on directing it myself. 'Are you sure?' they asked. But I was. Since 1971, with Max Stafford-Clark, Richard Eyre and Michael Blakemore, I had enjoyed a charmed run of directors. I had no reason on the grounds of achievement to forgo any of them. But I had developed a suspicion that the tendency of any director when faced with a new voice is to hunt around for parallels. Searching for a tone, they direct in the style of what it reminds them of. Rightly or wrongly, I believed my voice was original. At whatever loss of quality, I needed to take charge of making that clear. The popular notion, put about by directors, that writers shouldn't direct is nonsense. At any point in the British theatre there are always dozens of bad directors. Only a handful of them are writers.

With Michael Codron's blessing, after a quick holiday with Margaret and Joe on the Greek island of Rhodes, I set to work with the Court's vibrant new casting director, Patsy Pollock. It was a case of the right person at the right time. Patsy had been born to a hardscrabble life in the East End and had moved on through the fashionable world of sixties advertising to work as a stylist for Alan Parker and David Puttnam. I had shown the play to my old colleague Charlie Gillett, who had corrected some of its most obvious errors of tone. But Patsy's background meant that she also knew the culture of music inside out. She'd grown up with it. Patsy was as passionate as I was about the task of putting together a company of actors who needed to be able to play musical instruments and act at the same time, but who also, crucially, looked as if they might belong in rock 'n' roll's attractive, degenerate world. I can't remember a period of preparation I enjoyed so much, with Patsy, outspoken, diligent, hilarious, serving as a blast of working-class fresh air blowing the cobwebs off my preconceptions, as all sorts of human jetsam – actors, musicians, and God knows who – washed up in unending waves on the shores of the tiny Royal Court casting office.

Our outstanding challenge was to find someone who could play Maggie. My lasting hatred of the word 'self-destructive' stems from the fact that I have no idea what it means. Or rather, it's in such common and lazy use as to have no meaning at all, except presumably to convince you that the user somehow knows what they're talking about. When a politician takes no care to hide the fact he is sleeping with his research assistant, the word for what he does is 'stupid'. When a rock singer dies in a pool of their own vomit, the word for them is almost certain to be 'addict'. In my play, the central character, Maggie, is fond of a drink, and is also in a state of violent revulsion at what she sees her world becoming. As she keeps intoning satirically, 'The acid dream is over, let's have a good time.' But there is a purpose to her antics. Under the ragged surface of chaotic abuse, her ex-boyfriend, the lyricist Arthur, can detect a certain iron control. For the role of Maggie, Patsy and I therefore needed an actress who was too intelligent to buy into the newspaper myth of self-destruction. She had to be able to scare the living daylights out of every man she met, but also to amaze them with her acumen. There was only one candidate. But the problem we had was that Helen Mirren couldn't sing.

Like many first-rate teachers of music, Nick Bicât holds to the idealistic principle that there is no such thing as a nonsinger. We can all sing, we've just been taught wrong. In four switchback weeks of rehearsal, Nick certainly made his point.

Helen was such a good actress that, standing in front of a flat-out rock band and fixing you firmly in the eye, she could make you *believe* she could sing by the mesmerising power of her presence, even though the actual notes she was hitting were occasionally John o'Groats to the tune's Land's End. At the time she came to us, Helen had been travelling round Africa with Peter Brook and was very much a believer in onstage spontaneity. She had an insouciant approach which included telling stories about the unhappy effects of imagining she could enliven her appearance in a Royal Shakespeare Company performance of *The Wars of the Roses* in Stratford with a few spliffs. Helen's ways of not listening to direction were far more sophisticated than those of anyone I had previously encountered. Once she received me naked for a notes session in her dressing room. She discarded the *Evening Standard* which had briefly obscured her, clearly with the aim of putting me off my stride. She succeeded. Helen's fondness for hanging loose was fine by me – it was so unselfconscious and natural, and on stage it fed into the character – and it was also fine with Jack Shepherd, who was playing Arthur. He was an old hand who had dealt with far trickier people than Helen. He loved going out and jazzing according to whatever Helen threw at him that night. She was so accomplished that, whatever she did, she never let go of the play's intent. But her freedom, both professional and personal, did not go down so well with Dave King, the more senior actor who was playing Saraffian, the band's manager.

By the time of the play Dave was in his fifties, but in his day he'd been the only British song-and-dance man ever to hold down a prime-time show on American television. Like Perry Como or Dean Martin, he'd sat on a lounge lizard stool, often in a shiny suit and thin tie, singing standards and telling jokes.

He'd had a massive hit with 'Memories Are Made of This'. But he'd been thrown off the network after going to a bash for the programme's commercial sponsors and informing them over lunch that their product was crap. He was perfectly cast as a mohair-coated impresario whose happiest times had been in Tin Pan Alley in the fifties, before the middle classes got hold of pop music and made it meaningful. At the climax of the play, his speech in defence of the wartime looting of the bombed-out Café de Paris was beautifully delivered. But Dave also had a sense of physical threat about him which came through on stage and gave his performance a dangerous edge which was not entirely a matter of acting. Perhaps because his two teenage daughters, on whom in the days of his US stardom he had bestowed Cherokee names, were giving him a bad time at home, Dave did find Helen, a modern woman with a justified sense of her own value, an almost impossible threat.

After the first preview, Nick Wright made me laugh when he told me he had greeted a famous novelist coming out of the theatre aghast. When he had asked her whether she had enjoyed the evening, she had replied, 'Oh no, not at all. It was horrible. It was all sex and jokes and rock and roll.' As Nick said, to his ears it sounded like the recipe for a perfect evening. Just before the play's press night, Patsy Pollock went down the King's Road to visit Sex, the clothes shop just renamed by Malcolm McLaren and Vivienne Westwood. The slogan in its window read 'Rubberwear for the Office'. Patsy came back with a hot-off-the-press punk T-shirt, lemon-yellow, ripped right down the middle and scrawled with thick black handwriting, as my first-night present. On one side: 'Things We Like'. On the other: 'Things We Don't'. It seemed appropriate. When you see *Teeth 'n' Smiles* today in revival, it seems far more punk than hippy, catching the particular moment at which musical joy turned to musical fury.

For a couple of months afterwards, my social circles briefly expanded. I was asked to a party by Elton John's lyricist, Bernie Taupin, not someone I'd previously have expected to hear from. Because he was a friend of one of the cast, Keith Moon, the dissolute drummer of the Who, drove his Rolls-Royce into the side of the Royal Court Theatre, staggered through the stage door and walked downstairs to the stage where, in the middle of a performance, in full view, he greeted his old friend Karl Howman. Karl coped heroically while the audience treated Moon's appearance as an unpublicised but welcome add-on to the evening. Moon said later, 'Karl asked me to come and see the play. So I did.' And then Jerry Leiber and Mike Stoller approached me with an eye to asset-stripping the play and replacing the music with some of their own. They wanted to take the result to America. Since their library of songs already included 'Hound Dog', 'Jailhouse Rock' and 'Stand by Me', everyone told me I was mad to turn them down. But, for me, Nick and Tony's contribution was as vital to the feeling of the evening as my own.

Personally I was as happy as I'd ever been in my life. I adored my son, who sometimes seemed to look back at me as if he knew that he was, in some small aspect, a satirical version of myself. I was commuting up to the Yorkshire Dales where Margaret, on behalf of David Susskind, was producing the second of two cinema films about a vet, written by a man who called himself James Herriot but whose real name was Alf Wight. Once more, in between, I was back sitting on the steps outside the theatre in Sloane Square. After all those battles, it did seem to be where I belonged. If there was an artistic problem with the play itself, it was identified by the critic Ronald Bryden, who wrote an exceptionally perceptive review:

> *Everything in the play is a little too clever, too funny, too articulate to be true . . . The evening works too well as theatre, allows itself too much dazzle and enjoyment to put over satisfactorily the serious point it is trying to make . . . One can see why in the bleak and austerer chapels of the theatrical Left, Hare is mistrusted for his excessive brilliance and success. There is a kind of over-willed, show-off quality to his writing, an intrusion of himself on his creations by trying too hard to be magisterial, which distorts* Teeth 'n' Smiles *even more than* Knuckle *and brings to mind the young Auden of* The Dog Beneath the Skin . . . *All the same, it is the personal tensions in his talent, the tug between popularity and politics, display and distaste for his own cleverness which have made* Teeth 'n' Smiles *for all its impurities a success. Rage as it may, the far theatrical Left has nothing to teach him until it has realised that, without success, political purity is as impotent as cheap music.*

1975 was the first of two successive blazing summers which bathed the whole country in luxurious sunshine. In 1970, before air conditioning was installed at the Royal Court, a man at a matinee of David Storey's play *Home* had keeled over dead in the fourth row from a heart attack brought on by the stifling heat. John Gielgud had cried with laughter when showing us all a letter from a sympathetic member of the public seeking to reassure the actor that the corpse being carried from the stalls had, in his opinion, not spoiled the audience's enjoyment of the play one bit. In 1971, Anna Massey, Barbara Ferris and

Lynn Redgrave performing *Slag* had made me feel that the-atre could be tremendous fun. And now I was feeling it again. The old building was shaking behind me, plaster falling off the ceiling to the sound of Nick's music, and a young audience were pouring through the doors to hear Helen rip into lines like 'America is a crippled giant. England is a sick gnome.' An exceptional cast including Cherie Lunghi, Hugh Fraser, Mick Ford and Antony Sher, making his first appearance in London as a medical student who carries a dismembered finger in his pocket, were having a blast, while back at Hampstead, after four months of touring, *Fanshen* was doing a second London season. The BBC were even planning to transmit the play in full. We had done one performance already for agricultural workers at a farm in Tring and been gratified by their response. Now it was to be filmed specially on another farm at Aston Clinton in Buckinghamshire. But I was facing what Edward Heath laughably used to call the problems of success. *Fanshen* had acquired a reputation, and in response the original author was threatening to withdraw permission for the play to con-tinue unless I agreed to radical changes.

William Hinton did not hide his surprise that my play caught on. It was only because it was so widely noticed and gaining a significant audience that its tone began to bother him. Previous dramatic versions of the book, of whose existence I had never even heard, had disappeared without being widely seen. But now Kenneth Tynan and Shirley MacLaine, as unlikely a cou-ple of producers as you could imagine, were asking to present the play off Broadway. Alarmed, Hinton had submitted my script both to his daughter, who was a Red Guard, and to the Chinese embassy in Washington for their approval. Not sur-prisingly, such consultations had resulted in Hinton insisting on 110 specific changes to my text. Often it was a question of terminology. The word 'murdered' should not be used. The correct term is 'executed'. You don't 'summon' people. It's too commandist. A peasant would never say, 'I hate China.' It was unimaginable.

The BBC flew me over for a weekend of negotiation on his Pennsylvania farm. I could hardly deny that from his point of view Hinton was right to be concerned. He had discerned, quite correctly, that the play was indeed not saying the same thing as his book. As a Marxist and passionate believer in the Chinese revolution, Hinton had intended his account to be a ringing endorsement of land reform. As a non-Marxist, I had considerable reservations. I had aimed instead to write a classic play which opposed two points of view. I believed that in any society there will always be one political faction in government which will lay stress on the importance of production. They will argue that encouraging people to produce is the key to the good society. But another opposing faction will want to put more urgent stress on the fair distribution of that production. They will insist that no society can be good unless it is also just. Interestingly, when *Fanshen* was revived by the National Theatre in 1988 after nine years of the Thatcher ascendancy, it did not seem remotely dated. Rather, it seemed more pressing than ever. Whatever the political climate of the time, however we frame society's priorities, the abiding argument between plenty and justice is one that will never go away. The language of ideology changes, or, as today, seems to lose definition. But the fundamental dispute about whether abundance is more important than fairness does not. Thatcher argued, in her famous gloss on the parable of the Good Samaritan, that people could only do good if they first had money. Her opponents asked by what means of exploitation they had acquired that money in the first place.

The sessions I had with Hinton were warm but attritional. Understandably, he did not accept my terms of reference. As a Marxist, he found my use of the word 'justice' meaningless. Whose justice, he would say? In class terms, what does the word 'justice' even mean? I did believe that Mao had liberated millions of peasants from servitude. But I also had read enough evidence, even by the mid-1970s, to suspect Mao had delivered them into a different, more ambiguous kind of slavery. At the end of every scene, Hinton wanted an upward tick. Although he was ready to agree that my representation of what had happened in the Chinese village of Long Bow was indeed accurate and true to his own gruellingly thorough record, he always wanted to add a line, as false as anything Hollywood might come up with, which effectively said, 'But in spite of all this, things continued to get better.'

As my work reached a larger public, I would grow used to the pressures for censorship, offered for the best of exemplary reasons. When people tell you they value political art, what they often mean is that they enjoy political propaganda which corroborates what they already think. All kinds of groups, including socialists and feminists, would ask me to reconfigure work in order to show what ought to happen rather than what does. I grew used to having to argue to the literal-minded that drama is not and cannot be a cartoon form of exhortation. It is about people, it is not about types. Shakespeare did not intend *Macbeth* to be an indictment of Scottish monarchy. Nor is the characterisation of Lady Macbeth misogynist. The idiotic language of role models would take hold and grow like a creeper to try to stifle the life out of art and reduce it to sociology. For so many people making a living out of culture, playing with cultural politics turned out to be much better sport than the challenge of seeing and listening to what was being conveyed in actual works of art. With that rising tide of programmatic wordsoup which would threaten the vigour and authenticity of theatre in the new century, I would have no patience. Work, when fully achieved, seemed to me a more powerful manifesto than manifestos. Nor, on the other hand, was I willing to take credit when equally passionate interest groups sought to congratulate me on showing things in ways which, by sublime coincidence, just happened to flatter positions they already approved. But my arguments with Hinton were different, because they were on a much more understandable moral basis. He was the author, after all. More than that, he was the witness. On his return from China in the early 1950s during the frenzy of anti-communism, Hinton had twice had his notes seized, first by the US Customs, again later by the Senate. I did well to remind myself that the writing of his book had cost Hinton a long legal struggle and fifteen years of hard work. The adaptor had given barely six months.

At the end of the weekend, we had come to some decent compromises. Some of my favourite lines had gone from the play, but I had not been forced to include any substitutions. It was an elegant truce, and the play held up, unspoiled. The structure was so secure that it did no damage when a bit of plaster was knocked away. The writer who wanted the audience to understand had made peace with the writer who wanted them to believe. In 1975, none of us at Joint Stock realised how lucky we were still to live in a culture in which the principal public broadcaster would think nothing of devoting a whole evening on one of its two major channels to the political details of the

Chinese agrarian revolution. I'm not saying we took such seriousness for granted. We didn't. But nor did we appreciate just how quickly fashion would change.

11

007

On 15 October 1974 a group of artistic directors from all over the country, including Joan Littlewood and Richard Eyre, signed a letter to *The Times* in which they warned of the threat posed by the new National Theatre. They were concerned, they said, that when the organisation moved to its future home on the South Bank, not only would the newly expanded theatre with its three auditoria take up a disproportionate share of the Arts Council's budget, but, by the sheer scale of its ambitions, it might suffocate smaller and regional playhouses artistically as well. 'Mr Hall has said he wants to make the National Theatre "the nation's theatre". This is an effective slogan: but the nation has many good theatres already. Big is not always beautiful. The size and status of the new National Theatre must not be allowed to drain and enfeeble the other theatres of the nation. This, we suggest, is now a dangerous possibility.'

Anyone who had followed the National Theatre's story from the very beginning of the twentieth century was well used to routine attacks from the private sector. Even during Olivier's tenure, when Henry V himself was giving the enterprise some much-needed cover, there had been press outrage about the scandalous cost to the taxpayer of Robert Stephens's contact lenses in a play by Lope de Vega. Ralph Richardson's shoes for Ibsen were similarly rumoured to be overpriced. But as construction deadlines went by and the completion of the South

Bank theatre was postponed too many times to count, so a new front was opened, this time from the left. Since the founding initiatives of George Bernard Shaw and Harley Granville-Barker, the idea of a national theatre had been held to be progressive. Liberating theatre from the obligation to be commercial and giving it the immunity of art was felt to be an enlightened ambition. It was something every forward-thinking person had argued for. But now that a National Theatre was to be a reality, the left, for some reason, was doing a collective volte-face. The cause was being declared reactionary.

It made no sense to me. For a start, Peter Hall was planning to put on new plays. He was not interested in creating a fusty old Comédie Française, its sole mission to perpetuate the classical idiom of the past. At the Royal Shakespeare Company Peter had given Harold Pinter the same stage and the same status as Shakespeare. He intended to do the same again. The doubters were saying that it would be wrong for writers and actors from the fringe to join what was bound to be an establishment theatre. I took a far less defeatist view. I couldn't understand: why not join it and shape it? Did the opponents really believe that their own ideals were so feeble, their own convictions so shallowly held that they would be corrupted and softened the moment they came into contact with a larger organisation? Did they feel themselves that powerless? The South Bank would only become an establishment theatre if non-establishment artists turned down the chance to work there. And what exactly would be the profit in that? Why would we who had believed in a national theatre want to hand it over to the very people who believed in it least? There was no suggestion from Peter that he was, in any way, planning to inhibit anything we intended to say. We could write the plays we wanted and stage them in the ways we wanted. Why on earth would you refuse the chance to address as many people as possible? Howard Brenton said that for years he'd been playing pub piano. Now at last he was getting his hands on the Steinway.

Normally during this decade of no-holds-barred dispute, you could at least see your opponent's point of view. Since childhood, my automatic assumption had been to fear that, if people said so, I must be in the wrong. At school and at university, I had paid the price of a psychological deformity which had me secretly tending to credit my enemies before I credited my friends. But in 1976 the widespread odium Howard and I attracted by becoming the first playwright and the first director to have a production originate in the new Lyttelton Theatre mystified me. I could feel it – God knows, I could feel it everywhere I went in the British theatre – but, try as I might, I could not understand it. Least of all did I know why old comrades were using the word 'traitor'. Traitor to what, exactly? The case seemed to me open and shut. I could see that if you still held to the idea of a rough aesthetic, the plush seats might be wrong for you. A certain nostalgia might even hold you back. You might say, 'I love the fringe and I don't want to leave.' If you still believed in touring as strongly as I did, the National Theatre's ready abandonment of Hayden Griffin's sprung platform after we had done *The Party* was a depressing portent. For the following forty years, the National's neglect of the rest of the country would be a largely unremarked scandal. But why should those of us who believed that the best place to be radical was at the centre be declared to be wrong? We felt differently, maybe, from those who wanted to stay out. But we were not *wrong*. The fight I had just endured to take an anti-capitalist play into the capitalist theatre had given me much the most

bruising experience of my life. But I had not finished up thinking it misguided. Arguments about purity had always bored me
stiff. I'd heard too many such at Cambridge. There they had
been about literature. These days they were about politics, or,
worse, tribe. They were the very arguments which had disempowered British intellectual life for years.

To his many critics at the other end of the spectrum, Howard was presenting a dismayingly tricky target. The organised
right knew an enemy when they saw one, but try as they might,
they couldn't quite get their hooks into Howard. His poetry of
regret for the ideals of the organised left confused them, and
his desire to reanimate those ideals drove them nuts. Clearly a
socialist, Howard had never written a single word in favour of
Soviet communism. Nor, for that matter, had I. They combed
our work, sentence by sentence, looking for incriminating evidence, and found none. It enraged a whole slew of prominent
British journalists formed by the Cold War that younger writers should so smoothly uncouple socialism from dictatorship.
How could we do that, when for years their own self-certainty
as writers had depended on the pretence that such a feat was
impossible? Howard had written a play, *Magnificence*, in 1973
for the Royal Court, effectively about the Angry Brigade, in
which a domestic terrorist with a plastic explosive accidentally
kills both himself and an MP. It ended with a moving coda
from his best friend: 'Jed. The waste. I can't forgive you that
. . . What I can't forgive you, Jed, my dear, dear friend, is the
waste.' Howard's understanding towards the violent, combined
with his unequivocal disapproval of their violence, had sent
Fleet Street's opinion factory into a spin.

Now, for the National, Howard had written a new play
which I was to direct. After my production of *The Party*, Peter

had offered me a flattering carte blanche. I could do what I wanted. But I was only interested in Howard's play. *Weapons of Happiness* took its title from the Serbian poet Vasko Popa: 'All the bright weapons of happiness wait only for a sign.' The story is centred on the real-life figure of Josef Frank, who was one of the Czech communists executed by the Russians after the Prague Show Trials in 1952. Frank was accused of being in what was called at the time 'a Titoite–Trotskyite–Zionist conspiracy'. The play imagines what might have happened if he had survived. Howard has Frank living in South London and working in an everyday job in a crisp factory, trying at night to suppress his memory of the Soviet horrors he has endured. When his fellow workers try to involve him in a sit-in against the hopeless factory management, there is a lovely dramatic contrast between the scale of the two different fights. In the early 1950s, Frank is watching great forces of history at work as Stalinism tears into the whole of Eastern Europe at terrifying human cost. In the 1970s, we have only the pathetic British spectacle of exhausted industrial squabbles signifying what looks like terminal economic decline. The violence of one struggle is pitched against the absurdity of the other. In his writing Howard spared us neither the full power of Stalin's terror nor the ignominy of British class-bound union–management relations. But, more than that, in alternating between two superbly imagined worlds, he offered Hayden and me the perfect visual opportunity to create the kind of epic imagery of which we'd been dreaming.

Hayden and I started discussions, preparing a decor which would put to full use all the amazing resources of the new National Theatre. During the intervening time I had seen little of Kate Nelligan. We had the shared sensation of being loyal friends for life without actually ever seeing each other. In the circumstances, both of us generally thought it best to keep apart. Early in 1975 Kate had appeared with my friend Anna Massey and Eileen Atkins in George Bernard Shaw's *Heartbreak House* at the Old Vic. Uncertain of the director, Kate had asked me to attend the first preview, as someone she trusted, to give her informal acting advice on her performance as Ellie Dunn. I'd been amused to see that some of the other principal actors had asked their friends along as well. By chance, we were all sitting in a row, somewhere in the middle of the stalls, like sports coaches, comparing notes but each with our individual charges. It was that kind of production. I'd given what help I could – truthfully, she needed very little – and thought no more about it. Kate and I would chat on the phone occasionally about a script she was reading, or, more often, about a director she was finding impossible. Then, one afternoon in the spring of 1976, we ended up having tea together. Kate, still with her boyfriend Mark, had moved to live in Stockwell in a pretty pink-painted house, less than a mile away from my own family quarters in Richborne Terrace. We were in her front room and I was describing a television play I had written about a British black propaganda unit in the Second World War. I was relishing my disbelief at having stumbled on such an extraordinary subject when, with no notice, Kate burst into tears.

It was a mark of my young selfishness that, not just in affairs of the heart, I had always assumed that other people suffered less than I did. An essential part of a dramatist's job is to identify with others, to see things their way round. But because you do it all day, the danger is that you lose practice at doing it in the evening. As it turned out, in this particular case, Kate's tears had nothing to do with me or with the memory of our

259

time together. They sprang from her deepening fear that as a foreigner she would always be disliked and misunderstood in England. But in a careless way I had unthinkingly assumed that after us both being thrown for such a loop, Kate would have regained her equilibrium much more quickly than me. She had seemed stronger. And after all, it was she who had insisted we end our relationship. But the strange thing was that, thanks to Joe's existence, I had slid into happiness without even noticing. On the occasions when I had chatted with Kate on the phone, I had been too insulated to detect that our moods had been going in opposite directions. Sitting there watching Kate cry, I realised how completely happiness may cut you off from everyone else.

In the outside world, there was by now a certain hysteria attending Kate's fame. You couldn't have missed it. Kate was one of those people who, innocent of jealousy themselves, thereby bring it out more violently in others. Even on *Knuckle*, before she was widely known, I had noticed that the temperature tended to rise when she walked into a room. In her presence men's voices went up a note or two. They often became subtly unnatural, laughing too loudly or telling long stories which had no point. Some women, meanwhile, became defensive or fell silent. But by rumour things had been getting worse. The wife of one famous actor who was working with Kate had gone to the lengths of hiring a private detective to make sure her husband was involved in no irregularity for the whole of the theatrical run. The detective reassured the client by giving Kate a blameless all-clear, but nevertheless it added to her reputation as a transatlantic Lola Montez. Her refusal to make any secret of the fact that she dreaded the life of an English actress, skating around in the classics and wearing long skirts, did not make her any more popular with her peers who would have been grateful for half her chances. They called her spoilt. When she had been approached to be a Bond girl, she had laughed. She wasn't going to vamp and smoulder, however well paid. Inevitably, the word 'difficult', always more freely bestowed on actresses than on actors, and less deservedly, had become a sort of honorific permanently attached to her name.

It was when Kate was crying across the tea-table from me that I first thought it would be interesting to cast her in *Licking Hitler*. She was not perhaps the most obvious choice. While I had been writing the film, the idea had never occurred to me. Anna Seaton is a young woman with no experience of life who is sent into the English countryside in 1941 to work in a fake radio station which broadcasts damaging and sometimes obscene disinformation to the Germans. She arrives at a specially commandeered country house not knowing how to make a cup of tea, a detail I had picked up from reading about the similarly upper-class Jessica Mitford, who, in ignorance of even the most basic practicalities of life, had eloped with Esmond Romilly to fight in the Spanish Civil War in 1937. Kate was working-class, Canadian and sophisticated. Playing Anna, who was aristocratic, English and innocent, would be a stretch. But after her performance in *Knuckle*, I was bound to feel that the foreign edge she might bring to these very British roles gave them a sharp perspective not accessed so easily by natives.

Licking Hitler was the first properly achieved television script I had written. In the 1970s, television was regarded as a uniquely important medium. No playwright would dream of condescending to it, or of not giving it their very best work. *Armchair Theatre* and *The Wednesday Play* had initiated the practice of good dramatists and actors setting out to tell truths about the lives of all the people watching at home. Often socially engaged, many first-class plays and films, like *Cathy Come Home* or Trevor Griffiths' disturbing play about breast cancer, *Through the Night*, were shown to audiences not only much larger but also much more diverse than those in the theatre or cinema. It was noticeable that writers like David Mercer seemed happier to show a warmer side to their character. In his stage plays, Alan Bennett was barbed and clever, as though on his guard, bristling against attack. But when he wrote for television, usually with Stephen Frears directing, his guard dropped and his heart was on his sleeve. The size and spread of the audience provoked in dramatists a sincerity which, for depressing reasons, they were nervous to risk in the theatre.

After I had written *Slag*, I had at once been approached by producers wanting me to write for the medium. I was keen but I was also incompetent. My first attempt was a prescient satire on society's increasing dependence on prescription drugs. But by insisting on calling the play *Mandrax*, the name of a then popular sleeping pill, I gave the BBC a perfect excuse to reject it. They seized it eagerly, explaining that they couldn't go to air with a play sporting the name of a proprietary drug. It was against the rules of their charter. I felt nothing but relief. That was why, to their bewilderment, I refused to change the title. I had followed *Mandrax* quickly with another studio play, which did get made in 1973. It was directed by Alan Clarke. Alan was to die from cancer at the age of fifty-four, unaware that he was about to become one of a handful of British film-makers whose influence has grown until it reaches all over the world. He would have been amazed by his posthumous celebrity. He was a scruffy Liverpudlian with abundant charm, who lived like an indigent and drank like a fish. His apparent casualness in the rehearsal room disguised the amount of intense preparation he had done before the first day. Alan was the living proof of my own belief that you could only achieve freedom through discipline. You could only throw everything out when you had worked exhaustively to know why it was there in the first place. Normally Alan only took on working-class subjects. He felt very strongly about this bias, and for good reasons. But for once he was stimulated by a dramatist who came at the middle class from a route which was at least unfamiliar. Alan did everything he could to make my unseasoned apprentice writing look good. Originally called *Trailblazers*, but with its title changed at the BBC's anodyne suggestion, *Man above Men* was a half-domestic, half-social play about the isolation of judges and the cost of their ignorance, both on their families and on the accused who came before them. He cast Gwen Watford and Alexander Knox, another long-standing cinema favourite of mine, and gave them the emotional detail and social accuracy which marked Alan out from other gifted contemporaries in the old doughnut-shaped factory in Wood Lane. But in the end, the unwieldy process of a studio play, with video cameras swishing around the polished dance floor just like outsize versions of the vacuum cleaners I'd once failed to sell, left me convinced that tape was a doomed medium. Next time it had to be film.

A year or two later, Howard and I had conceded after some argument and agreed, against our better judgement, to *Brassneck* being made half on film and half on tape. We both knew that a television version made in such a bastard way was likely to be a bugger's muddle, but the chance to offer a play about civic corruption at 9.25 p.m. on BBC1 was too good to resist. The result, put out to a huge audience, was bang in the middle of the great traditions of public broadcasting. *Brassneck* played well with an electorate desperate to mix mockery of their rulers with some invigorating spite and anger. Its broadcast opened up a groundbreaking subject for television fiction. But things had got off to an embarrassing start when we were allocated a director sunk in personal despair and without a sense of humour. Since the play was meant to be a comedy, we had requested of the BBC that he be replaced. He was furious. Displaying a level of vitality he had not evidenced hitherto, he stormed to the producers and demanded angrily, 'Oh, writers are in charge now, are they?' – as though that were self-evidently such a terrible idea. Luckily we acquired Mike Newell as his replacement. Technically adept, Mike brought to the subject an enormous horse-laugh as well as the panache it needed. But under the pressure of time, the impossible ambition of attempting such a mammoth epic overwhelmed him, and we authors disgraced ourselves further when, in the general panic, we broke the first rule of author–director etiquette and gave a few notes to some actors without the director present. This branded us once more as thoroughly bad people. My abiding memory of the whole experience is of Mike running hours over schedule, at one in the morning in the studio gallery overlooking the action, with six cameras at his command and shouting at them like dodgem cars: 'Go in, Number One, anything you can get.' When I went down to the studio floor to thank one of the more senior actors who had completed his role, he shook my hand and said, 'Just to let you know: I didn't believe a word of it.'

My approach to *Licking Hitler* was thankfully proving to be much more peaceable. The idea had occurred to me because at some stage I had been working on an unfulfilled project to make a film about Simon Wiesenthal, the famous Austrian Holocaust survivor who had become the public face of post-war

Nazi-hunting, without perhaps being too careful about where else credit for the most significant achievements in that field might properly belong. I had been sitting researching in the Wiener Library in Devonshire Street, off Portland Place. It had an old-fashioned reading room, with proper leather seats and open shelves, and was dedicated principally to literature documenting the experience of the Jews in the Second World War. As I worked, in the opposite chair there wheezed an asthmatic old man in a grey three-piece suit, hair plastered down, surrounded by piles of books. He was the very image of the elderly scholar, complete with watch chain and National Health spectacles. Without introduction, he looked up and said, 'You do not know who I am, but I have sat as close to Adolf Hitler and to Winston Churchill as I am to you now.'

Such a magniloquent line of introduction must, I suppose, have been rehearsed many times. But I was the leaping fish who loved the hook. The man told me his name was Sefton Delmer. In the 1930s he had been the Berlin correspondent of the *Daily Express*. Coming back to England as a fluent German speaker, he had been recruited by the Political Warfare Executive to pioneer their first steps into black propaganda. As we fell to talking for an hour or more, Delmer implored me to read his book *Black Boomerang*, which gives an account of all the wicked things his fake radio station got up to in the space of two years. Its plausibility depended on German soldiers believing that they were accidentally overhearing the casual, indiscreet conversation of two German officers. Not only did the operation take on obvious tasks of enemy demoralisation. As you would expect, it relished broadcasting military disinformation and general pessimism about the outcome of the war. It exaggerated Allied advances and denied their setbacks. It sought to sow dissent between conservative elements in the German army and the radicals whom they distrusted in the Nazi party. By pretending to support Hitler, it sought to undermine him. But it also stretched further, taking on more doubtful work. Among other things, it targeted specific soldiers and officers, undermining their morale with obscene gossip about their wives having sex back home while they were at the front. Broadcasts took special pleasure in inventing outbreaks of venereal disease among named individuals.

Learning of the scale, malice and extreme pettiness of this work was, for me, like the opening of a door. All my life I had suspected that the Second World War had been misrepresented in fiction. Almost nothing I had seen at the cinema had smelt right – or convincing. What I had watched as a child was not art but propaganda. Yes, of course defeating Nazism had been a good cause, perhaps the last military cause Britons were ever to agree on. But the ridiculous piety surrounding the way in which we'd licked Hitler had made me suspicious that there were corners of Allied behaviour which weren't going to hold up too well to scrutiny. Now here, after all the years of puffery, was proof. The same people who had allowed or run black propaganda during the war had gone on to high office in Whitehall and government afterwards. The moral nullity of this bizarre operation seemed to illuminate what in the film I would call 'the national habit of lying'. In my view, it reflected as much on life after the war as during it.

The extra anticipation I felt was at the opportunity to put a woman's experience at the centre of a war story. This was important to me. In 1950 Herbert Wilcox had directed his wife Anna Neagle in an analgesic film, *Odette*, about the special agent Odette Sanson, who had flown into France to liaise for the Special Operations Executive. In 1958, there had been a rather better film, *Carve Her Name with Pride*, with Virginia McKenna playing Violette Szabo. But these were about exceptional women who'd both had exceptional wars. In 1975 my old prep-school friend Christopher Hudson had scripted a story about D-Day which had proved to be a welcome antidote to the 'Chocks away' school of film-making. *Overlord* followed the random story of a hapless young recruit sacrificed on a Normandy beach. I too wanted to draw on common experiences. I wanted to portray that special wartime phenomenon: violent juxtaposition. Dissimilar people from different backgrounds had to learn to adjust to each other far more quickly than in civilian life. As Alan Ross observes in his book *The Forties*, it was 'the unbearable partings and comings together in dark confined places' which compensated for 'the suffering and boredom and fear of war'. But it wasn't just the content of the film which excited me. At university I had never wanted to make a life in theatre. When I started, it had been second best. Here, at last, was my chance to hear my own clapsticks for the first time.

Before I could find someone willing to make *Licking Hitler*, I first had to revive *Teeth 'n' Smiles* in the West End. It turned out less than happily and taught me a painful lesson about how easy it is to mislay magic. I made a total mess of it. In 1975 our season at the Court had played to full houses, and we had wanted to transfer straight away. But Helen Mirren was already committed before we started rehearsals to spending the winter in a long run of a new farce by the octogenarian Ben Travers. She had reluctantly agreed that when she had finished, she would come back and do mine again. But by the time she returned, Helen was understandably exhausted and had misplaced her zeal. She had the air of not wanting to revisit old work. Whereas at the Court she had been able to hypnotise an audience into believing she could sing, at Wyndham's with a far cooler audience Helen seemed much more exposed. Nick Bicât began to mutter darkly that everyone can sing but only if they have the will. Jack Shepherd had left the venture and something of the play's soul had gone with him. His casual delivery had given the production much of its ambling charm. As if that were not enough, I had compounded our problems by imagining it was a good idea to give a reporter from the *New Musical Express* free access backstage to do a prominent four-page story on this unusual attempt to bring the cultures of rock music and theatre together. When it was published I knew that I'd made a mistake. It quoted Dave King in his dressing room referring to Helen Mirren as 'that cunt'.

Even in those days I had learnt enough to recognise that a director is always in trouble when having to assume the role of schoolmaster. When actor/director turns into pupil/teacher the outcome cannot be anything but doomed. In the 1980s, at Joe Papp's request, I would even fly the Atlantic to try and get a couple of warring actors who were at daily loggerheads to reconcile. 'But, David,' one of them said, oblivious of my three-thousand-mile journey, 'you don't understand. We don't *want* to get on.' Dave was the same. When I asked him if he wanted to come out for a drink and talk about his problem with Helen, Dave replied in words which were henceforth etched on my heart: 'Not very much.' Later I would read Samuel Johnson: 'Kindness is in our power, even when fondness is not.' Never going to be fond of Helen, Dave was doubly determined not to be kind. The production closed in six weeks, with no trace of the abundant feckless joy it had spread so effortlessly at the Court.

Worse still, it marked the end of my professional relationship with Michael Codron. Today I regard myself as the lucky beneficiary of an enlightened system. Not only did the state contribute to the cost of my education, the government also intervened through the Arts Council to subsidise me at the moment when I most needed help. I was, briefly, welfare-dependent and proud of it. In return, I and many others like me were to compensate the taxman many times over. The state's later earnings from my plays and films would prove the wisdom of their decision to volunteer to jumpstart me. But such a narrative excludes the contribution of my first producer. In the 1990s, because he was serving on the board of the National Theatre, Michael was, for sound ethical reasons, disqualified from transferring my plays which originated there. I felt bad. Michael had believed in me at a time when few others did. I was his discovery. He had gone out on a limb, capitalising my flops without complaint. Michael would no doubt feel that virtue was its own reward. But, when the hits came, he deserved some of the other kind as well.

Four days after opening *Teeth 'n' Smiles*, I was rehearsing *Weapons of Happiness*. Like *Knuckle*, it had not been easy to cast. Alec Guinness, Paul Scofield and Max von Sydow had all turned down the central part of Josef Frank. Most of all, I wanted to complete a childhood circle and approach Dirk Bogarde, but he had not been on stage since 1958, when two weeks' Anouilh in Oxford had nearly carried him away with pleurisy. Bogarde had turned down the chance to open the Chichester Festival Theatre, and was unlikely to want to open the Lyttelton. Warily, I went instead to Frank Finlay, whose most celebrated performance had been as a chippy Iago to Olivier's more extravagant Othello. Frank seemed happy to take on this original new play, though perhaps as suspicious of a young director as I was of such a well-established actor. For once, the actor auditioned the director. In the event we got on fine, and as Howard observed, Frank made the character of the wrecked old man curiously elegant. Opposite him I put Julie Covington, whom I had known since she was nineteen and training to be a teacher. As the factory workers I brought in a fine company of young actors, whose authentic London accents would try the Lyttelton Theatre's acoustics to destruction and, in the case of American tourists, beyond. There would be a lot of complaints. Hayden had finished designing a spectacular set which had an entire London factory being replaced by Soviet tanks rolling into Prague. Towering light-boxes of Stalin swept by to make way for the dome of the London Planetarium. Rough theatre this was not. On this occasion, I believed, the spectacle matched the play's breadth and helped it breathe.

After so many years of delay it was inevitable there would be problems once we got inside the building. Of the three theatres, the 890-seat proscenium house, the Lyttelton, opened first. The rest of its early repertory transferred from the Old Vic, like an off-the-peg succession of touring shows, road-tested and ready to go. Peggy Ashcroft and Ralph Richardson were having no problems at all. But it was the lot of *Weapons of Happiness* to be the first show to open afresh and, as luck would have it, the most ambitious, pulling right back to the massive steel dock doors and revealing the whole stage. For several days in the middle of July we sat in agony in the darkened stalls watching as machinery failed. Hayden's complicated design, intended to exploit the fabulous new facilities, had simply exposed them. It was clear nothing worked. By two o'clock on the afternoon we were due to give our first preview, we had not even got through the play on stage, let alone set it or lit it. Having consulted Peter

Hall, I called the company together and told them that sadly we would have to cancel our first preview. But minutes after I announced this decision Peter appeared in person in the stalls. He said he had no wish to undermine me, and of course such an important question must be answered by a company decision, but did we realise that it would be a gift to a hostile press if an audience were turned away? Nothing could do the reputation of the National more harm. He accepted that the actors had been tested beyond endurance, but even so, he felt that on this occasion they should put the good of the whole National Theatre first.

Actors in the theatre respond much better to appeals to public-school sentiment than they do on a film set. It was therefore only a matter of minutes before all the actors agreed with Peter that they must put on some sort of show that night, however poor. The house was going to be packed – this was a big opening, after all – and they wanted to show that they were troupers. But in response to what I regarded as blackmail from a management which had let me down, I felt betrayed. I had made the only sensible professional judgement and been ignored. However, as the afternoon dragged on and as large pieces of scenery failed to move sideways, upwards or forwards, morale sagged and actors began to sidle up to me unobserved to tell me they were having second thoughts. It would do huge damage both to them and to the play to open when we were unlikely to be able to get through. They had changed their minds. Eventually they stopped work and formed a delegation. Could I go upstairs and please tell Peter we were calling the performance off?

Needless to say, when we did get to preview, one day late, we were all full of foreboding. There had indeed been the predicted bad publicity in the right-wing press. Journalists were eager to insist that our failure to open on time was emblematic of the lavish inefficiency of the whole enterprise. The foyer was packed with rubberneckers, come to see the scene of the crash. Lindsay Anderson, as if called into a disaster zone by sonic whistle to act as the very opposite of an emergency service, was standing in the bar on the second night declaring to anyone who would listen that the National Theatre was going to be a fiasco. He had always said it and – hey! – he was right. But when we finally got to present it, the play cast its spell, and the performance ended with an image which was unanswerable. The failed organisers of the factory sit-in leave town and head for the Welsh hills. For this last tentative utopia, Hayden had designed a staggering white snow-cloth which covered the whole enormous area. After all the characters had gone and the hillside was left empty, very slowly, from the high fly tower of the Lyttelton there came a fall of snow, intermittent at first, and then in a thick curtain which drifted down and settled silently on the floor. The audience were still happily gasping in disbelief as, relieved, I bolted backstage to talk to the actors. But as I came through the pass door, Peter Hall was already lying in wait in the wings. He said he needed to give me some notes about what he saw as the dangerous inadequacy of Frank Finlay's performance. He had ideas on how to improve it. I told him, after the week I had just been through, this was hardly the time. I was listening at him rather than to him. Unforgivably, as Peter persisted, I lost my temper, wrongly imagining that he was trying to pay me back for having given him a bumpy twenty-four hours. As far as I was concerned, Peter had done his best to wreck the opening of the show by intervening with the actors, more in the interests of public relations than of art.

Why the hell should I now listen to him? I think I may even have told him to get out of my way.

It was certainly one of the more shaming episodes of my life, for which there is an explanation but no excuse. For some time I had been living on my nerves. A pack of Pepto-Bismol rarely lasted me a day. A yoga teacher would have located my centre of gravity in my larynx. Although, as for many lucky sufferers, asthma and eczema were leaving me in my late twenties, they were being replaced by a toxic mix of indigestion and indignation. Peggy had rebuked me after *Knuckle*, saying that my harshness with myself was 'all inverted conceit, in an odd sort of way'. But lately my hypertension had developed physical symptoms. My lasting memory of my first ten years at the National Theatre is of sticking my head down the lavatory to rack the terror out of my guts yet again. Once during technical rehearsals, when someone came into the empty auditorium and asked where I was, Rory Dempster looked casually at his watch and said, 'Oh if it's seven o'clock, you'll usually find David being sick in the Gents.' A jangly physical state was made worse by a quite unnecessary paranoia which my artistic team did nothing to discourage. My plastic security pass for the new building was numbered 007 and might just as well have added 'Licensed to Whinge'. Hayden's choleric muttering had reached the point where it could be heard from the Thames. He and Rory were being given such an impossible time by technical departments unable to deliver on their promises that, to keep our spirits up, we had resorted to disloyal rhetoric, calling ourselves Charabanc Productions. The company's motto, we liked to say gaily, was 'Just Passing Through'. At the end of the week the Lyttelton's technical manager, who was, after the theatre's opening weeks, little more than a human shadow, was removed by ambulance to have rectal surgery under merciful anaesthetic. He stayed in bed for a week.

Whatever the pressures, this had been a poor way for me to reward my benefactor. To his credit, Peter never seemed to mind. He'd had an awful lot of rows in the wings with an awful lot of people by then. But more seriously, it meant that the entirely justified message he had wanted to give me – that after all our technical gridlock my attention should be redirected to Frank's performance – went overlooked. I was further thrown after a couple of previews by a typically mischievous visit from Laurence Olivier, who, rather to my surprise, was enjoying the show. Never much of a man for politics, he was nevertheless gifted with a matchless sense of occasion, and, no question, this seemed to be an occasion he liked. He greeted me in the interval by raising his arms above his head and saying, 'Success! Success! I smell it in the air.' I waited nervously. 'Wonderful play! And Frank!' he said, 'Frank! Never been better. It's the performance of his life.' I agreed, saying Frank was indeed on the way. But I knew Olivier well enough to be sure that he would have a kicker up his sleeve. I waited. 'Only one problem with Frank, you know.' Sucked in now, I had no choice but to reply. What was the problem with Frank, I asked. Olivier smiled, content. 'Frank? Can't do it on first nights.'

Olivier walked away from the conversation even happier than when he arrived. It turned out unsurprisingly that he was right, and Frank was indeed not at his best when the press were in. But it didn't matter. For the general audience the play survived and prospered, and, once the machinery worked, Hayden's decor set standards of fluency and beauty to which all designers subsequently aspired in that large, rather cold proscenium house. As Kate, who had never met Howard Brenton, commented after standing at the back for a performance, 'Listening, you knew you were in the presence of someone profoundly generous.' But for those within the profession in search for a peg on which to hang the anger of their coming disillusionment, *Weapons of Happiness* represented a perfect spike. Its mix of poetry and despair about the unlikeliness of British revolution was calculated to bring out the worst in those who were about to feel the most pain. Political plates were beginning to shift throughout the western world. Socialism, had we but known it, was heading for the rocks, and so the wounds of disagreement about a mere play chosen, as it happened, to open a new theatre in South London ran deeper than you could possibly believe. Those who had invested all their hopes in the word 'alternative' were looking for a new word and it wasn't 'national'.

One director who ran a radical theatre in the East End told me that after the play she had stood weeping on Waterloo Bridge, because she had experienced exactly the same feelings as when Joan Littlewood had seen Harry H. Corbett, a treasured member of her East London company, playing on television in *Steptoe and Son*. The working-class actors this director most loved were betraying their provenance by appearing on the National Theatre stage in a play which, because it was anti-Soviet, she regarded as giving comfort to the enemy. It was, for her, a symbolic moment: the miserable death of a great theatrical movement, killed from within by its own foot-soldiers. For me, her attitudes smacked of a snobbery with which, coming from my background, I was never going to sympathise. Justifying his refusal to denounce Stalin's purges, Sartre had notoriously remarked, '*Il ne faut pas désespérer Billancourt*' – which you can loosely translate to mean 'Never lower the workers' morale by telling them the truth.' Needless to say, I felt the opposite. The truth strengthens us. But Ken Tynan, who was still fighting to get *Fanshen* performed off Broadway, wrote in his diary that *Weapons of Happiness* was 'an insulting evening which moved me to boo for the first time in a decade . . . The mixture of arrogance and condescension was impossible to stomach. It almost made me long to be a critic again.'

I did not yet know of the German saying '*Viel Feind, viel Ehr*' – many enemies, much honour – but if I had, I would have regarded myself as one of the most honoured workers in the British theatre.

12

Birmingham University

Arriving at the Royal Court in the last days of 1968, I had not just been young, I had been naive. For all my surface attempts at worldliness, the simplest remark caught me off guard. On my very first morning, the director Peter Gill had observed how much he was looking forward to his forthcoming lunch with the actress Jill Bennett. Hopelessly innocent, I replied, 'Jill Bennett? Oh, is she nice?' Peter looked at me as if I were from Mars and said dismissively, 'No, of course Jill's not nice. But she is fun.' I was twenty-one, and the idea of choosing to eat with anyone who was not nice had never occurred to me. But it was an early statement of Bill Gaskill's which struck me harder. In his office one day he was speaking about his closeness to the young Harold Pinter. Pinter had been a struggling actor working under the name of David Baron when the two of them had been best friends. They had done everything together – that is, until Harold became a playwright. I asked him why they were no longer friends. Bill shook his head, as though the sadness of the years were beyond reach. 'I can't explain. You're too young. All I can tell you: it becomes impossible.'

It was the example of living among such quarrels, spoken or unspoken, which made me determined to remain loyal to my friends. Not that it needed much determination. It was simple. I admired them: that's why they were my friends. It had been an early principle of Joint Stock that each of the founding members was going to maintain an active role, so when the others insisted that it was time that I took my turn to direct, I wanted to make sure I was continuing the relationships which were most important to me.

The company, which had started out with just one producer, one director and one dramatist, had been transformed by its production of *Fanshen* into an unwieldy co-operative with long communal meetings to decide policy and practice. The process was proving to be time-consuming and exhausting. Understandably, it was beginning to get on everyone's nerves. Some of us longed for the day when we might be allowed to do something without talking it to death before we began. When John Osborne read that the company was preparing a play about horse-racing, he mocked us for our approach. In the 1950s, he said, all actors would have *gone* to the Derby. The last thing they'd have done was go to *research* it. The very triumph of *Fanshen* – it would soon have to be revived yet again with yet another new cast – had created its own problem of identity. None of us could ever quite decide whether we were a theatre group who had done a show about collectives, or a collective theatre group. But whatever the aggravations, nobody could deny that the method worked. Edward Bond named us 'the Royal Court in exile', but truthfully we had discovered a distinctive approach to the creation of new plays which few companies could afford or emulate.

Fanshen had been followed by a piece of reportorial theatre, group-written and authentic. The actors had talked to a bunch of British mercenaries on their return from fighting in the civil war in Angola. The resulting show, *Yesterday's News*, pioneered what would one day become the increasingly popular form of verbatim theatre – a play made up of other people's words. It

was riveting. And next had come an original Caryl Churchill project called *Light Shining in Buckinghamshire*, which took
us back into the territory of radical politics. It was about the
Ranters, that most extreme of English movements who were
on the far wing of Cromwell's republican revolution in the sev-
enteenth century. They believed that all things should be held
in common, and they lived their beliefs. To our surprise, it was
the first time Caryl had seen actors' exercises or improvisations.
For her, the experience was eye-opening, like being a child, she
said, taken to their first pantomime. Caryl adhered to what, by
trial and error, had become the regular Joint Stock schedule.
First, there was a workshop, packed with research to which the
actors contributed freely. This was followed by a lay-off period
during which the playwright was sent away to write alone
before formal rehearsals began. When I was press-ganged into
directing, I was keen to see what happened if we applied this
technique to a play not drawn from written source material. I
wanted a change from documentary. Why not for once try to
write straight from the human imagination? For this purpose,
I turned to my first colleague, Tony Bicât.

By now Tony's feelings were almost entirely for film. For
the BFI, he had made a Howard Brenton short, *Skinflicker*,
about an English group of terrorists, and was these days working in television on a sharp contemporary series called *Second
City Firsts*. He was frankly sceptical about theatre ever moving
on to accommodate the kind of dreams we had had when we
started Portable. Like so many people in so many other fields
in the late 1970s, he was beginning to feel that a particular
moment for change had been lost. Tony was further reluctant
to write for Joint Stock because he believed neither Max nor
Bill had any respect for his work. I didn't care. I felt a debt

to Tony which I wanted to pay back. Both Howard Brenton and I had prospered in good part thanks to Tony's selflessness. Now I wanted to do something for him. From this mixture of motives came *Devil's Island*, ambitiously set in 1937, 1977 and 1997. Three men and three women evolved, becoming different people at different times, starting in the Spanish Civil War. Tony was an early fan of J. G. Ballard, spotting him way before his cult eminence. He aimed to write a technically innovative, futuristic piece about a Britain in which all the most unacceptable citizens would be exiled together to a devil's island. The play set out to challenge the director's ingenuity. Of all 1970s dystopian works about the hopeless future ahead, this was, underneath, the most uncompromising. When, a couple of years later, Caryl Churchill deployed the same structural idea – people from one period become different people in another – in another Joint Stock show, *Cloud Nine*, the satiric effect was intentionally far gentler.

Margaret had long believed that Tony was potentially the most popular of the Portable writers, because his mixture of wit and mellow characterisation was attractive in a way which might one day reach all kinds of audiences. He wrote about people. By the turn of the year we were off on a tour of leisure centres and arts centres, where Tony's pleasing modesty and quietness went down well. For the first time in a Joint Stock production, the women's parts were as good as the men's, with Jane Wood, Suzanne Bertish and Gillian Barge all seizing them gratefully and having a whale of a time. But in a major miscalculation, Tony and I were talked into moving the play's London opening from the fringe theatre where it was tentatively scheduled onto the proscenium at the Royal Court, where, we were assured, it would blossom. It was a costly mistake. It turned out that at a time of strong feelings, when audiences wanted plays to be instantly decipherable and clearly partisan, I had not done Tony any favours by setting his subtleties down in such a mainstream house.

My life was now punctuated by long writing periods in Peggy's Kemp Town shack. In Trafalgar Lane, the weather always seemed to be bad. Salty rain ran down the dismal windows and the electric light stayed on all day. I loved the smell of the wood-yard opposite and the sound of the circular saw. I would write for as long as I could in my hutch, then go out to drink and eat at night, alone and with a book. Brighton became my precious place of retreat, a sort of home from home where I worked not only on polishing *Licking Hitler* but on a new stage play which I saw as a deliberate companion piece. 'Delighted you are emotionally exhausted', wrote Peggy, 'as a play which doesn't emotionally exhaust an author is – <u>useless</u>.' But while I was writing with a growing certainty that I was this time onto something really interesting, Margaret's life was taking a similarly positive turn. Her tactic of zig-zagging out of the BBC had paid off again. Once more she had been invited back in, and having produced exactly one film, was now, at the age of thirty, being put in charge of the weekly one-off strand on BBC1, *Play for Today*. In the next chaotic couple of years Margaret would go on not only to produce one of television's most popular plays of all time – *Abigail's Party* by Mike Leigh – but also one of its most controversial. Since the mid-1950s, the promotion of the single play had been one of the best features of public television. But soon, with the making of Roy Minton's film *Scum*, which dramatised the rough culture of the British borstal system, it was about to become the bumpiest as well.

Most people who had run the BBC since the war had come

from journalistic backgrounds. It had long been clear that few of them had any understanding either of the arts or of drama, and even fewer a feel for it. Their bungling interferences and attempts at censorship were notoriously inept and dangerous, usually coming about because they wanted to apply the rules of newspaper reporting to works of fiction. With the honourable exception of Hugh Carleton Greene, who shared with his novelist brother Graham a family fondness for making trouble, and of the visionary David Attenborough, the most senior bureaucrats were lacking in courage when called upon to stand up to government. But my good fortune was to be summoned by David Rose, who ran a drama empire of his own from some studios in the Edgbaston suburb of Birmingham. They were housed at Pebble Mill in a famously ugly building which would all too soon die of concrete cancer, only to be replaced by something fancier called the Mailbox, which was even uglier. David had made his reputation as the producer of *Z-Cars*, the first of television's realistic police series. By moving a hundred miles from London, David, whether by luck or calculation, enjoyed a degree of freedom from the excessive supervision which sometimes made film-making needlessly difficult in the BBC's headquarters at Wood Lane. By the time the senior executives in London discovered they had made a film on the questionable topic of wartime black propaganda – a shameful operation which had hitherto been swept under the carpet – it was too late. *Licking Hitler* was already scheduled for transmission. When it went out, eight million people would watch.

BBC Pebble Mill became my second university, an admirable place of learning where the company of your peers, if you were willing to listen, improved both your mind and your skills, and the place where almost every serious film writer or director trained or practised. On any day in the canteen, while they were recording *The Archers* downstairs, you might be able to sit and talk with Stephen Frears, with Ken Loach, with Willy Russell, with Alan Bleasdale, with Mike Leigh, with Alan Clarke, with Peter Terson, with David Rudkin and with Alan Plater. Of all the places I have ever worked, this was the most collegiate. We took a sympathetic interest in each other's work, and we gave advice when it was asked. To the same degree that the Royal Court was shark-filled and competitive, Pebble Mill was democratic. It was what a Hollywood studio was intended to be. Everyone had headed to the West Midlands for the same reason: to prosper under the protection of a regime which could be trusted to leave us alone to do our best work. If from today's perspective the personnel seems overly male, the one thing it was not was overly white. It was Pebble Mill, positioned as it was in the second city, which alone had championed the portrayal of a multiracial Britain. It was thanks to David Rose, and to his resident producers Peter Ansorge and Barry Hanson, that the screen was beginning belatedly to look like the street. In 1973, Tara Prem had written *A Touch of Eastern Promise*, the first television play with an all-Asian cast. This had been followed by at least two series, *Gangsters* and *Empire Road*, which achieved quiet revolution by putting black and Asian actors at the centre of the drama and refusing to present them as familiar stereotypes. Norman Beaton became the most popular in-house actor. Pebble Mill was the only television outfit in Britain where you would find yourself working in the same building as Horace Ové, Mustapha Matura and Michael Abbensetts. Put BBC Birmingham beside any other media organisation in Britain and it was years ahead of its time.

There were only two difficult issues in my years at Pebble

Mill, and they were both resolved on the day of my arrival. Would I be allowed to direct my own work and would I be allowed to make it on film? Obviously I had no experience as a film director, and, worse, the greater part of *Licking Hitler* was set indoors. It was only reasonable that people were therefore asking why the whole thing couldn't be made, like most subjects in that period, much more cheaply in a studio with video cameras. We only needed, they said, to go outside once or twice to pick up the odd film insert. But there was something in the tone of my own conviction which moved David Rose to take a risk on me. I argued that the subject of the film was propaganda. The form had to fit the content. I was intending to make *Licking Hitler* look as though it had been made in the 1940s, so that it might most closely resemble the national cinema of uplift that it was setting out to undermine. The camera, if it moved at all, would move only in that contemporary style. Further, the film was about isolation. A terrified woman was growing up far from her friends and family in a closed environment with a bunch of crazed misogynists. In the course of the story she would tap into her own unrecognised resources of character to challenge the morality of what she was doing and of what was being done to her. The more hermetic we could make the atmosphere, the better. I had waited my whole life to make a film. Every childhood visit to the cinema in Bexhill had been a preparation. I was ready.

When the final film was shown, Stephen Frears loved to tell me, rather more often than perhaps was necessary, that its authority was a fluke. Anyone could make a first film. Just wait, he said, until I made my second. That's when the problems would really start. He was right. If you fling yourself ignorantly at a day's filming, the sheer intensity of your longing can initially get you through. You've dreamt of it for so many years that if you know what story you want to tell, its realisation becomes a formality. That's why careers behind the camera so often falter. It's only as you go deeper that you begin to real-ise how little you know, and how much technique you lack. Almost all film-makers jump confidently out of the landing craft, but only a gifted handful make it up the beach.

After *Licking Hitler*, a tide of similar films would soon fol-low in slightly cringing homage. The murkier corners of the war began to be routinely re-examined from a woman's point of view. But those of us who made *Licking Hitler* had the satis-faction of knowing that we would be the first. This was what made my period of research in the spring of 1977 so rewarding. Every week I was speeding on trains all over a sunlit Britain from Cornwall to the north of Scotland, on my way to meet the elderly survivors of the generation who had taken part in the eccentric and sometimes scabrous tasks of propaganda. In ten years, nearly every one would be dead. Without exception they seemed pleased to see me, grateful that after all these years of neglect someone wanted to throw a light on their peculiar contribution. They would describe trips ferrying German actors back and forth from detention camps for their broad-casts with the freshness and assurance of people who knew that what they had to say was both shocking and unfamiliar. At the same time, I was casting. Kate, fresh from a commanding performance under Maximilian Schell's direction in an Odön von Horvath play, *Tales from the Vienna Woods*, was a given. And to portray the working-class Scottish genius of propa-ganda, in came Bill Paterson whom I'd seen being hilarious in the Theatre Upstairs playing forty years more than his true age in a comedy by Billy Connolly called *An' Me wi' a Bad Leg Tae*.

For the Head of the Political Warfare Executive, very loosely based on Richard Crossman, who later became a minister in the 1964 Labour government, I chose the Billy Wilder favourite Clive Revill. And to play another important character, this time based on Ian Fleming but transposed for the purposes of my fiction from his real-life role in Naval Intelligence, I cut the hair off Hugh Fraser, who had played bass guitar in the band in *Teeth 'n' Smiles*. As a newcomer to film, Hugh was blank and expressionless for the first few shots. On questioning, he explained that someone had given him the useful tip that film acting was about doing nothing. 'Doing nothing, maybe,' I said. 'But not thinking nothing.' From then on, Hugh was great.

Birmingham itself was a rebarbative place at the end of the 1970s, a nightmare of lousy post-war development, where to drive a French or German car into the BBC car park was still to invite contempt. You were spitting in the eye of the locals. But the city became warm and rewarding once you got past its sullen facade. Because the sun hit the glass of my office so hard in the afternoons, I positioned some grobags on the window shelf, and puffed up with pride when Percy Thrower, the legendary presenter of *Gardener's World*, came by to tell me my tomatoes were doing much better than his in the office next door. In April, before filming, I went up to Oldham for a day's patient education at the hands of Mike Leigh, who extended me the kind of comradeship which made Pebble Mill so creative. Characteristically, Mike was filming in an undertaker's. He was having to deal with a corpse on a marble slab. The actor's stomach was visibly moving. When I pointed this out, Mike said he knew, but that lying dead was a skill. The daily rate for people who could really do it, clothes off, was too much for the BBC to afford. But even after Mike's eight-hour crash course, I walked onto my first film set a couple of weeks later in a state of sublime ignorance. When at the end of the day I revealed to Ken Morgan, the most talented of BBC lighting cameramen, that it had been the first time I had ever looked down a camera, he shrugged and said, 'Well it didn't show.'

To make up the composite country headquarters of black propaganda, Aspley Guise, we used two different locations. One, Compton Verney, near Stratford-upon-Avon, was uninhabited, but the other, Edgcote House, near Banbury, was a private home. The patrician owner sat apparently content at rushes as Bill Paterson's character, over many repeated takes, described it as 'this bloody awful English house'. It was an amazingly disciplined shoot throughout, everything accomplished in seventeen days during one of those blazing English Mays where spring turns to summer in front of your eyes. Driving in to work at dawn put me in a confident mood which lasted all day. When I went into the editing room, the storytelling was so planned in my head that I threw away no more than fifteen shots. It turned out to my astonishment that, besides writing plays, there was a second thing to add to the list of what I could actually do. I could direct film. The actors I had chosen, all from different backgrounds, had been perfectly matched. Kate, Bill and Brenda Fricker, who had once lived with Margaret and me in the Chase, liked each other from the off and their gears clicked as if they'd been acting together all their lives. There was nothing more rewarding than to have a brief rehearsal at the end of the day, to roll out of bed before daylight next morning and, on the basis of the actors' insights, to improve the scene on the spot. The huge advantage of being a writer-director was that some of the film's most potent moments, particularly when Anna Seaton finally turns on her persecutor Archie Maclean, came from this freedom to rewrite as we went along. The solidarity in the whole group was symbolised by one touching comic gesture. Kate realised that in the improvised dressing rooms, where only a string and a curtain separated the sexes, our most elderly actor, well into his seventies, could tilt a mirror to watch her changing. Without ever saying anything, she regularly prolonged the process of undressing each day to allow him this pleasure.

Given our proximity and our joy in the filming, Kate and I held off from each other for a reasonably long time. My wife had trusted me to work with my former girlfriend and the moment came when I betrayed that trust. Kate and I were artistically in love, and the other kind became a formality. After perhaps ten days of fulfilling work, we fell into each other's arms as if we'd never been away. It was completion. I was back on my favourite drug: intimacy with someone whose dreams were even bigger than my own. The end of the shoot passed in a blaze, partly because we knew we were making a good film, but also because we were together again. Both things seemed natural and both things seemed natural together. If we couldn't have happiness, we could at least have pleasure. But this time there was a subtle difference, a fault-line which would widen over time and cause everyone caught up in the damage more distress than at times it would seem possible for any of us to handle. Second time round, Kate never for a moment imagined she and I had a future together. I might be her passion but I was not going to be her partner. Whereas, over the next few years, as things got worse for myself and for my family I became incapable of imagining any future at all.

It was inevitable that as soon as I called 'Cut!' for the last time on *Licking Hitler*, I would want to cast Kate as Susan

Traherne in *Plenty*. The play I'd been writing in such excitement was, after all, a companion piece to the film. At the end of *Licking Hitler*, which is mostly devoted to a young woman's war, the story flashes forward in a coda to her experiences in the peace that follows. In contrast, *Plenty* disposes of a young woman's war in a scene or two, and chooses to concentrate instead on the disappointment she feels in post-war Britain. I had been fired up by reading a book about the Special Operations Executive, which had flown British agents behind enemy lines. Among them had been a great many women. But, fascinatingly, over seventy per cent of those women had divorced in the years after the war. It was as if their own gallantry and that of their colleagues had given them impossibly high expectations. Nothing could live up either to the intensity or to the nobility of what they'd been through. Everything thereafter was a disappointment.

When I'd finished a draft of the play in March, I'd given it to Peter Hall and asked if we might do it at the National. The first scene of the play is set in 1962, before the action winds back to restart in 1944. In his enthusiasm Peter had rung Harold Pinter to tell him that David Hare had given him a play which began at the end. In panic, Harold had come running into the theatre and grabbed a script. He had begun writing *Betrayal*, his play which works backwards, running entirely from finish to start. He couldn't believe that another dramatist might have got there before him. Harold was reassured to discover that *Plenty* is bookended by only two scenes out of order. Meanwhile Peter and I had started discussing directors. He wanted John Schlesinger. I didn't, because, still a complicated prig, I'd disliked his thriller, *Marathon Man*, which I saw as lurid and exploitative. It had disgusted me. There was one of those brief periods of theatrical confusion during which Diana Rigg appeared to be cast in the leading role, and when Bill Gaskill, at my wish, appeared to be about to direct. But when, walking together down the middle of the Mall, Bill confided that perhaps he wasn't too keen on the play after all, I decided I might as well direct it myself. Why not? In the intervening time, Diana Rigg's husband had declared the prospect of sharing his life with somebody playing a stage role so driven and discontented unbearable. So it was no great problem, as soon as I had a spare moment from filming, to put it in an envelope and send it to Kate.

In my notebook some two years earlier I'd written the four words 'A woman over Europe', and had that insane jag of excitement you get when you know you're in business. By coincidence, at roughly the same time both Fassbinder in Germany with his film *The Marriage of Maria Braun* and Diane Kurys in France with *Entre Nous* would have similar ideas of telling post-war history through the eyes of a woman who had survived the war. Today Cate Blanchett likes to say that she has played Ibsen's Hedda Gabler, she has played Blanche DuBois in *A Streetcar Named Desire* and she has played Susan Traherne in *Plenty*, so as far she's concerned, she's played the three best female roles in the repertory. Certainly there is something in the play's technique of skipping through an eighteen-year period of a woman's life, without too laboriously explaining what has happened between each scene, which presents an actress with almost unique opportunities and challenges. Yes, there's the full range of emotion from rage to humour that you'd hope to find in any grand leading role. There is the expected succession of bravura moments. But what makes Susan different is that I aimed for a half-filled-in quality which would be deliberately suggestive and which would give the actress particular freedom to take the role in any direction she chose. As always, in the right hands what is not shown can be as powerful as what is. I had started with a painterly image. A woman is sitting on some packing cases in an empty room with light coming in from behind her through high windows. She is rolling a cigarette, and a naked man, smeared with blood, is lying at her feet. Expectation is the most overlooked element in the arts and the least understood. If you achieve it, there is a way of whetting an audience's appetite, rarely used, which can set a bar high from the first moment. *Plenty* is a play which sets out on a long journey to explain its opening scene.

Kate wrote back to me in response to reading *Plenty* because she had already gone off to Stratford, where she was due to play Rosalind in *As You Like It*. It was a job which she was approaching with some foreboding. It represented the kind of respectability which she most dreaded. She felt that the first act, during which Susan is comparatively sane, was special, 'so much more and different from other plays'. But she also felt that the second act, more given to Susan's madness and sedation, tailed off. 'I think the end is not worthy of the beginning . . . It becomes like other plays.' I knew that if I cast Kate I was going to have to rewrite a bit anyway, because she was a few years too young for the range of ages as I had them originally. But my artistic love affair with Kate had long mutated into a mission. Her words 'I can only say now that it is by far, by a long way the best play you have written' fired me up to do whatever was necessary.

One way or another, there were at least three other reasons why 1977 was turning into a distinctive and interesting year. Some time previously, on the trip to New York which had done so much to determine the texture of *Teeth 'n' Smiles*, I had tried to go to the Public Theater to see a play by a writer I had never heard of called Wallace Shawn. Unable to get in because the box office had wrongly told me it was full, I'd asked Peggy for a script on my return. *Our Late Night* was so original, both in its humour and method, that I'd shown it to Caryl Churchill and to Howard Brenton, both of whom liked it as much as I did. It turned out that Wally, unable to make a living, was struggling to survive as a playwright at all, so he and his girlfriend Deborah Eisenberg had been astonished to find not just that Peggy wanted to represent him – he had never dreamed of such a thing – but also that in Britain at least he had a devoted following among his fellow playwrights. Isolated in the American theatre and regarded as waywardly avant-garde, Wally was thrilled when he visited England to be greeted by an admiring fan club of his peers who seemed to have no trouble with the supposed difficulties of his work at all. Max Stafford-Clark liked both him and his writing as much as I did. We had resolved that whatever else Joint Stock did, it would premiere Wallace Shawn in England.

The immediate problem we had was that his next play was a triple bill. The first and third plays were unexceptionable and beautifully written, but in the middle was a riotous sex farce about an orgy at the YMCA. Not just sexually explicit, *Youth Hostel* was also, at least in my opinion, the only unembarrassing piece of pornography ever to be written for the stage. Hitherto Max and I had spent our time pushing at political boundaries. This time we would be pushing at the erotic as well. No New York producer had yet been brave enough to take it on. When it opened at the Institute of Contemporary Arts in Max's hilarious production, the ceaseless frenzy of coupling and uncoupling spread infectious laughter. One of the four actors calculated that they averaged seven orgasms each in thirty-five minutes. But at the centre of all the high jinks was a moving young woman whose true, unspoken feelings for one of her fellow orgiasts were being hideously damaged. Moral enough, you might think, but not enough apparently to satisfy the press, who at once tried to drag the play into one of those insane feeding frenzies which make British journalists and politicians feel they're alive. They reacted like old women in Bexhill faced with Marty Wilde. The *Evening Standard* refused to name any of the actors 'because their parents might come along and spank them', and the *Daily Telegraph* reported that the play 'was as likely to give offence as anything I have ever seen in the theatre ... There is no attempt at anything that could be called artistic endeavour.' But it was *The Times*'s revelation that 'Unveiled in standing, lying or canine positions, orally fondled and stimulated by a vibrator, here are the most generous portions of erectile tissue yet slapped on the London fringe stage' which caused Michael Alison, a Conservative shadow Home Office minister, to call on the Attorney General for a public prosecution. He also threatened that, should a public prosecution fail, he had friends who would be only too happy to bring a private case. There followed in the House of Lords a debate in which the arts minister, Lord Donaldson of Knightsbridge, was forced to defend the whole principle of subsidy to the arts against what would in the following decade become increasingly crude and political attacks.

Many years later, Wally would claim that it was a playwrights' letter to the newspapers which I organised in defence of the serious purpose of his play which gave him the will and courage to go on writing. Since he went on to produce, over the next twenty years, some of the best American plays of the twentieth century – *My Dinner with Andre*, *The Fever*, *Aunt Dan and Lemon* and *The Designated Mourner* – then, if it's true, it remains one of the things I'm proudest of in my life. The gutless ICA, by contrast, caved in quickly, perhaps frightened of losing their Arts Council grant but also under the influence of their founder, Sir Roland Penrose. As Picasso's biographer, Penrose, husband to the exceptional war photographer Lee Miller, was a self-proclaimed big skittle in the surrealist movement and therefore by elective category unshockable – before his reincarnation as pillar of the British art establishment, at least. But Penrose's public announcement that he had prudishly cut his links with the organisation he had founded after the war for the dissemination of avant-garde art helped persuade the ICA to shorten the run of the play, even though sales at the box office had, for ignoble reasons, gone through the roof.

It was deeply depressing to find there were rebels-turned-blimps wanting to turn back the advances they had championed. It was even more depressing that there was anyone willing to listen to them. But there was also a redeeming element of farce which made these shenanigans hard to take seriously. As in Mary Whitehouse's attempts in the early 1980s to prosecute the director of Howard Brenton's play *The Romans in Britain*, it was almost impossible for the so-called moral guardians even to describe the reasons for their horror without sounding ridiculous. Their cause was discredited the moment they opened their mouths. But later in the year, Margaret found herself taking on a parallel but far more serious fight, which seemed to foreshadow an ominous change of mood in government. On taking over at *Play for Today* she had found on the shelf a script which had been gathering dust since 1975. She made its realisation her

most urgent priority. Roy Minton's *Scum*, directed with towering integrity by Alan Clarke, brought to mind the James Cag-
ney film *Angels with Dirty Faces*. It belonged in a tradition of
tough but big-hearted cinema. A young recruit, badly wronged
in his last place of detention, arrives in a borstal and, rather than
give in either to the screws or to the most powerful inmates,
fights his way to the top of the tree, where he imposes a new and
healthier order. The portrayal of the borstal was unflinching
but true, the violence not overstated. Yet just two weeks before
the film was due to be transmitted, Margaret and Alan were
told that there were questions about whether it would ever be
allowed to go out. The head of BBC1, Bill Cotton, hated it, and
the BBC's managing director of television, the authoritarian
Alasdair Milne, liked and understood it even less.

In 1956, after the national humiliation in Egypt, Clarissa,
the wife of the prime minister Anthony Eden, is said to have
remarked that 'For the last few weeks I have really felt as if
the Suez canal were flowing through my drawing room.' It
was not so different for us. For those few months at the turn of
1977, almost everything Margaret and I did was aimed towards
getting *Scum* shown. For a while, we thought about little else.
Margaret was fighting as hard as she could within the building, managing at least to get a hearing from the Chairman of
the BBC governors, Michael Swann. And it fell to me to fight
outside the building, providing a public face for a campaign
in which I passionately believed. The fact that the film was,
in the words of the *Observer*, 'one of the finest pieces of work
ever made by the BBC Drama Group' counted for nothing. In
matters of censorship, Milne had form. One of those dangerous
people who mistake ruthlessness for efficiency, he had always
loved banning things. He had already stopped Dennis Potter's

harmless comedy *Brimstone and Treacle* being broadcast on the grounds that it was 'nauseating' and 'quite simply diabolical'. But the special piquancy of the threat to *Scum* was that the borstal system being criticised in the film was run by the Home Office. By something less than a coincidence, it was the Home Office which was also responsible for the licensing of the BBC.

You didn't have to be a conspiracy theorist to know that this was political censorship of the most blatant kind. It was hard to say which would be worse. It was possible that *Scum* was being banned because of a direct order from the Home Office, which didn't approve of what it saw. But even if there were no such order and the BBC was doing its master's business unprompted and banning the film out of sheer cowardice, what did that say about the craven character of those in charge? What, indeed, did it suggest about the future independence of public broadcasting? Unable to attack the film's basic veracity – even their 'expert advisers' told them that everything that happened was perfectly plausible – Milne and Cotton took instead to attacking its compression, saying that because so many unflattering things were shown to happen in such a short space of time, the film gave a misleading impression of the daily life of a borstal – just as, presumably, they would have said *King Lear* gave a misleading impression of the daily life of a king. Further, they claimed to be worried that because the film was shot in realistic style, a lot of it hand-held, the audience might be confused into thinking they were watching a documentary. Dishonest snobs, *they* knew it was a fiction. But would the great unwashed? It all added up to one charge: *Scum* was too good to be shown.

Any objective observer would say that it was a rare and extraordinary achievement to make a work of art of which society's guardians were frightened. This, after all, is what political art is meant to do. But you could hardly ask Alan Clarke or Margaret to leave it at that. As Alan said on a discussion programme when asked what he wanted for Christmas, 'I'd like a television transmitter.' After screening the film for the press, and finding it acclaimed as 'one of the most polished and most compelling pieces of film-making that television has ever sired', both producer and director were in despair, but also determined not to let the row become, as it threatened to, the defining event of their lives. When the campaign to transmit the film ended in failure, Milne, tone-deaf to anything at a human pitch, had the nerve to send Margaret a message reading, 'I admire your courage but not your judgement. You have had your fun. Now get back to work.' I'm not sure that even Milne would have had the nerve to send such a message to a man. It was at this moment that Margaret began to feel that her own stay at the BBC might turn out to be brief. She had gone there because, above all, she valued the freedom. Under a different regime, producing *Play for Today* had been the best job in television. But the BBC's egregious refusal, in the case of *Scum*, to assert its independence from government had created a disastrous precedent which would license nothing but trouble in the coming thirty years.

The sense that times were changing decisively was reinforced by an incident at the end of the year in the Beverly Wilshire Hotel. Clive Goodwin had gone to Los Angeles to negotiate terms with Warren Beatty for his client Trevor Griffiths to write the film *Reds*. It was about the American journalist John Reed, who had been swept up in the Russian Revolution and written his account, *Ten Days that Shook the World*. On 14 November Clive returned to the hotel from a lunch at which he'd had one glass of wine. In the lobby, he

began to have a blinding headache. He told the hotel reception-
ist that he was feeling very ill. When he began to vomit and fell
to the ground, hotel security decided that Clive was drunk. Not
bothering even to smell his breath, they called for the police
to have him taken away. The cops handcuffed Clive, dragged
him through the lobby and laid him out on the pavement, then
drove him to the Beverly Hills police station, where they threw
him in a cell for drunks. He was found dead in there the next
morning. When a leading actor threatened to sue the LA police
for the murder of an innocent man who'd been having a brain
haemorrhage, he was told that if he brought his suit, every
cocaine-using film star in Hollywood would be busted.

Back in London, a wake was held at the Essoldo Cinema
on 4 December, organised by Clive's friends and defiantly sec-
ular in tone. Margaret and I went with Joe. We all wore jeans.
There were performances by radical poets and singers. In books
about the 1970s, often written by people too young to have lived
through them, the period is represented as one of chaos and
decline. History belongs to the victors. I can only say that's not
how it felt at the time. But for all of us on the left gathered
in the King's Road that day to remember the bright spirit of a
friend who had been killed at the age of forty-six by being mis-
taken for a drunk, there was a strong foreboding that Clive had
left us before our best hopes came crashing.

13

The Underlining

Clearly I was driving for a wall. The question was if and how I was going to avoid it. Early in 1977 I'd read that to celebrate the bicentenary of the founding of the United States, fellowships were to be offered for five American artists in different fields to come to the UK, and for five British artists to go to the US. It occurred to me once again that a change of air was what I needed. I could hardly go on as I was, betraying my wife and unable to accept the limits of a relationship with a woman who was secreted in the English countryside rehearsing Shakespeare. But once I had applied successfully and the date of my departure at the end of April 1978 drew near, I realised I was sending myself into exile. I was dealing with my problems by the unlikely expedient of dodging them. I was going to be away for a year.

In my heart I was convinced that, artistically, *Plenty* was an underlining. For the first time in ten years as a dramatist, I had not the slightest idea what I would do next. Evelyn Waugh said that 'At forty every English writer starts to prophesy or acquire a style.' I was just thirty, but once *Plenty* was finished I was sure it was the play for which I'd long been heading, the one that would somehow accommodate much of what I had to say about the country I'd grown up in. I'd lived through a certain period of history, and now here it was. I'd managed to transport the feel of it onstage. The story of one woman's disillusionment provided as powerful a metaphor as I'd hoped. Furthermore, the fleet-footed style of cinema-as-theatre which I had struggled with in *Knuckle* was this time under proper control. I'd written a play whose effects were achieved by juxtaposition: the aim of all epic writing.

A few years earlier, it had been Bill Gaskill who taught me one of the most valuable theatrical lessons of my young life. He had been to see a successful production about the threat of renascent British fascism. It was a play I had enjoyed a good deal for its general exuberance and courage. But Bill returned dissatisfied. In particular, he said, there was a short scene in which the central character had to make a phone call. A stage manager had carried on a small table in order to help him do so. On it was a telephone, and hanging from the telephone was a short piece of wire, which tapered out and clearly went nowhere. 'Now that', said Bill, 'is not what I call political theatre.' His point struck home and has stayed with me ever since. Nobody should imagine art has much to do with good intentions. The job of the playwright is to cast the material in a way which is potent and beautiful. The mark of your sincerity will not be in the righteousness of your thinking, but in your ability to transform your thinking so that it truly belongs in the medium you're working in. For Bill, the ugliness of a dangling wire was a sign that the playwright wasn't properly engaged. The scene was not playable, because the practicalities of staging it revealed that it had not been thought through. With *Plenty*, after nearly a decade of apprenticeship, I felt some correspondence between my intentions and the means with which I had realised those intentions.

I had known for a long time that my private behaviour had become deeply dishonourable but I was beginning to apprehend a little of the reasons behind it. Margaret had always been ahead of me, emotionally tuned and aware in a way I had never been. After our decision on the sofa in Battersea, way back in 1970, when she and I had first discussed getting married, we had both woken the next day discomforted. But I could now see that my uneasiness at least had been down to the uncertainty of my motives. My professional wish had been to free myself up for the adventure of becoming a playwright. When I was young I was so self-critical that I had assumed I was also self-aware. Wrong. I had blithely mocked a friend who argued that self-knowledge was the purpose of life. Self-knowledge, I had said, was simple. Knowing how to act on that self-knowledge was what was difficult. Wrong, again. In some obscure part of myself, I had imagined that by at last putting my private life in better order, I would unclutter myself to get on with my work. Although the strategy had been at all times unconscious – as though that were an excuse – the idea that I would undertake one thing principally in order to undertake another was a crime against the person I married. And in the way of things, it had had the very opposite effect. By a vicious generational irony, I was as guilty of trying to contain desire as my parents had been. Today everyone who had come close to me was paying the price.

Up till this moment, I'd shown a well-founded dislike of artistic theorising. When Pip Simmons, Howard Brenton and I had attended an international theatre shindig in the early 1970s in Florence, the official conference report, coming through our letter boxes months later, had noted that the British delegation seemed happier drinking wine and lolling in the Tuscan sunshine than discussing the coming crisis in European theatre. It was true. Writing plays was hard. Talking about what shape you would like unwritten plays to take was easy. The more deeply I fell in love with the difficulty of art, the more I despised the laziness of art-talk. But I had begun to feel that my break with the governing pieties of fringe theatre needed to be made explicit. I was so widely suspected for what I was assumed to believe that there didn't seem any harm to be done by confirming those suspicions. Perhaps then my many critics on the left might realise that my dissent from orthodoxy was not down to bad character but to sound reasoning. They had done me damage behind my back. Who knows? Maybe the time had come to confront. If I found most people on the right shitty in their attitudes, I had also discovered that too many people on the organised left were shitty in their behaviour.

I spent a lot of time constructing a considered talk for a spring theatre conference in Cambridge. Because I had always hated these kind of events, I took care to prepare as thoroughly as possible. In the lecture, entitled 'The Play Is in the Air', I presented a series of propositions which ought to have been self-evident but which, for good reasons, in the feverish atmosphere of the time, were not. A play, I argued, is never what happens on stage. It's what happens between the stage and the audience. The excitement and fun of theatre is never in the play itself but in the transaction. Unless that transaction is live and suggestive, you might as well write a pamphlet. Why bother detaining hundreds of people for up to three hours to drive them towards a conclusion which is already known? It was no longer sensible, as Marxists did, to demand of an artist that they must 'declare their allegiance'. Throughout my whole time as a writer I had been told that the purpose of art was to raise consciousness. But, I pointed out, 'Consciousness has been raised in this country for a good many years now and we seem further from radical political change than at any time in my life.' The question we had to answer was why.

Audiences, I argued, have minds of their own. They are not passive consumers who walk away from the auditorium, lesson learnt. Discerning playgoers arrive with preconceptions which they test from their own experience against what they see on the stage. Of any play, the audience asks, 'Is this how it is? Is this true? Am I convinced?' It was worse than pointless to offer a didactic evening. It was actually counterproductive. Using the theatre either to lecture or to parade your virtuous beliefs excludes the audience and leaves them with nothing to do. They hate you for it, because it insults their intelligence. Worse, it insults their experience of life. A good play is there not to close minds but to open them.

Such notions, you might imagine, ought to have been unexceptionable. But even as I laid them out on paper I knew they represented a break from the Germanic mode into which fashionable thinking had fallen in the previous ten years. Rehearsals for *Plenty* were already in their second week back in London when an unwieldy group consisting of me, Margaret, Kate and Joe all piled into a car together to go and stay for the weekend with Reg and Annette Gadney in their house in Wendy, not far from Cambridge. We passed a cold Saturday night in one of those country vicarages where, when you woke in a gabled bedroom, the ice was as likely to be on the inside of the windows as on the out. Reg was an ex-Guards officer who, when not writing excellent thrillers, taught general studies at the Royal College of Art. By chance, he had been house manager at the National Film Theatre on the afternoon in 1968 – I was in the audience – when Jean-Luc Godard, detained in the Paris uprising, failed to appear and instead sent a telegram ordering the British Film Institute to give his £100 away to the first poor person they saw in the street. 'Talk to him of images and sound.

You will learn much more from him than from me.' Reg had been one of my most supportive friends, but because he knew me so well he warned me at supper: 'David, you're fine when you feel the audience is friendly, but with a hostile one you go to pieces. Don't go to pieces.'

Small wonder, then, that driving in on Sunday after a vigorous morning's walk felt like travelling towards an execution. Reg says today that he feared for me even before we arrived, because I already looked like a starved dog. When we got out at King's College, the audience waiting for my lecture could hardly have been worse suited. Some of them came from street theatre groups and were still in costume, fresh from playing cartoon capitalists, with top hats, masks and painted faces. Over their shoulders, they might as well have carried bags marked 'Swag' and filled with dollar bills. Others were still dressed as clowns, complete with baggy trousers and spotted tops. There were a good many attendees from the world of marionettes and mime. It had never been my intention to tell believers in the fringe that the party was over. I was making a subtler point: if political theatre were to enjoy more impact in the future than it had in the past, the nature of the party would have to change. It was a defence, not an attack. I had not lost my political faith, I was seeking to reconsider how best to deploy it. But among an audience who had come to celebrate themselves rather than to think, I was faced with no choice but to bear Reg's admonition in mind and to plough on saying unpopular things in an unpopular way. I tried to keep my eye fixed on Annette, Kate and Margaret since they alone looked friendly. I was half-heartedly interrupted a few times, but otherwise received in more or less abject silence.

A dragon in shallow waters is the sport of shrimps. The

conference organiser asked for comments, but the feeling in the hall was that nobody was much interested to jump over the bar. They all went under it. One virulent objector shouted the question 'Did Piscator die for this?' – surely one of history's more erudite heckles – before walking out without waiting for a reply. The heckler was apparently unaware that a good part of the German theatre director's radical career had been spent, like too many others', in the vain search for a Broadway hit. A few people joined in, taking advantage of my presence more broadly to disparage what they felt to be the general failings of my work. There was an overwhelming consensus that whatever questions I had posed, no one was in the mood to join in the hunt for answers. My sense of isolation, already strong, was further reinforced. Journalistically, I would be represented as having broken with a movement I'd helped to create. The academic historian Catherine Itzin noticed that the lecture 'left many members of the political theatre movement reeling as if from an unexpected, undeserved blow'. And yet in the following decade, as the climate of the country moved sharply rightwards, the questions of effectiveness I had raised would seem more urgent, not less. Under the pitiless scrutiny engendered in an antagonistic political climate, the whole subsidised theatre, underprepared, would be alarmed by the urgent need to find answers. Looking back, my analysis had only one thing wrong with it. It was premature.

The time I had spent meanwhile preparing *Plenty* had been educational. Many years later, having seen Cate Blanchett, Meryl Streep and Kate Nelligan play Susan Traherne, Mike Leigh would ask me bad-temperedly when he was going to see an English actress play the role. I gave him no answer because I had none. But with the seasoned advice of Gillian Diamond in the National Theatre's casting department, I had for the premiere assembled a first-rate team. Lindsay Duncan was to make her London debut in the second act, in the small but valued part of Dorcas, a self-confident young girl looking to fund an abortion, while, much to everyone's surprise and to some people's dismay, Julie Covington had agreed to play Alice, Susan's bohemian best friend. Just a year earlier, every bar and radio station had vibrated to the sound of Julie's unequalled recording of 'Don't Cry for Me, Argentina'. Her thrilling timbre had made the song a worldwide hit. As usual, Tim Rice and Andrew Lloyd Webber had put out an LP of *Evita* to familiarise the audience with the songs before they followed up by presenting the show on stage. They had taken it for granted that Julie would move on to take the lead. But rather than sing out in defence of a South American dictator, Julie had chosen instead to play second banana to Kate Nelligan in a stroppy new play at the National Theatre. She had, she said, 'trouble with Evita's politics'.

It takes courage to refuse such a certain pathway to stardom and I felt both grateful and, in some way, responsible. After all, it was my play Julie had preferred. I owed a debt to her. It had better be good. But I felt equal gratitude to Stephen Moore, who was joining to play the part of Brock, the young diplomat who meets Susan in Brussels after the war and who marries her in England some years later when he fears for her sanity. I was becoming used to what was already a familiar problem. For as long as I continued to write central female roles, casting the lead presented little difficulty. The scarcity of such opportunities guaranteed that the greatest actresses of the day would queue up in Europe and in America to play them on film or in the theatre. For years to come, I would be super-served. But male actors, to the contrary, were spoiled and correspondingly reluctant. They were unused to the idea that on occasions the conventional power relationship might be reversed. It was not just a question of the size of the part or indeed of the billing. It was about the way I portrayed the world. I once asked the Swiss actor Bruno Ganz to put his head in a woman's lap. Afterwards Bruno was smiling. I asked him why. The posture implied submission. 'I'm fine with it, David,' he said, 'but I'm amused because you know full well no American leading man would agree to do such a thing.'

Perhaps Kate resented my excessive sense of gratitude to the two other players. She was certainly extremely impatient in rehearsal when Julie was struggling with her elusive and slightly underwritten part. For whatever reason, something of my hitherto perfect artistic accord with Kate was starting to fray. Sporadically we fought, in a way which was no less toxic for being a matter of tone. Kate had endured a torrid time at Stratford, unhappy in a preconceived *As You Like It* in which Rosalind had been required to slot in as little more than a suede-clad puppet. Used to the full and proper collaboration which is routine on new plays, Kate had been far too independent to climb into the half-timbered straitjacket of the RSC house style. She hated herself for doing what she called 'leafy acting'. Although I had frequently visited her in her rented cottage outside town, she had forbidden me to attend. She had also, to the understandable disappointment of the management, declined to take up a contract for a projected London season. She was their star and she was leaving early. During her time away, she had broken up with her longstanding companion, Mark Cullingham. Mark wanted to try his luck as a television director in Los Angeles. Together they had sold their house in Stockwell, and so, for the time she was doing *Plenty*, I had found Kate a room to live in with Caroline Younger, who by now had moved to Notting Hill. Kate was happy not to be tied down by property or indeed by anything else.

I was forced to concede that for various people at the National Kate seemed, in the time since we had done *Licking Hitler*, to have crossed a line from being rumoured to be difficult to actually becoming it. A part of my day was spent going round the costume shop, the publicity department or the stage management smoothing ruffled feathers. I was used to it. In those days I ruffled feathers myself. 'It's just her manner,' I'd say. 'Take no notice.' Those who backed Kate's cause called her 'intense'. As she said in an interview later, it was not her ambition which made her unusual. All actors are ambitious. It was her ability to focus her ambition. But the blame for rehearsals sometimes becoming scratchy lay just as much with me. Probably more so. My moodiness began to answer hers. I was becoming aware that as an artist, whatever my shortcomings, I had always been free. Richard Eyre had remarked on one occasion that as a director I was the most reckless he'd ever produced. Sometimes he'd had to hold himself back from interrupting because, he claimed, I was never frightened to say anything to anyone, regardless of the consequences. I scared him. Now, moving towards doing a play which meant so much to me, I felt at a disadvantage. I was no longer free, because my heart was in hock to the leading lady. At some level I resented the loss of control. Rehearsing *Plenty*, I had begun to feel constrained, and to chafe at that constraint. At times, I even took my anger with myself out on the precipitator of that anger. It was understandable, but it was also disgraceful. On any shared artistic endeavour, achieving one clear agenda is hard enough. To have a second is always disastrous.

Neither of us, I think, would look back nostalgically to that rehearsal period. It was sometimes bad-tempered, and progress was in fits and starts. Probably Kate and I were both at our worst: Kate, because for the first time in her professional life she was really scared. She was facing the challenge of being the first person to play as demanding a leading role as exists in the repertory. And me, because I was panicking as my romantic life closed in unhelpfully on my professional. But in the last couple of weeks, as we were able to pull the tendons of the story tighter, the play began to cohere. We woke up one day, without warning, to find that the play was lifting the whole company up. You looked about you and everyone was smiling. A few people invited from upstairs at the National Theatre to come and see run-throughs in the rehearsal room left thoughtful and silent. When we went into the theatre and saw the decor arrive, we began to work with a quiet concentration which marks out people who know they're about to do something good. In 1999 the designer Maria Björnson tried to reconceive the play for a new generation, but she told me that the images of Hayden's original vision were still so clear to her that she could do nothing to improve them. They were stuck in her retinas, and all she could do was summon them up once more, this time with slight variations. The moment when Susan lies back on the bed with a joint in her hand in a hotel room in Blackpool, and the walls around her fly away to reveal the sunlit fields of France stretching away for miles, was as perfect a visualisation of a theatrical idea as I'd ever seen. Although the route to achieving the play had been uncomfortable, the moment we could all surrender to it made everything worthwhile.

From the first preview of the play it was clear that a section of the audience would never accept it. We had never imagined how personally parts of a British audience were going to take the play's analysis. You could feel that the public were at war the moment the play began. Lindsay Duncan's hilarious performance as a girl too bone-headed to realise the moral implications of termination had had us all in stitches in the rehearsal room. But when she walked out into the Lyttelton she was received in appalled silence. Depressingly, during the West End revival twenty years later, there were men as loudly offended by the scene in which Susan uses a man to get herself pregnant as they were in the late 1970s. But less obviously sexist objections to *Plenty* centred on the feeling that the play was moralistic, the work of a man who believed himself superior to other people. Perhaps in the first production Kate and I, both gung-ho for Susan and her indictment of post-war Britain, did press her case a little too hard. On occasions the production became overly strident. Our shared anger showed through to a degree which alienated those who were not on Susan's side. Balanced properly, *Plenty* is a play which presents as equally costly all choices in a society which is institutionally hypocritical. Yes, you will suffer if you accept society's hypocrisies and endure them without complaint. But you may well suffer an even higher price, as Susan does, for spending a life in permanent dissent. Already I had met enough people who had become victims of either course, and I knew no right way to proceed. For any intelligent audience, *Plenty* indicts its own author long before it indicts anyone else.

From when I had first presented *Plenty* to him, Peter Hall had been broadly approving. But when he came to see it at the first preview, his response changed. Next morning, in his office, Peter told me that in performance *Plenty* had revealed itself as one of those landmark plays which serve as a permanent point of reference. He said simply, 'Well done. This one's going to last.' He told me he could not have been more proud. I casually reported his approval to the actors – 'Peter likes it' – and thought no more about it. I had no inkling at that moment of just how crucial Peter's support was going to become. He, like me, was dismissive of people who, as a way of rejecting the play, were already muttering that Susan Traherne was 'unlikeable'. What did it mean? As Peter said, audiences pretended to be shocked on stage by behaviour which was frequently nowhere near as bad as their own. A cheerful double standard obtained. Adultery and deceit were greeted with frowns of disapproval by people who themselves were strangers to neither in real life. And if Susan *was* formidable, so what? So was Hedda Gabler. So was Medea. Were they 'likeable'? Why were men so frightened of a strong woman?

On the South Bank, with its policy of a rotating repertory, plays had only four previews before they opened to the press. Almost as soon as I walked into the foyers on the first night, my stomach lurched. I was sure that the cards were going to be stacked against us. When the play began, it was clear that if anyone wanted to give themselves over to the flow of the story, they were going to have to ignore a certain stratum in the audience. It was April already but high society seemed to be in the grip of a devilishly targeted flu which at times bordered on laryngitis. In selected parts of the house there was a listlessness, not uncommon in the Lyttelton, which made everyone else conscious they were watching some very small figures shouting at the far end of a very big room. How on earth could I have imagined that *Plenty* would be welcomed by the very people it was about? The disconnection appeared complete. When Susan launched into her unsparing satire about the

national shame of Suez, you could feel some spectators wanting to get up from their seats and wring her neck. When the
smoothie British diplomat Charleson argued the importance at
all times of good manners over truthfulness, you could feel a
moment's widespread relief that there was one person in the
play who talked sense. Yes, I had been convinced that the stage
of the National Theatre would be the ideal place from which to
address the nation. But what if the nation, or that section of it
which patronised the National Theatre, was determined not to
listen? Peter's horror at the tenor of the evening resulted in him
ordering that the schedule of names for complimentary first-
night tickets be comprehensively redrawn. No author or actor
in future would have to endure the resentful crowd of political
fixers who felt entitled to attend because they had long ago contributed a word of support to the building of the theatre. But
for *Plenty* the cleansing of the establishment list came too late.
I walked away from the theatre furious and disbelieving. How
could any play so destined to go right go so miserably wrong?

   There were only five days left until I was due to fly to Washington DC to begin my year of absence. Margaret and Joe, we
agreed, would follow later. In advance, I had made no practical arrangements. I had a visa and a bank account and nothing else. I was stepping into a void. I had always been addicted
to a quick exit, but this was ridiculous. How could I be running away at what was, for Kate and me, the most dangerous
moment of vulnerability? What on earth had I been thinking?
On the Monday after opening the play I had a farewell lunch
with Kate to lick our wounds. Advance bookings were poor.
She knew that in response to scepticism towards the play on
the first night she had overcompensated. As a result her performance as Susan had turned a touch too febrile and rattled. In

several passages she had looked short of technique. But in the restaurant I found her calm and defiant, looking forward to the run and confident that once there was a rhythm to the performances the play would soon find its public. It was too good not to, she said.

By Thursday of the same week, I was down in Chapel Hill teaching young boys and girls, check-shirted, fresh off the land, about the history of the British theatre. It was blossom time in North Carolina, the most exquisite time of the year, and the air was scented with bougainvillea. Colleges and dormitories glowed with colour. My pupils all looked about fifteen, with piercing blue eyes and tufts of sprouty blonde hair shooting straight up from suntanned faces. They were intensely well-mannered, keeping up a polite and gratifying interest, as if they knew that it was the only time they would hear a word about the subject before they returned to their farms. The English professor, Kimball King, who had invited me on campus because he knew as much about modern theatre as anyone alive, said the pupils were young but they were also impossible to fool. He was right. My week at the university was my only scheduled commitment in return for the full year's fellowship. The bicentenary fellowship didn't oblige me to *do* anything. The other fifty-one weeks gaped ahead, unfilled.

I went down to a Chapel Hill car lot and, for $1500, randomly bought a 1964 Ford Galaxie, a monstrous gas-guzzler which sat on the road like an ocean liner. The average car wastes ninety-nine per cent of its energy propelling itself. Only one per cent propels the passengers. This one drove as if it wasted ninety-nine point nine per cent. Its fins stretched to infinity but it comfortably sat two. The salesman had the sense of humour to say, 'Good choice.' On the flight over, I had conceived an absurdly bad idea for a film. It was to be called *Stella* and it was about a woman working in government who discovers, when he turns up in a car crash in the wrong state, that her husband is a bigamist, leading one life with her in Washington at weekends and another while working on the NASA space programme during the week in Cape Canaveral. For that reason I decided, when my week's teaching was up, to drive south to Florida, and take a look at one of the film's potential locations.

To give them their flavour, road movies, especially American ones, tend to stress the romance of life on the road. But what I valued was the tedium. I loved it. I was never happier than glazing over, surrendering to an impotent, pointless rage about the unspeakable unfairness of things. What was the point of writing? Nobody wanted to hear from me. After so many years of apprenticeship and maddened purpose, it was pleasant to sit in a Ford Galaxie and stare for days at an unvarying road, with nothing but a steady rise in humidity to make me feel I was getting anywhere at all. As I wound down the window, I listened to the radio and began to wonder whether, in the time I'd been away, the whole continent had been infantilised. When exactly had Can Do turned into How To? There were tips all day on How To enjoy yourself, or How To choose a holiday, as if American citizens were no longer capable of doing anything without first being given a manual. Worse, there was a complete contrast between the USA's founding philosophy and a new fearfulness which seemed to be stressing that life was really dangerous, so watch out. The national motto had once been Take Risks. Now it was Take Care. When I got to Daytona Beach, where I based myself in a massive empty concrete hotel, I found there were no doors on the toilet stalls in Dunkin' Donuts. That was because people liked to go in there to shoot up. It would be a couple of years before Michael Mann would make his superb cinema debut, *Thief*, in which James Caan dies discovering how completely the lone entrepreneur has had their heart kicked out by the corporate. But for now there was no work of art to make sense of things. It was impossible to work out, in my general gloom, whether it was America which had changed or me.

Daytona owed its prosperity to the hundred thousand students who used it for spring break. But that was March. This was May. It counted as out of season. Occasionally I would say something, like 'Can I have some coffee please?' or 'Can you tell me where there's a bookshop?' But otherwise I was pretty well silent from the start of the day to the end. It didn't bother me. I had no hankering to speak. Some days, serving myself in an automat, I didn't open my mouth at all. It occurred to me that perhaps I was having a nervous breakdown, walking the wide, breathtaking twenty-three miles of beach or staring at the typewriter in despair. I'd always had a goal, a task. Now I had none. Tom Stoppard says that being blocked is not a question of not being able to write. It's a question of never being satisfied with anything you do write. By that standard I was blocked, and would remain so for the rest of the year. *Stella* was one idea so lifeless, so terrible that not even Kael's 'treacherous power of art' could do anything to transform it. I knew less than nothing about America. Why on earth did I think I could write about it? But, worse, how on earth could I write at all when the last play that I'd written looked certain to be ignored?

I honestly don't know how long I stayed in Florida, paralysed by self-pity, wondering whether anyone would one day come to rescue me. At every important junction in my life, a Bexhill boy, I had always gone back to stare at the sea. Well, this was the moment when it finally came home to me that I had done everything wrong. How could I have been so stupid? Back in London Margaret and Joe were getting on with their lives. How could I have come this far without realising how selfish I had been? Peggy had often told me that the people she despised most in life were those who were unwilling to pay the bill. 'Do what you want to,' she would say. '*But then pay the bill.*' I had deceived myself into believing that my aim was to balance out the love I felt for two women to whose loyalty and brilliance I owed so much. But in seeking to please everyone, I had satisfied no one. On the contrary. I was plummeting down and pulling down everyone with me. When I drove back up the East Coast to New York to stay with my cousin Rosi, my legs gave way. I parked the car in a midtown lot and was walking up Sixth Avenue when the pain became so great that I was incapable of moving. Maybe this mysterious paralysis was physical, the result of driving for five days, or maybe it was psychosomatic. Who knows? Whichever, I sat down on the edge of one of the low brick walls outside the Time-Life building and stayed there for several hours, hoping the pain would pass. Next day, I still couldn't walk.

Rosi lived with her witty but volatile husband Pierre, who had taken over the Marlborough Gallery following the shakedown from an expensive lawsuit brought by the estate of Mark Rothko against Pierre's uncle, Frank Lloyd, who was now exiled in the Bahamas. The daughter of my uncle Bumper and aunt Eileen, Rosi was one of those clever women who'd looked round England when she was young and got out as fast as possible. She'd become personal assistant to Ted Rousseau, who was curator in chief at the Metropolitan Museum. Pierre and Rosi lived on the Upper East Side and had a spare room in which I could sleep at nights and work by day while they were

out. The room's only disadvantage was that right beside the
bed was a massive Francis Bacon depicting what looked like
someone being sick in the lavatory. I woke to this vast canvas
every morning. Pierre couldn't sell it, so he'd dumped it in the
spare room. When I nervously remarked to Pierre that it wasn't
very good, he just shrugged and said, 'Everyone knows. Francis
can't paint women.'

As a guest, I felt compelled to do a reasonable job of dis-
sembling. I didn't want my problems to show because I didn't
want to discuss them. Besides, I knew from my time at school
that I enjoyed occupying other people's lives. For a while, I ate
what was given and went where I was told, in the company
of Pierre and Rosi's friends. After what felt like a lifetime of
wrong choices, it was pleasant to make none. But in June I had
to fly briefly back to England for two reasons. Margaret was
pregnant again. She had been to the hospital, where they had
pointed to a black dot and said, 'Look, do you see the child?'
In reply, she had said indeed she did see it, but what was that
other black dot? In response, the scan operator had vanished
for fifteen minutes. She had gone to get a doctor, it turned out,
because she was under instructions not to tell mothers they
were expecting twins, for fear of a bad reaction. Margaret had
anyway been feeling that her time at the BBC was not going
to run much longer. There had been executive interference
on a couple more films. With two children on the way, it was
important we were all together all the time. Margaret asked
me who I thought should take over running *Play for Today*. I
pointed out that our friend Richard Eyre was signing off from
his superlative tenure at the Nottingham Playhouse with a
group-written play, ten years before its time, about the unscru-
pulous methods used by powdered milk manufacturers to sell

their doubtful products to perfectly healthy mothers in Africa. Why didn't Margaret press his cause?

My second reason for returning was, of course, *Plenty*. From Florida, I'd become anxious, picking up only the vaguest indications. Now I heard the full story. The board of the theatre, and in particular its chairman, Max Rayne, had been alarmed to find what poor business the play had been doing since its opening. It was a flop, he said. Take it off. But Peter had dug in his heels, insisting that an important point of principle was now at stake. He was prepared to accept that when the National did work which it considered bad, it was reasonable to shorten its run. Of course. But *Plenty* was work which everyone in the theatre believed in. If they couldn't now stand up for things which were either ahead of their time or uncommercial, what on earth was the point of a National Theatre? Unless your values were seen to be demonstrably different, you might as well stick with the commercial. Peter confided to me that he'd be able to protect the play by presenting it just seven times a month, rather than ten, and by playing it mostly at weekends. If he nursed it, he said, he was sure its fortunes would change.

By now I was in such a state that I'm not sure I even heard what Peter said. I certainly didn't guess that Peter's readiness to put his job on the line on the play's behalf would be the turning point of my professional life. Margaret and I installed Kate to house-sit in our absence from Richborne Terrace, then flew back with Joe to Cape Cod, where I planned to continue my purposeless fellowship by renting an A-frame on the beach at Wellfleet. We stayed there for a month, me all the time bashing away in a futile bid to animate a dead screenplay. When the stately Galaxie got bogged down in a rainstorm in the sand and we spent hours digging it out with spades, it seemed all too apt. In July we started slowly to move westwards, taking four weeks to cross America. When we broke the speed limit in Colorado, a creepy policeman was willing to let us off if Margaret sat with him in his police car for five minutes. In the mountains we fed on the plentiful pink trout fishermen would otherwise have thrown back. We were heading for Los Angeles with the idea of spending the rest of the year there, mainly because I had been happy in LA thirteen years earlier and Margaret was interested to see it. But nobody had explained to us that in the late seventies it was impossible to find living space in LA if you had a child. Nobody was willing to rent. There were signs everywhere – 'no dogs, no children' – and estate agents told us not even to try. So it was a paradox that the only place willing to accommodate a doubly pregnant woman, her husband and our three-year-old son was a swingers' apartment block in a dockside village in Marina del Rey.

It was certainly a different way of life from the one we were used to. We were by the ocean, but that was the best you could say. From time to time at dusk we would go down to the communal Jacuzzi, where all our neighbours were preparing for a night of action. Nobody minded Joe's presence. Oddly, they rather welcomed him. But by eight thirty Margaret and I would be the only pucker-skinned couple heading back upstairs in the formation in which we'd arrived. After a week or two, it became melancholic. Los Angeles was not prising itself open to us, and we both had a strong sense that this was not where we wanted our children to be born. So in the middle of September we got back in the car and headed up to stay at the El Cortez Hotel in San Francisco. We had dinner with Jessica Mitford, whose ignorance of the basics of tea-making had once so inspired me. Then we set off east, this time going as fast as possible. By chance our first night's stop was in Reno, where my aspiring producer Shirley MacLaine was in solo cabaret at one of the casinos. Afterwards she told us that no one had been round to see her for weeks, and asked would I please give her notes? I refused, saying that I knew nothing about song and dance, it was not my field, and, really, we'd both had a lovely time and the show was perfect. At this, Shirley became so insistent that, mistaking her vehemence for sincerity, and being myself at the time more than slightly unhinged, I remarked that if I had a single problem it was perhaps with that speech from *Some Came Running* where a woman complains: 'You've got no right to talk to me the way you did, Dave. I am a human being and I've got as many rights and feelings as anybody else.' Shirley asked me what exactly was wrong with that speech. It was one of her fans' favourites. It was one of the highlights of the show. People loved it. 'Yes, of course, I can see that, Shirley, but isn't it just a touch, well, *sentimental?*'

Next day, getting out of Nevada as fast as our wheels could carry us, Margaret and I speculated freely as to whether Shirley would ever speak to us again. When we got to New York we hit a more serious problem. There was a newspaper strike. Usually you could rent an apartment by buying the *New York Times*, but in September 1978 it was not publishing. The sole source of news about rentals had become the *Village Voice*, which, in the mad rush of the homeless, was now selling tens of thousands of extra copies. There was, however, we were told, one stand on Christopher Street where the *Voice* was available the night before publication. We duly stood there among a bunch of desperate people wise to the same dodge, and grabbed the first copies as soon as they were thrown off the truck. But by the time we went to see Jerry Gretzinger, the landlord of what seemed to be an absolutely perfect tenth-floor loft on Broadway between Broome and Grand, right in the heart of SoHo, he had already half-promised it to someone else.

It was the sight of Margaret's stomach beneath her winter coat which changed Jerry's mind. A deeply considerate and friendly man, who ran a handbag factory in one third of the loft and lived in another third, he could not allow a pregnant woman to leave the premises without knowing that the last third of the loft was hers for as long as she wanted it. He was not going to be the person who turned her out onto the street. By the following week we had left the thirty-ninth motel of our trip and were installed, Little Italy glowing like a Vincente Minnelli musical at one window and the ever-changing colours of the Empire State Building visible from another. The news I was getting from London had turned from being good to being incredible. Peter's strategy had worked better than even he could have imagined. The first indication of a change in mood had come earlier that summer when Fred Zinnemann sent me a letter to tell me that *Plenty* was the best thing he'd ever seen at the National. The second indication was when, in July, Mike Nichols had invited me to his house in Connecticut to discuss making a film of *Plenty*. He had been watching an Ibsen play in the Olivier, got bored and wandered instead into the Lyttelton to see a play of which he'd never heard, but by which he was now possessed. Even Peggy wrote: 'It's taken you a long time to become the Darling of Gods, so caution, caution. You've another thirty years of writing, so there's plenty of time.' But most certain evidence of a reversal of fortune came in a string of increasingly excited letters from Kate. 'I can't begin to tell you what's happening here.'

In November I sold the car for $1200 – a $300 hit for fifteen thousand miles – and I flew back to London to see *Plenty* for the last time. It was not just that the place was packed to the rafters, with long queues waiting all day for returns. More importantly, there was a quality of anticipation in the house when the play started which was completely new. I had always believed that expectation was four fifths of the battle. Well, here it was, tangible. *Plenty* had turned into one of those ideal theatre evenings in which not a word, not a thought, not an image is lost. Kate stepped forward at the end and there followed the kind of ovation I had hitherto heard only in the movies. I was reminded afresh how lucky I'd been to have a bona fide great actress around when I'd been writing these roles. The Portable dream was in some way fulfilled: a play could be made by its audience and no one else.

I was not there on the last night, but someone told me of the impromptu curtain speech Kate made in response to an audience who would not let her go. It was curiously phrased and so, for me, deeply moving. Kate thanked everyone who had supported the play and also everyone who had supported the author, who, she said, 'has come from among you'. When I heard that phrase, I knew exactly what she was saying. She was saying goodbye.

14

Like Everyone's a Writer

The last nine months of my marriage were spent mostly in New York. I would do my best to work uptown in Rosi's apartment, then at four o'clock in the afternoon I would give up and walk the more than ninety blocks down to our home in SoHo. In defiance of Nietzsche, no great thoughts were conceived. Instead I would take in the minute racial variations from block to block, drinking in the life of each immigrant group, their shops, their houses, their conversation on the sidewalk. I knew to within three feet exactly where the Czech quarter turned German. Bill Gaskill had asked me to adapt Tolstoy's novel *Resurrection* for the Olivier Theatre, but I was refusing to accept all the wise counsel I had received from everyone that *Stella* was a dud. My work wasn't impressing me. Why should it impress anyone else? From time to time I would go and see Joe Papp, who seemed to be pleased that I was living in New York. He behaved in a proprietorial way, as if my being in the city meant he were somehow my host. Anything I wanted, he said. But after a ninety-minute *tour d'horizon* on any subject but *Plenty*, Joe would tell me the reasons why he wasn't, at the moment, going to do it.

Our life in SoHo was effectively communal. Upstairs, on the top floor, Dave Brubeck had his studio, and from time to time we'd see him in the elevator. Jerry Gretzinger's door was open most of the day, and so was ours. His children, Nell and Aaron, would run through to see us, and Joe would run through to see them. There was still enough of old artistic SoHo left to make it feel interesting, although people were beginning to talk more frequently about property prices. We were just on the cusp of change. At a time when private life in the UK was still often furtive and repressed, English friends would come over to the US because they could be themselves. We had a gay friend who went to the bathhouses every Friday and Saturday night and he would come in for coffee in the morning to report on the previous night's Saturnalia. But the heterosexual opportunities in the late 1970s weren't significantly fewer, if that's what you wanted. Studio 54, the nightclub adored by people who wanted to be celebrities, was represented in the newspapers as being the city's keynote institution. More properly, that honour should have gone to Plato's Retreat, one of several places anyone could go for a nice middle-class commercial orgy. The likely draw-back was that the first person you would meet there would be a British theatre director.

Feelings of decadence were reinforced by a growing friend-ship with Tennessee Williams, which would continue well into the next decade. We had met at a cocktail party where Myrna Loy, the world's most attractive seventy-five-year old, had charmed me rotten. Margaret and Lynn Redgrave had carried the party on to dinner, and Tennessee and I had hit it off straight away. Tennessee was never happier than when enjoying his own often incomprehensible jokes. Every day he got up early to write, then began drinking white wine before lunchtime. By the time I got to him he was more than half cut, but deter-mined every night to keep going as long as possible, preferably until a final drink at 3 a.m. 'How are you doing, Tennessee?' I would ask around midnight, when conversation had slurred to a halt. Like a Southern belle, he would curl his pinkie, throw back his head and reply, 'Why thank you, David, I'm doing just as well as I possibly can.' He would then peal with cheerful laughter. When we got to know each other better, he would insist on dining at Sardi's, a theatrical restaurant in midtown where the food was appalling. He ordered cannelloni, which he left untouched. But he felt Sardi's was the last place where he was properly treated. Tennessee liked eating there because they made a fuss. Waiters stood in a line while he passed. And quite right too. The larger part of his conversation was about how completely he'd fallen out of fashion. He felt it so keenly that he was inconsolable, however hard you tried. He ignored praise. Once Tennessee got into his riff about how his plays could no longer be mounted in New York because the critics hated him so much, it was impossible to get him out. I didn't mind. The reliable grievances of one of America's greatest dramatists shut out of the city where he had made his name reinforced my own feelings of companionable gloom. Later my junior friendship with John Osborne was played out to the same harsh melody: 'I knew it would end badly, but not this badly.'

We had put Joe into a friendly kindergarten in Washington Square. I liked walking west for a change and it was a pleasure to take him across in the sunshine before I rode the subway uptown. But one morning in December I returned to our loft to find Margaret in labour. She was only eight months gone. I took her downstairs and helped her into the back of a cab. It was still rush hour and St Luke's Hospital, where she was being looked after, was right up by Columbia University at the other end of the city. Margaret was stretched out on the back seat of the taxi about to give birth, while the driver, oblivious, played his radio so loud that he didn't hear her screams. When after forty minutes we reached our destination, Margaret was in too much pain to get out. The moment the driver finally realised what was holding her up, he immediately started defending his route. 'I came through the park. It's the quickest way.'

Within fifteen minutes our second son, Lewis, was born and within ten more our daughter, Darcy, followed. Premature, neither was in the best shape. Darcy weighed four pounds fourteen ounces, her hip was broken and she was having trouble breathing. When, after a few days, Lewis was able to keep his temperature up in the open air and therefore no longer strictly in need of intensive care, we explained, embarrassed, that because Margaret had come to the States already pregnant, we had only been able to secure insurance for emergencies. Time in a regular ward would cost us. 'Oh, OK,' the doctors said at once. 'We'll keep him in emergency.'

Margaret's sister Sarah flew out to join us, and we became a family of six. There was thick snow that Christmas as the babies gained weight and came home, Darcy wearing a Pavlik harness for four months while her damaged hips healed. The first flakes of a snowstorm would usually arrive in the afternoon, and there was no more gorgeous prospect in Manhattan than to stand at a tenth-floor window looking down to a daffodil-yellow stream of taxis making their way out of town before the snow got too thick for them to work. I found the spectacle of the city brought to a silent halt by nature overwhelming. That month, in a frenzy of determined domesticity, I even started going to pastry class, so that I could practise millefeuille, folding the butter and the flour together in layers on a cold slab. Everyone would be waiting at home for the resulting croissants. But when the turn of the year came, I found the resources finally to face the failure of my novice screenwriting. A fellow playwright, Mike Weller, read *Stella* and told me that the purpose of writing was to get things out. He didn't know what had motivated me to write the film, but whatever it was, it showed every sign of staying in. He was right. I'd wasted the greater part of the year. Very well. On the train to Nottingham in 1974, I had made a promise not to burden the public when I had nothing to say. It was time to make good on that promise.

The week after I threw *Stella* away, Bill Gaskill appeared in New York to tell me that my adaptation of *Resurrection* – I had done only half the first act – was never going to work. It had been a bad idea. Whatever had attracted him to the book was not in the play. Bill was one of a flock of friends that winter who passed through our apartment, using our residence in Manhattan as a welcome chance to visit. Peter Hall came by, observing that he had never seen such small children in such a large space. He was in town because Peter Shaffer, who lived in New York, had finished a play about Salieri's jealousy of Mozart. It was entitled *Amadeus*. But Peter used the chance now to offer me the artistic directorship of the Olivier Theatre. He wanted to hive off his twelve-hundred-seat open stage and have just one person run it. But this time Mephistopheles had targeted the wrong Faust. Would I direct John Gielgud in *King Lear*? No. I had already resolved I would rather be a blocked writer for the rest of my life than not be a writer at all. By chance, a few days later, an article appeared about the future of the British theatre in the *New York Times*, with half a page of photographs. Jerry came running in excitedly. 'Have you seen this? The *Times* says you're a playwright.' I looked at him, not understanding. 'But Jerry, I told you that's what I did. What do you think I do every day?' Jerry shook his head. 'Yeah, but I thought you were a writer like everyone's a writer. It never occurred to me you were really a writer.'

The act of clearing my desk liberated me. David Rose, with the soul of a great producer, had written me a timely letter to say that he had shooting dates for a *Play for Today* in July, and why didn't I just write it? He couldn't imagine anything better. All he cared about was that I should be working at Pebble Mill again, and he promised to do whatever I wrote, sight unseen. I sat down and began something new, a fable, a Rohmer-ish *conte morale*. The subject was a young man's pursuit of an unattainable woman. A young journalist is unable ever to find out whether the object of his love is indeed as struck with him as she claims to be. Every time he sees her she seems to have a new job. First she's working in an art gallery, then she's teaching dance. Pretty soon she's having a nervous breakdown. It's impossible for our hero to be sure whether she's ever told him the truth, or whether the curious circumstances that have repeatedly kept them apart were actually intentional. At the end he's seen to be living out his days in a loveless marriage, discontent and dreaming of leaving. For whatever reason, within eight days of my starting work there were fifty pages. This one, like *South Downs*, was pain-free and from my subconscious. Perhaps I was finding it so easy to write because longing has always been my subject, or perhaps it was simply because it wasn't *Stella*. David Rose read it the moment I finished it and told me how excited he was.

All the time we'd been away, Kate had been living in our house in London, and when we returned at the beginning of April it was full of fresh flowers to welcome us home. The idea was that Margaret and I would now settle down to some kind of normality, a married couple with three children. Margaret, an outstanding feminist to her fingertips, had been in her element in Lower Manhattan. Americans had responded both to

328

her directness and to her generosity, so that she had become the centre of a spontaneous, disparate community of warmth and laughter, of which she had taken memorable black-and-white photographs. Her many admirers in New York seemed to know and understand this Scot better than the English ever could. The plan now was that she should go back to work. A number of overdramatic but well-meaning people treated me as though I were the prince from over the water, asking what I was going to do to help save the British theatre, which was going through one of its periodic crises of confidence. I told everyone who asked that I had no plans for new initiatives or new structures. I had already played a part in founding two companies which had made waves in the small world of the theatre. But now I wanted to try and write plays which might reach out beyond that world. I had concluded that it was the most radical thing I could do.

My relationship with Kate was clearly finished. She was living with another man. So that was that. But I could also sense that not only had Kate's personal circumstances changed, her attitudes were shifting as well. She was stepping backwards from the *folie à deux* which had powered us both for so long. Firstly, she expressed regret that she had not taken her chances to become a film actress. When she had been at the age when Hollywood wanted her, the offers had come thick and fast. Now she was beginning to feel that turning them down had been a mistake. She had left it too late. She wasn't English, she was Canadian and emotionally she had belonged all the time on the other side of the Atlantic, and in the cinema, not in the theatre. She felt she had lived too long in the wrong country and it had made her unhappy. In public, in the *Sunday Times*, she was quoted as saying, '*Plenty* has spoilt me for ever. I'll never get a chance of that range again in British theatre.' But in private she believed there was another downside. The formidable roles I'd cast her in had convinced people that was who she was. They had created an impression of coldness, of distance. People sometimes approached her gingerly, and in her view that was because the parts and the player had become mixed up. People were expecting Susan Traherne and were intimidated. Kate was far too sensible and too sensitive to blame me directly. She knew perfectly well that she'd already played three good parts and now that I was planning to make a new film, she was eager to play a fourth. She knew there were plenty of actresses who would have loved the chance. But she had also reached the point where she felt trapped in my idea of her. That had been the meaning of her curtain speech. I belonged in England. She didn't. There was a side to her which the public wasn't seeing.

On our return, Margaret and I found the country in the grip of counter-revolution. This being England, when *fanshen* came, it came from the right. Some popular propaganda about the unions not collecting rubbish and leaving bodies unburied in the winter months had convinced a large section of the electorate that bracing self-punishment was now in order. In love with a worst-case scenario and always up for moral correction, the British public had decided that in Margaret Thatcher they saw the ideal instrument for the job. Just four weeks after we got back, the new prime minister, Britain's first woman leader, was voted in on the back of a widespread panic which made no sense to us. Maurice Saatchi, the PR architect of her victory, went on to claim that 'Time for a Change' was the most powerful slogan in politics. But I never thought it as potent as 'We Can't Go On as We Are'. It's true that the country had staggered for the last decade, reeling around, shedding identity, raggedly trying to work out its uncertain future. But, my God, staggering was a great deal preferable to what lay ahead. From the moment Thatcher assumed office on 4 May it was clear to anyone who had spent the last year abroad that whatever the disease was thought to be, the cure was going to be far worse. On the back of a blowhard theory called monetarism, a fifth of British industry was about to be destroyed. A group of jackass intellectuals would seize Downing Street, push their wild ideas and damn the consequences. Within ten years, anything which resembled a community would be under sustained ideological attack. Thanks to a successful policy of divide and rule, policemen confronting a picket line would feel free to taunt striking miners by waving their overtime slips at them. If the lowering of the cranes for Churchill's funeral had been the most moving public image of my lifetime, this image of abject class treachery was by far and away the most shaming.

In that fateful early summer of 1979, this latest development, the election of a hardline prime minister, looked like just one more twist in our continuing island story. Nothing had prepared us for quotations from St Francis on the steps of Downing Street – 'Where there is discord, may we bring harmony' – being offered straight to camera as a ruling-class piss-take. The effrontery was new. But the change of tone did not alert me, or indeed anyone else I knew, to the first shudders of a hairpin reversal that would last for at least thirty-five years. Of all the things that might happen, we had least foreseen that capitalism might have the ability to renew itself from within, kicking up a gear by freeing up markets and tearing up workers' rights. It had been ingrained in every aspect and in all the evidence of my upbringing that the gains made in the 1940s towards free education, free health and decent standards of welfare were permanent gains, lasting standards of improvement, the majority of the people finally imposing themselves on the minority. There was no other way in which history made sense. People had fought for exactly this and returned from war to secure it. Like so many socialists of my age, I had insufficiently appreciated the values of the welfare state because all I had been able to see were its shortcomings. Many of us in our nightmares had imagined violence, the seizure of the country at the end of a gun by plutocrats or the military. But for those of us who were committed to believing in the essential wisdom of electorates, the idea of the country agreeing to hand itself back to the *laissez-faire* barbarism of the years before the war was unimaginable. Aiming to encourage industry and hard work, Margaret Thatcher was shocked at the end, according to Michael Portillo at least, to discover that she had encouraged only selfishness. Even she was forced to accept that the effects of her philosophy were wildly at odds with its intentions. As one wise commentator put it, committed to making a country in her father's image, she succeeded only in making it in her son's. Up till now, for those of us born in 1947, the direction of travel, however erratic, had been towards social justice and equality. From this point on, it would be a retreat.

There was a curious parallel in my private life. Margaret and I tried to settle, but at some level we both knew that there was never going to be any such thing as normal. It was gone. In New York we had lived in a community full of visitors, people coming and going all the time. The doors of the apartment were open and so were we. Life had felt temporary, provisional, shared. We were pinballs, knocked about each day by whoever we bumped into. Now we were back in England, we were facing reality. It was just us. At a certain point, it became clear to Margaret that I had been lying to her for over two years. I told her that Kate and I had indeed resumed our relationship some time previously, and that I had sustained the deception for a very long period. Since Margaret had openly invited Kate into our lives and liked her, the impact of the news was devastating. The fact that it was over counted for nothing. We reeled around for a few weeks with me spending most of my time in Birmingham preparing the film, even though most of its shooting would take place in London, some of it in the very flat I had lived in at Cambridge Circus. The grotesque appropriateness with which I had entitled the film *Dreams of Leaving* did nothing to palliate the injury I was doing to Margaret.

Our marriage ended in miserable circumstances in Rye in Sussex, ten miles from where I had been born. We had gone to stay with Peter Jenkins and Polly Toynbee, two *Guardian* journalists who had invited our whole family for a weekend in their cottage. Polly and Margaret had recently become good friends. On the Saturday afternoon, we had gone to our room to have a rest while the children slept across the corridor. It was the most sustained time that Margaret and I had spent together since the discovery of my other life and the full extent of my deceit. From the first day we had met Margaret and I had felt immense esteem and unforced admiration for each other, as well as love. Now, Margaret said, in her eyes that esteem was gone. It would never return. In that case, I said, we would have to break up, since I was finding its loss unbearable. I would rather we lived apart than lived diminished. Margaret agreed.

Having resolved to bring our marriage to an end after nine years, Margaret and I went down to dinner with Peter and Polly. Peter Jenkins, a man who at the best of times behaved as though *Guardian* columnist were an office of state, set off from

the head of the table on a bumptious name-dropping monologue in which he was invariably the hero. Misguided prime
ministers like Harold Wilson and Edward Heath featured for
Peter only in so far as they were willing to listen respectfully
to his advice and marvel at how much better it would have
served them than what they had actually done. A politician's
purpose in life was to provide red wine-driven anecdotes for
Peter's nightly self-celebration. Bottle after bottle went down,
Peter entirely insensitive to our unhappiness and far too deep
in his own narrative to care. For me, his fluffy voice, whistling
oblivious through archaic dentistry, was impossible to bear. On
Sunday morning, after an entirely sleepless night, the Hare
family left early. In the thirty-five years since that unendurable
weekend, I admit I have never opened the *Guardian* and seen
the words 'Polly Toynbee' without groaning. Her trademark
censoriousness has always brought back memories of utter
bleakness and despair. Of course any sane observer would say
it was hardly Polly and Peter's fault that our marriage ended in
their house. But I am no sane observer.

At the end of the weekend I made life far worse for Margaret
by suggesting that perhaps we should not break up immediately. I had a film to make. Could we delay until it was in the
can? Rightly, she told me to get out. The only excuse I can offer
for my callousness is that in abandoning my wife and family, it
occurred to me more than once that I was in danger of becoming my father. All my life I had felt myself hurt by a father who
had been absent. Now, in my turn, I proposed to absent myself.
Anyone determined to think ill of me would henceforth say,
'He left his kids when two of them were six months old.' The
wife of a fellow playwright remarked, 'Oh they're allowed to
leave now, are they?' In artistic matters I had been free in my

judgements. After all, there was art I liked and art I didn't. But in matters of personal behaviour I had never presumed to judge others, nor had much wish to. As someone who had long been abstemious, I now went cold turkey. Since childhood, I had known that adults were at risk from feelings over which they had little control. Few people were able to do what they ought. They did what they could. To judge them for their personal lapses was to judge them for being human. I knew that I had always been drawn to Oscar Wilde as much for his philosophy as for his wit. It was Wilde who insisted that morality was never a matter of telling others how to behave. It was how you behaved yourself. Only the sinner was in a position to judge the sin. And in my case, my judgement on myself was far worse than anyone else's could ever be.

As it turned out, as my children grew up I grew close to them, far closer than my own father was to me, and did my best to take care of them. Our lives became so happily intertwined that I scarcely noticed how intimate our arrangements were. I took them for granted. So did everyone else. Margaret wanted me to be their father and so did I. When I watched Lewis, aged four, bounce off the fender of a slow-moving car on Brighton seafront, I thought my life was over. I came very close to losing my temper only once, as it happened, when we were making the film of *Saigon* in Bangkok. I had brought my three-year-old daughter to be with me during the shoot. It was sometimes inconvenient, and sometimes I had to lean on other people's kindness when I had too much to do. One day, the whole cast and crew were gathered round the pool. I was watching Darcy in the water when another divorced father, beer in hand, asked me whether I wasn't overcompensating. I asked him what he meant. 'I mean, bringing your daughter all the way to Bangkok. Isn't that too much the guilty husband?' I had to hold down sudden white-hot anger. 'Has it not occurred to you', I said, 'that I might have brought Darcy here because I adore her company?'

I moved out as soon as I was told to, and went, like other strays before me, to lodge in the house of Caroline Younger. Caroline was the calm port in the storm, who, after the odd misfortune of her own, regarded those of others with practical good sense and kindness. I was quick to find out which of my friends identified with human suffering and which didn't. There were welcome and unwelcome surprises. Anna Massey, Roger Dancey and Stephen Frears were unfailingly loyal and wise. In particular, I dreaded telling my mother what had happened, and when I did finally pluck up courage she reacted as I knew she would, at once sounding distraught but not altogether unready. I went on to say I knew, it was terrible, I was so worried for the family I was leaving. At this point Mum confounded me more than she had ever done in my life. She said, 'You don't understand. I'm not worried for them. I'm worried for you.'

Meanwhile, I needed a leading man for my film, and Stephen Moore recommended to me a young actor he knew who had been doing great things at the Liverpool Everyman. I asked whether he could play a romantic lead. Stephen said he had never been required to so far, he was seen more as a character man, but he was a good-enough-looking chap, so why didn't I meet him? Bill Nighy claims that on our first encounter I warned him that, while filming, I might occasionally turn white and be sick, and not to take it personally if it happened while he was acting. All I remember is the pretty fringe like a pelmet over Bill's forehead and, already, the air of cheerful self-irony which was ten per cent reminiscent of the raffish actor Denholm Elliott and ninety per cent blindingly original. I thought he was perfect, and still do. In all I was to work with Kate five times. With Judi Dench, four. With Bill, so far, ten.

In *Teeth 'n' Smiles*, the manager Saraffian describes his singer Maggie as a minor cult. He adds, 'I'd rather have leprosy than a minor cult.' While we were filming *Dreams of Leaving* one of the crew who had worked on *Licking Hitler* said to me, 'Why don't you stick to those period things? You're good at those.' When the film went out, some people couldn't see the point of it, while others were provoked. Tony Bicât's sister Tina wrote me a cogent letter saying, effectively, 'Yes of course, we all dream of leaving, so what? Most of us can't.' But the title itself caught on, and all too soon I knew by the film's persistence in strangers' conversation – 'Are you the man who wrote *Dreams of Leaving*?' – that I had a minor cult. When I went into book-shops, other writers always seemed to be using the title. Both the Human League and the Clientele released songs called 'Dreams of Leaving'. Another group took the last lines of the film and made them into a song which rose briefly in the charts.

> *Our lives dismay us*
> *We know no comfort*
> *We have dreams of leaving*
> *Everyone I know*

Soon, Margaret and I would begin new lives. But for now I had done the only thing I knew how. For better or worse, for-give me, I had gone back to work.

Our Child Will Understand

1979 represented a low point for our whole family. When I was once asked by an interviewer if I had suffered for my art, I said yes, a good deal, but not nearly as much as those around me. We all had to get going again from a standing start, and with no momentum. I went off to Linden Gardens in the dingier part of Notting Hill, where, by spending every penny I had, I secured a deposit for a mortgage on a gloomy flat with a leaking skylight and resolved to live alone. On the floor above worked a prostitute who came downstairs one night with a knife between her shoulder blades. A dispute with her pimp. After a year of almost zero productiveness I went off to Australia for three weeks, having agreed to write for the 1982 Adelaide Festival. I calculated that I would force myself to finish a new play. If I failed . . . well, Australia was a long way away. On the trip home, I stopped over with Joe, aged seven, in Mumbai for a week and I was handed my subject. Disgracefully, *A Map of the World* remains to this day one of only a handful of plays in the English-speaking repertory with a leading part for an Indian actor. Roshan Seth played Victor Mehta, first in Adelaide and Sydney, then in London and later in New York. Margaret meanwhile had found a new job as Head of Drama at Central Television, where she commissioned and oversaw some standout television including *Made in Britain* and *Auf Wiedersehen Pet*.

Four years after it was written, Joe Papp gave way to the pressure of his friends and mounted *Plenty*, first off Broadway, and subsequently on, in a production stronger than the first. Papp said he only produced the play because he was so tired of people telling him to. He resented the fact that he had to go abroad to get the political writing he so badly wanted from American dramatists. Kate had by now acted on the feelings of misery England brought out in her and moved to New York to start over. Suddenly, with the Plymouth Theatre neon-lit by a sign reading '1983: The Year of Plenty', both of us were enjoying a delirious kind of open-hearted acceptance, unknown in England. As Kate said to me, 'Even you can't pick a hole in this.' A subsequent film starring Meryl Streep on shining form brought the story to a much larger audience. But it wasn't until I went off to Brighton for four weeks in 1984 with Howard Brenton to write a play about a demented press magnate who is out to destroy everything in his sight that I began to feel some of my shattered confidence returning. One day, walking on the promenade and seeing Michael Heseltine a few feet away heading towards the Conservative Party conference, Howard remarked to me how easy it would be to take a pop at him. There was no visible security. Next day we woke to find the IRA had bombed the Grand Hotel. We rushed to the seafront to see its facade collapsed like a wedding cake. Margaret Thatcher's behaviour that morning, as she organised clothes from Marks and Spencer for her shell-shocked colleagues, was exemplary. As Howard said, 'She may be a terrible prime minister, but she'd make a great tank commander.'

The production of *Pravda* was exhilarating, and for Howard and me it was our last collaboration. Thanks to a historic performance from Anthony Hopkins, we went out with a bang.

The play's subject matter – the undignified surrender of British journalists to Rupert Murdoch and Robert Maxwell – ensured that the guerrilla skirmishes both Howard and I had frequently engaged in with our skewed dystopian press were transformed by our theatrical declaration of war into outright bloody conflict. But it was too late for the newspapers to do much damage. Somehow my series of conversations with Howard in Brighton had not just resulted in a play. They had also cleared my head to unlock a steady flow of work. In less than ten years I would write *The Bay at Nice*, *The Secret Rapture*, *Racing Demon*, *Murmuring Judges*, *The Absence of War* and *Skylight*, all at an indecent speed which at one point would have been impossible.

I was particularly influenced by a letter from Philip Roth, who became a good friend in the years he spent living in London. I would often join him for lunch and be amazed that one of America's greatest novelists could be found eating most days in the Notting Hill branch of Spudulike.

Saw Pravda last night. You are lucky to have Mr Hopkins and he is lucky indeed to have you. I remember when I told you about the right-wing ideologues on the West Bank you mentioned the excitement of writing about a monster. Well, it's all there. Your excitement comes through in his incredible performance. I wish you'd write a play with only monsters. You are not a nice boy David and even if you persisting [sic] in pretending to be in Real Life, you should yield to the muses who know better than anyone, and stick to the wicked. I mean this and I'd be delighted to give you old Doc R's prescription any time you want to have a meal . . . Anyway, congratulations for this. I like these monsters you create.

341

In 1989 I went to direct *The Secret Rapture* in New York, first at the Public Theater, then on Broadway. Immediately after it transferred to the Ethel Barrymore Theatre my father died in Bexhill Hospital. During his last years he had attempted something which would pass for intimacy. 'Nobody tells you,' he said more than once, 'nobody tells you what old age is going to be like. It's bloody awful.' I flew back to the UK after the opening of the play to console my mother, only to find news awaiting me that the play was to close after only ten days of full performances. Wallace Shawn advised me: 'Broadway has very low standards, but somehow you don't even meet those.' At the weekend I flew back to New York to console the cast and to share sorrows with Joe Papp, who did not yet publicly admit to the cancer from which we all suspected he was suffering. Because he was contemplating the approach of his own mortality, my stillborn production devastated him as much as me. I was mortified to have disappointed him at such a moment. I flew home for my father's funeral in a cramped chapel outside Battle.

By the end of that year, it was clear that my mother was yielding to the Alzheimer's which had already shown itself while my father was alive. Nancy was letting go. We had an unhappy Christmas where I found her fully packed and dressed, sitting on the side of the bed waiting to go home, at 3 a.m., after just eight hours staying in my house. After Dad's death she was well looked after by the Botwrights, her loving neighbours in Newlands Avenue, but after a while they warned us they could no longer vouch for her safety. So we moved her first to a residential home in the Park in Nottingham, near where my sister lived, and afterwards, when the disorientation became more severe, to a nursing home. When we sold her house it seemed pathetically small, the tiny crucible of huge feeling. The plumber to whom we sold it then arranged his surplus lavatory cisterns in rows in the back garden – a social offence for which he would have been run out of town in the 1950s. The world had changed, but Newlands Avenue had changed faster.

By 1991 Peggy Ramsay had long been prey to the same disease. She had persisted in going in to the office even though she had little idea what was happening, preferring to watch tennis on the television instead. Her identification with John McEnroe was by now complete. She loved him best for his hot temper, and most of all when he lost it. 'People say he's aggressive, but Caravaggio *killed* his opponent at tennis.' When her secretary locked her in her room, saying she had to read a play – 'This one's by David, you have to read it' – she was found a couple of hours later fast asleep on the sofa. Her loyal office had rung me in despair, saying that since I was one of only two people she trusted I might be able to persuade her to go into hospital. She loved me, it was up to me to protect her. She was refusing to go on the grounds that no one she knew who had ever gone into a hospital had ever come out. When I went to try and change her mind, she resisted me so fiercely that I said, very well, she could come and live in my house. Peggy leaned on my shoulder as I took her downstairs to the basement which I had prepared for her, but her condition deteriorated so rapidly that soon she was leaning on my shoulder again as I, feeling a traitor, led her into the hospital she dreaded. She'd been right. She died of bronchopneumonia within a few days. A few weeks later I came home at midnight to find twenty-six messages on my answering machine, all from different people, to tell me that Joe Papp had gone. Coming so soon after Peggy, it was unbearable. Caryl Churchill rang me to say, 'David, everyone who believes in us is dying.'

In the middle of all this, I met Nicole Farhi. I walked into a party following the first night of a play, and across the room I saw a woman whose eyes laughed at me as though she knew me already. She was a fashion designer whose combination of integrity and style defied everything that is usually implied by the word 'fashion'. She was also the cousin of my old friend Moris Farhi, who had acted in *How Brophy Made Good*. Five years previously I had written a film in which an Englishwoman sits envious and content in the bosom of a French Jewish family in Paris eating *pot au feu*, finding in them a warmth she cannot find in herself. On the eve of my marriage, watching a French Jewish family tuck into the seafood spaghetti, I realised that as so often, I was writing something, then living it. But unlike Gustav Mahler writing music about the death of his children, then having it happen, or Philip Roth giving his hero a heart attack and soon having one himself, my artistic prefiguring was wholly benign.

My mother came down from Nottingham for our wedding, for what was to be her penultimate visit to London. She was so charming and gentle to everyone that the other guests did not notice she was ill. In the coming years, during which my sister Margaret was close to her, it was hard for us to give her a birthday party every February and know that afterwards only Margaret and I would remember it. On one visit in June 1998, I wrote down exactly what Mum said to me, a series of remarks in the form of a Beckett monologue, which nevertheless revealed exactly where her wandering mind was focused.

I'm married to a nice, dear man.
Go quickly and I'll say nothing and you'll say nothing and
our child will understand.

I get myself so dead I really can't play with these things.
I can't get a name to give to you.
Did you have a bad father?
I've got the money but I haven't got the money.

But on occasions, Nancy could also rage. The most insistent theme of her conversation for many years was her desire to leave Woodthorpe Manor nursing home and go back to live with her mother in Paisley. She had had enough. She wanted to go home. Only Euphemia understood her. When she first began to ask for this, she would apologise afterwards. In the back of the car after a lunch with Margaret and me at which she had asked for little else, she said, 'I'm sorry but I have to say these things.' Later, however, she ceased to apologise. One day when she was sitting on a bench alone with me in the park, I had said repeatedly that, sadly, I could not take her back to live with her mother because her mother was no longer there. On this occasion Mum turned to me and, very unusually, looked me straight in the eye. 'Well then damn you. Damn you to hell.'

On 7 November 2001 Mum was given a flu jab. The following day, she was alone in her room when she lay down on her bed and died. She was ninety-one. For her funeral eight days later, Bill Paterson gave me his recording of Robert Burns's poem 'Ae Fond Kiss', which includes the lines:

I'll ne'er blame my partial fancy,
Naething could resist my Nancy.

In my eulogy, I remembered how deliberately she'd given my sister and me the freedom which she herself had been denied in her upbringing. It was as if she had stepped aside in order that we might go ahead. Mum wanted us to have something she never had – or feared to have. 'There is in the narrowness of her expectation something which burnt peculiarly bright, peculiarly pure. In modesty, she found grace. Expecting less than us, she somehow therefore gave more. If the struggle of life is to hold on to what is best in us, Mum won that struggle triumphantly.'

After the wake, Nicole and I drove back to London in silence. The formative events described in this book reached their proper conclusion on a day of streaming winter sunshine on the outskirts of Nottingham. Always expecting trouble round the next corner and absolutely certain I will miss the flight when only ninety minutes early at the airport, I am my mother's son. In my recessiveness and apprehension of the wine waiter's disapproval – 'And a nice Bordeaux' – am I my father's? How can I tell? To answer that question I would have to have known him, and the chance has gone. Almost a hundred years ago my dad stole walnuts under the spreading tree in Chigwell. Today I walk the hills and imagine new ideas.

Acknowledgements

PLATE SECTION CREDITS

Howard Brenton © Snoo Wilson

Pen and ink drawing © Richard Cork, 1966

Royal Court: the playwrights of the 1971 season © *Sunday Times*

DH with Tennessee Williams, Manhattan, 1978 © Arnold Weissberger

Band and vocals for *Teeth 'n' Smiles*, 1975 © Roger Perry

Fanshen, the first production © John Haynes/Lebrecht Music & Arts

Bill Paterson, in *Licking Hitler*, 1977 © BBC Photo Library

Kate Nelligan as Susan Traherne in *Plenty*; National Theatre, London, April 1978 © Nobby Clark / ArenaPAL

DH with Kate Nelligan, *Dreams of Leaving*, 1979 © Nobby Clark / ArenaPAL

All other photos courtesy of the author.

Two short sections of the book, about Lancing and New York in 1965, were previously published in a different form in *Areté*.

With thanks to Ann and Lindsay Todd, Tom Stoppard, Philip Roth and the Peggy Ramsay Foundation for permission to quote from letters.